Polycarp & John

Christianity and Judaism in Antiquity Series

Gregory E. Sterling, *Series Editor*

VOLUME 12

The University of Notre Dame Press gratefully acknowledges the generous support of Jack and Joan Conroy of Naples, Florida, in the publication of titles in this series.

Polycarp & John

The Harris Fragments and Their Challenge to the Literary Traditions

FREDERICK W. WEIDMANN

UNIVERSITY OF NOTRE DAME PRESS
Notre Dame, Indiana

Manufactured in the United States of America
Reprinted in 2010

The author and publisher are grateful to the British Library for permission to reproduce photographs of fragments in the Harris collection of Coptic papyri, OR.7561, nos. 55, 56, 63, and 64, British Library, London.

Library of Congress Cataloging-in-Publication Data

Weidmann, Frederick W.
Polycarp and John : the Harris fragments and their challenge to the literary traditions / Frederick W. Weidmann.
p. cm. — (Christianity and Judaism in antiquity series : v. 12).
Included bibliographical references and index. ISBN 0-268-03851-1(cloth : alk. paper)—ISBN 13: 978-0-268-03826-7 (pbk : alk. paper)—ISBN 10: 0-268-03826-0 (pbk : alk. paper). 1. Martyrdom of Polycarp. 2. British Library Manuscript. Oriental 7561. 3. Manuscripts, Coptic—England—London. 4. Polycarp, Saint, Bishop of Smyrna. 5. John, the Apostle, Saint. 6. Christian martyrs—Biography—History and criticism. 7. Church history—Primitive and early church, ca. 30–600. I. British Library. Manuscript. Oriental 7561. Selections. II. Title. III. Series: Christianity and Judaism in antiquity ; v. 12.
BR1720.P7W45 1999
272'.1'092—dc21 98-50200

∞ *This book is printed on acid-free paper.*

Christianity and Judaism in Antiquity Series (CJAS)

The Christianity and Judaism in Antiquity Program at the University of Notre Dame came into existence during the afterglow of the Second Vatican Council. The doctoral program combines the distinct academic disciplines of the Hebrew Bible, Judaism, the New Testament, and the Early Church in an effort to explore the religion of the ancient Hebrews, the diverse forms of Second Temple Judaism, and its offspring into religions of Rabbinic Judaism and the multiple incarnations of early Christianity. While the scope of the program thus extends from the late Bronze and Early Iron Ages to the late antique world, the fulcrum lies in the Second Temple and Early Christian periods. Each religion is explored in its own right, although the program cultivates a History-of-Religions approach that examines their reciprocally illuminating interrelationships and their place in the larger context of the ancient world.

During the seventies a monograph series was launched to reflect and promote the orientation of the program. Initially known as Studies in Judaism and Christianity in Antiquity, the series was published under the auspices of the Center of the Study of Judaism and Christianity in Antiquity. Six volumes appeared from 1975–86. In 1988 the series name became Christianity and Judaism in Antiquity as the editorship passed to Charles Kannengiesser, who oversaw the release of nine volumes. Professor Kannengiesser's departure from Notre Dame necessitated the appointment of a new editor. At the same time, the historic connection between the series and the CJA doctoral program was strengthened by the appointment of all CJA faculty to the editorial board. Throughout these institutional permutations, the purpose of the series has continued to be the promotion of research into the origins of Judaism and Christianity with the hope that a better grasp of the common ancestry and relationship of the two world's religions will not only illuminate the ancient world but the modern world as well.

Gregory Sterling
Series Editor

To Yvonne

Contents

Preface

The rediscovery of an ancient text for modern scholarly consideration is always an exciting occurrence. My own encounter with the Harris Fragments on Polycarp would have been most unlikely were it not for the influence of Professor Bentley Layton of Yale University. The lion's share of the work for this presentation and study of a "new" ancient text on Polycarp of Smyrna began as a dissertation written under his direction at Yale University. Besides Professor Layton there are many colleagues, from Yale and elsewhere, whose advice and criticism during the dissertation phase of my work are evident (at least to me) in what follows. Among these are David Brakke, Leo Depuydt, Stephen Emmel, Rowan Greer, Leander Keck, Rebecca Krawiec, Abraham Malherbe, Wayne Meeks, Paul-Hubert Poirier, Robert Ritner, James Smith, and Craig Wansink. Thanks are due also to the staffs of several libraries within Yale University for their kind assistance, especially those of the Divinity School Library, Sealy G. Mudd Library, and Sterling Memorial Library.

Without the opportunity to see the text firsthand, my work would have been significantly hampered and limited. To Dr. Vrej Nersessian and the staff of the British Library's Oriental and India Office Collections for making me welcome to study these ancient papyrus fragments, I extend sincere thanks.

More recently, my work has been supported through a research grant from the Society of Biblical Literature, which has been most helpful in securing printed resources, as well as technical and clerical assistance. Several colleagues within the Society of Biblical Literature, particularly members of the Intertextuality in Christian Apocrypha Seminar, have offered helpful comments and assistance. Among these are David Cartlidge, Dennis MacDonald, and Christopher Matthews.

I have been fortunate to be supported in a number of ways by the administration, faculty colleagues, students, and staff of Union Theological Seminary in New York, to whom I owe a great debt of gratitude. The staff of the Burke Library, including Seth Kasten, director of Reader Services; Drew Kadel, reference librarian; and Caroline Bolden, coordinator of interlibrary loans, have been particularly long-suffering. Further, I want to thank Gay Byron, who has acted as my research assistant on this project, for her careful work and good humor.

The University of Notre Dame Press has been supportive of—and patient with—me as I worked to bring the current manuscript to completion. Professor Gregory Sterling, editor of the Christianity and Judaism in Antiquity Series, and Professor Harry Attridge both read early drafts and made helpful suggestions. Particular thanks are due to them and to Rebecca DeBoer, Jeannette Morgenroth, and Ann Rice of the Press's editorial staff.

My family has supported this work in any number of ways. My brother, K. Timothy Weidmann, proofread a final draft of the manuscript and offered helpful suggestions. From Yvonne and our children, Joshua and Katie, I derive encouragement and strength more than they can know. Finally, I want to express my deep gratitude to that individual who supports me and shares her love with me on a daily basis—it is to Yvonne that I dedicate this book.

List of Abbreviations

Abbreviations used are those found in the *Journal of Biblical Literature* 107 (1988) 583–596, except:

ABD	*Anchor Bible Dictionary* (New York: Doubleday, 1992).
AH	Irenaeus, *Adversus Haereses*
AJn	the *Acts of John*
BIF	*Bulletin de l'institut francais d'archéologie orientale* 1 (1901)–
Boh	Bohairic; the Bohairic version of MartPol
FrgPol	The ancient work attested by the Harris Fragments on Polycarp
GIBM	C. T. Newton et al., eds., *Collection of Ancient Greek Inscriptions in the British Museum* (Oxford: Clarendon Press, 1874–1914)
HE	Eusebius, *Ecclesiastical History*
IvE	*Die Inschriften von Ephesos* Ia (1979)–
Jh	*Jahreshefte des österreichischen Archäologische Institutes in Wien* 1 (1898)–
MartPol	Polycarp's martyrdom as recounted in MPol and HE 4.15
MPion	the *Martyrdom of Pionius*

MPol	*Martyrdom of Polycarp*, Ps-Pionian version (i.e., *not* HE 4.15)
NT	the New Testament
OT	the Old Testament (Hebrew Bible)
Vir	Jerome, *De Viris Illustribus*
VPol	Ps. Pionius, *Life of Polycarp*

Introduction

The Occasion for This Book

The paleontologist Stephen Jay Gould writes, "Science tends to be difficult, subtle, ambiguous, and biased by all manner of social and psychic prejudice—although surely directed in a general way toward an increasingly better understanding of a real world 'out there.' But every once in a while, we do achieve the reward of a simple, pristine, and undeniable fact—and then we can rejoice."[1] The Harris Fragments on Polycarp (FrgPol)[2] are just such an "undeniable fact."

FrgPol provides an important and unique complement to the ancient literature associated with Polycarp, bishop of Smyrna, and with the apostle John. At a time when the traditions about John are receiving renewed attention[3] and scholarship on the *Martyrdom of Polycarp* and related documents is being increasingly sharpened and codified,[4] the "new" witness of this ancient text is particularly pertinent.

1. Stephen Jay Gould, "A Lesson from the Old Masters," *Natural History* 105.8 (1996) 19.
2. The abbreviation "FrgPol" will be used to indicate the literary work attested by these fragments.
3. See, for example, R. Alan Culpepper, *John, Son of Zebedee: The Life of a Legend* (Studies on Personalities of the New Testament; Columbia: University of South Carolina Press, 1994), and M.-É. Boismard, *Le Martyre de Jean L'Apôtre* (Cahiers de las Revue Biblique 35; Paris: J. Gabalda, 1996).
4. See, for example, both the extended article and book by Boudewijn Dehandschutter, "The Martyrium Polycarpi: A Century of Research," *ANRW* 2.27.1 (1993) 485–522, and *Martyrium Polycarpi: Een Literair-Kritische Studie* (Bibliotheca Ephemeridum Theologicarum Lovaniensum 52; Leuven: Leuven University Press, 1979), and the extended article

More broadly, FrgPol contains a particular understanding of martyrdom which is unique within the whole body of extant literature on early Christian apostles, apostolic figures, and martyrs. The following text edition, translation, commentary, and supplementary chapters are presented with the hope of accomplishing two major objectives: (1) making the unique narrative of the Harris Fragments on Polycarp available to the scholarly community and, more generally, to all interested in early Christian literature; and (2) locating the narrative within the literary traditions on Polycarp, John, and the greater body of literature about apostles, martyrs, and related figures. For the student of early Christianity these fragments are truly a treasure which provides the opportunity for a greater understanding of the world of ancient Christianity.

1. Polycarp's Martyrdom and the *Martyrdom of Polycarp*

Polycarp was martyred in Smyrna, between the mid-150s and the mid-160s CE.[5] The so-called *Martyrdom of Polycarp* (MartPol) is an account of his martyrdom, along with a report of the martyrdom of eleven other Christians, written in letter form and sent from a Christian community at Smyrna to a Christian community at Philomelium. MartPol is known through two separate text traditions, the Ps-Pionian (MPol) and the Eusebian. The former is preserved through menologia for the month of February. The latter is found in Eusebius' *Church History* (HE), sections 4.15.3–45, in which Eusebius of Caesaria includes a recounting of the

by William Schoedel, "Polycarp of Smyrna and Ignatius of Antioch," *ANRW* 2.27.1 (1993) 272–358. Just published is a commentary by Gerd Buschmann, *Das Martyrium des Polykarp* (KAV 6; Göttingen: Vandenhoeck and Ruprecht, 1998).

5. For recent discussion and bibliography on the debate over the date of Polycarp's martyrdom, see Dehandschutter, "The Martyrium Polycarpi: A Century of Research," 497–503; Schoedel, "Polycarp of Smyrna and Ignatius of Antioch," 354–355; and Schoedel, "Polycarp, Martyrdom of," ABD 5.392a–393a; not mentioned in any of the above is the short and helpful discussion in Gary A. Bisbee, *Pre-Decian Acts of Martyrs and Commentarii* (Harvard Dissertations in Religion 22; Philadelphia: Fortress Press, 1988) 119–121. See also T. D. Barnes, "Pre-Decian Acta Martyrum," *JTS* 19 (1968) 510–514; and Dehandschutter, *Martyrium Polycarpi,* 191–219. The discussion in J. B. Lightfoot, ed. and tr., *The Apostolic Fathers: Clement, Ignatius, and Polycarp* (1889–1890; reprint, Peabody, Mass.: Hendrickson, 1989) 2.1.646–722, remains important.

letter, slightly abridged,[6] along with some of his own comments.[7] It appears that the full text of MartPol "claims to be the work of eyewitnesses (MPol 15:1) written within a year of the event (MPol 18:3)."[8] Provided that evidence of later editing and interpolation is acknowledged, the scholarly consensus is that MartPol was, in fact, written shortly after Polycarp's death.[9]

Besides the Greek texts of MPol and HE 4.15, there are several ancient versions of MartPol. Latin versions exist both in Rufinus' translation of HE and in an independent form.[10] There is a Slavonic version which seems to rest on the Ps-Pionian tradition. Of the versions in other languages, B. Dehandschutter concludes that "none of these versions—Armenian, Syriac, or Coptic—has any independent value, all being adaptions of the Eusebian text" of MartPol.[11]

It ought to be noted, however, that the Coptic version in the Bohairic dialect (Boh), though clearly indebted to the Eusebian text tradition, includes significant, unique characteristics.[12] Among these are a change in

6. Relative to MPol.

7. The relationship of HE 4.15.3–45 to MPol is debated by scholars. Leslie W. Barnard, "In Defence of Pseudo-Pionius'Account of Saint Polycarp's Martyrdom," *Kyriakon: Festschrift Johannes Quasten* (ed. Patrick Granfield and Josef A. Jungmann; Münster: Aschendorf, 1970) 192–204, argues for the relative genuineness of MPol, rejecting a scholarly movement begun by observations recorded in Eduard Schwartz, *De Pionio et Polycarp* (Göttingen: Dieterich, 1905), and Hermann Müller's monograph, *Aus der Uberlieferungsgeschichte des Polykarp-Martyrium: Eine hagiographische Studie* (Paderborn: Bonifacius, 1908), and essay, "Das Martyrium Polycarpi: Ein Beitrag zur altchristlichen Heiligengeschichte," *RQ* 22 (1908) 1–16. This movement found a thorough statement in Hans Frhr. von Campenhausen, *Bearbeitungen und Interpolationen des Polykarpmartyriums* (Heidelberg: Carl Winter, 1957), in which the author locates several layers of interpolation in MPol and identifies the account in HE as containing narrative more original than that of MPol.

8. Schoedel, *Polycarp, Martyrdom of Polycarp, Fragments of Papias* (*The Apostolic Fathers: A New Translation and Commentary*, ed. Robert M. Grant, vol. 5; Camden, N.J.: Thomas Nelson and Sons, 1967) 48.

9. Schoedel, *Polycarp, Martyrdom of Polycarp, Fragments of Papias*, 48; Barnard, "In Defence of Pseudo-Pionius' Account of Polycarp's Martyrdom," 192–194. The abbreviation "MartPol" is employed herein to refer inclusively to the text traditions extant in both MPol and HE 4.15; for a parallel edition of the texts of MPol and HE 4.15, see Dehandschutter, *Martyrium Polycarpi*, 112–127.

10. Dehandschutter, *Martyrium Polycarpi*, 48–52; Lightfoot, *Apostolic Fathers* 2.3.358; also John van Bolland, ed., *Acta Sanctorum* vol. 2 ("Januarii Tomus"), esp. 701–707.

11. Dehandschutter, *Martyrium Polycarpi*, 275–276.

12. For the text and a modern Latin translation of Boh, see I. Balestri and H. Hyvernat, *Acta Martyrum* II "Textus" (1924; CSCO 86, Scriptores Coptici 6; Louvain: L. Durbecq, 1953) 62–72, 363–364, and Hyvernat, *Acta Martyrum* II "Versio" (CSCO 125, Scriptores Coptici ser. 3, no. 2; Louvain: L. Durbecq, 1950) 43–50. This supersedes the Coptic text

presentation (it circulated independently from HE); a change in—or, at least, assertion of—genre (it bears the titular heading, "martyr-account"); and the inclusion of additional comments about Polycarp,[13] found at the beginning and end of the narrative.[14]

Conventionally, a simple reference to "the Martyrdom of Polycarp" may refer directly to the Ps-Pionian text, or more generally to the martyr-account as contained in both/either the Ps-Pionian and/or Eusebian text traditions.[15] Within this study it is necessary to make available to the reader a greater level of precision. Hence the distinct abbreviations, MartPol, MPol, HE, and Boh, as indicated in the discussion above and in the preceding list of abbreviations.

2. Polycarp in Ancient Christian Literature

Besides MartPol, various ancient Christian works remember Polycarp. Primary among these is Polycarp's own letter to the Philippians (Pol. *Phil.*).[16] The occasion of the letter involves a request from Christians at Philippi for Polycarp's instruction on a matter of community discipline[17]—an apparent indication of the reputation and authority Polycarp enjoyed among Christians even outside his own city and province. In addition, the Philippians requested copies of the letters of Ignatius, bishop of Antioch, which were in Polycarp's possession.[18]

---

found in Amélineau, "Les actes coptes du martyre de St. Polycarpe"; further, Amélineau's French translation is unreliable due to its reliance on the text of MPol (and not HE).

13. Derived in large part from Irenaeus, *Detection and Overthrow of Pretended But False Gnosis* (AH) 3.3.4 (= HE 4.14.3–8).

14. Reference to, and citation of, Boh is included throughout the Text Edition (ch. 2) and Commentary (ch. 4).

15. For an example of the ambiguity of meaning of "MPol" as referring to the Ps-Pionian text tradition and/or the martyr-account more generally, see recently Dehandschutter, "The Martyrium Polycarpi: A Century of Research."

16. If Polycarp's student Irenaeus is to be believed, Polycarp wrote many other epistles and treatises as well (Irenaeus, "Letter to Florinus," preserved in Eusebius, HE 5.20.8).

17. See esp. Pol. *Phil.* 11.4–12.1.

18. Pol. *Phil.* 13.2. On the question of the chronological relationship between the drafting of Pol. *Phil.* and Ignatius' martyrdom, as well as the possibility of two separate Philippian correspondences, see recently Schoedel, "Polycarp, Epistle of," ABD 5.390a–392a, and the monograph by P. N. Harrison, *Polycarp's Two Epistles to the Philippians* (Cambridge: Cambridge University Press, 1936).

The passing of Ignatius through Asia *en route* to his martyrdom in Rome accounts for the personal association of Ignatius and Polycarp. After leaving Smyrna, Ignatius wrote separate letters to Polycarp and to the Smyrnaeans, and mentions Polycarp in other letters as well.[19] Among other pieces of information, these letters contain the earliest references to Polycarp as "bishop."[20]

The so-called *Life of Polycarp* (VPol), ascribed to Pionius,[21] provides a sustained, independent treatment of Polycarp from his early youth through his ordination and activities as bishop of Smyrna. It is extant in one manuscript, the tenth-century Codex Parisinus Graecus 1452 (a collection of "lives, martyrdoms, and eulogies of various saints for the month of February"), in which it immediately precedes MPol.[22] A leaf of text is missing at the end of chapter 28 and beginning of chapter 29.[23]

---

19. Ign. *Eph.* 21, Ign. *Magn.* 15. J. Ruis-Camps, *The Four Authentic Letters of Ignatius, the Martyr* (Orientalia Christiana Analecta 213; Rome: Pontificium Institutum Orientalium Studiorum, 1980), has argued against the authenticity of the letters to Polycarp and to his Smyrnaean congregation (as well as Ign. *Phld.*) based largely on internal evidence; for a rejection of the hypotheses of Ruis-Camps, see William R. Schoedel, *Ignatius of Antioch: A Commentary on the Letters of Ignatius of Antioch* (ed. Helmut Koester; Philadelphia: Fortress Press, 1985), esp. 5b–6a.

20. Polycarp does not call himself "bishop" in Pol. *Phil.* Besides the letters of Ignatius, Polycarp is also mentioned in the *Acts of Ignatius* 3—for the text, see ch. 2, register of parallels, (b) 6–8; for a recent survey of the secondary literature on the *Acts of Ignatius,* and an argument in favor of a second-century date for at least part of these *Acts,* see Bisbee, *Pre-Decian Acts,* esp. 133–151.

21. The Smyrnaean martyr who was killed under the emperor Decius and is the central figure in the *Martyrdom of Pionius* (MPion), and who may also be identical with the Pionius named in the postscripts to MPol (MPol 22.3, and the "Moscow Epilogue" 5); for discussion and bibliography, see Dehandschutter, *Martyrium Polycarpi,* 63–64, 277; Schoedel, *Polycarp, Martyrdom of Polycarp, Fragments of Papias,* 80–81; Hippolyte Delehaye, *Les passions des martyrs et les genres littéraires* (2d ed.; Brussels: Société des Bollandistes, 1966) 33–45, and Lightfoot, *Apostolic Fathers* 2.3, esp. 426–427. For discussion of the "Moscow epilogue . . . this special appendix" in the so-called "Moscow manuscript" of MPol, see Schoedel, *Polycarp, Martyrdom of Polycarp, Fragments of Papias,* 81, and recently, Dehandschutter, *Martyrium Polycarpi,* 33.

22. Lightfoot, *Apostolic Fathers* 2.3.423; see recently, Dehandschutter, *Martyrium Polycarpi,* 28. In the secondary literature the author of VPol is commonly called "(Pseudo-) Pionius," while the text tradition of MPol (as distinct from HE 4.15) is called "(Pseudo-) Pionian" (based on the proximity of MPol to VPol in the Paris manuscript and the mention of Pionius in MPol postscripts); however, it is well to remember the caveat offered by Dehandschutter, *Martyrium Polycarpi,* 277: "One must recognize that this theory is largely conjectural . . . There is no reason to identify the Pionius of MPol 22 with the author of the Vita, an anonymous writing that does not refer explicitly to the Martyrdom."

23. Lightfoot, *Apostolic Fathers* 2.3.423, 461.

The noted nineteenth-century scholar J. B. Lightfoot provided the assessment of VPol which has remained most influential among students of early Christianity. Lightfoot maintained that VPol was compiled "not earlier than the middle of the fourth century," and "is altogether valueless as a contribution to our knowledge of Polycarp."[24] Others, including the prominent New Testament scholar B. H. Streeter, would salvage all, or at least parts, of VPol for consideration.[25] Of course, regardless of the value of the information VPol conveys regarding Polycarp as a historical figure, it is important as a work within the literary tradition about Polycarp and his Smyrnaean church.

Lightfoot himself mined VPol for proof that there had existed within early Christianity a kind of collected works by and about Polycarp, a so-called *Corpus Polycarpianum*. In conjunction with the study of other manuscript evidence pertinent to the literary tradition, Lightfoot recorded the following observations about VPol:

> In chapter 3 the author promises a list of the earliest bishops of Smyrna. This never appears. Again in chapter 12 he states his intention of inserting [Polycarp's] Epistle to the Philippians; but we hear nothing more of it. Again in chapter 20 he defers his account of Polycarp's scriptural expositions till a later point, but we find nothing more about them or at least nothing which satisfies this pledge.[26]

A *Corpus Polycarpianum,* should it have existed, would have included, presumably, the texts of VPol, MPol, and Pol. *Phil.*, a list of Smyrnaean church leaders, and an account of Polycarp's interpretation of Scripture.[27] It should be noted that one might also have expected to find within it

24. Lightfoot, *Apostolic Fathers* 2.3.429, 431; similarly, Delehaye, *Les passions des martyrs,* 43–44; recently, Dehandschutter, *Martyrium Polycarpi,* 69–71, 277.

25. P. Corssen, "Die Vita Polycarpi," *ZNW* 5 (1904) 266–302, argues for authorship by the martyr Pionius; Cecil John Cadoux, *Ancient Smyrna: A History of the City from the Earliest Times to* 324 *A.D.* (Oxford: Basil Blackwell, 1938) 306–310, argues for a third-century date—"after 190 . . . no later than about 300," 306—based on considerations of theology (anti-quartodeciman) and the lack of any mention of John (which, according to Cadoux, would have been very unlikely after HE was published); B. H. Streeter, *The Primitive Church: Studied with Special Reference to the Origins of the Christian Ministry* (New York: MacMillan, 1929) 95–98, 271–278, argues for the "historical value" of, at least, the report about the apostle Paul and the early Smyrnaean bishops in VPol 2–3. For further discussion of VPol and the statements of Irenaeus about Polycarp, see ch. 5.

26. Lightfoot, *Apostolic Fathers* 2.3.424.

27. Cadoux, *Ancient Smyrna,* 307–308.

a fuller account of Polycarp's revelation to Pionius, for, according to the postscript of MPol: "I, Pionius, wrote from the aforementioned copy, after having made a search for it according to a revelation shown to me by the blessed Polycarp, just as I will explain in the sequel." As is argued persuasively by Dehandschutter, whether the author of VPol or anyone else in antiquity ever compiled a *Corpus Polycarpianum* cannot, at least given our present knowledge of extant literature, be known.[28]

Regardless of the identity of the Pionius in the postscript of MPol and, more generally, the Pionius associated with VPol and the *Corpus Polycarpianum,* it is important to consider the *Martyrdom of Pionius* (MPion) within ancient literature on Polycarp.[29] MPion records the trial and execution of Pionius of Smyrna, "teacher"[30] and "apostolic one,"[31] who was martyred under the emperor Decius. According to Robin Lane Fox, it was "ninety-five years" after Polycarp's execution[32] that Pionius, accompanied by a small circle of followers, "knew, one day before the anniversary of Polycarp's martyrdom,[33] that it was necessary that on that day[34] they would be seized" (MPion 2.2). Those responsible for MPion, perhaps including the martyr himself, were eager to associate Pionius and his death with Polycarp.

According to Dehandschutter, the compilers of MPion "certainly knew" MartPol.[35] Indeed, even among the vast body of early Christian martyrdoms and related works in which Polycarp is not named, there are several which indicate some reliance on MartPol, including, for example, the well-known *Martyrs of Lyons and Vienne,* and *Acts of Carpus, Papylus, and Agathonicé.*[36]

28. Dehandschutter, *Martyrium Polycarpi,* 66–67, 227.

29. For a recent treatment in favor of the martyr Pionius as the copyist identified in the MPol postscripts, see Robin Lane Fox, *Pagans and Christians* (San Francisco: Harper and Row, 1986) 472–473; for further discussion and bibliography, see n. 21 and n. 22 above.

30. MPion 19.6; see also 1.2, 4.7. In MPion 4.7 Pionius states, "and I am struggling not to change the things I first learned, and later taught"; cf. FrgPol (c) 11–16. For Polycarp as "teacher" see (d) 4–6 and ch. 4, comments on (c) 16–21 and (d) 4–6; also MPol 12.2 = HE 4.15.26 = Boh 68.15 and MPol 16.2 = HE 4.15.39 = Boh 70.29.

31. MPion 1.2. For Polycarp as "apostolic" see MPol 16.2 = HE 4.15.39 = Boh 70.29; see also below, comment on (e) 14–21, Obs. 3.

32. Fox, *Pagans and Christians,* 472; regarding the date of Polycarp's martyrdom, see above, n. 5.

33. Lit., "Polycarp's birthday."

34. Lit., "on this day"; however, the following sentence clarifies that it is the anniversary day, not the day preceding the anniversary, on which the foreknown arrest is to occur.

35. Dehandschutter, "The Martyrium Polycarpi: A Century of Research," 501.

36. For discussion and bibliography, see ibid., 501–502.

Polycarp is mentioned by Christian writers such as Irenaeus, Tertullian, and later, Jerome.[37] Chief among these is Irenaeus, a native of Smyrna, who claims to have heard Polycarp teach.[38] Irenaeus' comments have been influential in establishing the date of Polycarp's martyrdom[39] and in reconstructing Polycarp's early Christian influences and ecclesiastical training, including, of course, his relationship with John.[40]

Besides those writings discussed above, consideration of Polycarp is included in various synaxaria, menea, chronicles, histories, and other writings from the ancient period.[41]

3. The Harris Fragments: A Unique Work on Polycarp

In the Harris collection of Coptic literary fragments owned by the British Library are four papyrus leaves which contain a text, written in the Sahidic dialect of the Coptic language, about Polycarp, bishop of Smyrna. The fragments are catalogued as Or. 7561, nos. 55, 56, 63, 64. In their reconstructed state they provide six pages of text of which no one page is complete.

Modern Description of the Fragments on Polycarp

Early in this century the eminent Coptic scholar, Walter Ewing Crum, published a brief description of FrgPol. In comparing it to MartPol, he wrote: "This interesting text is wholly different in detail from the Greek Martyrdom (Letter of Smyrneans)."[42] More than fifty years later, in his *Catalogue of Coptic Literary Manuscripts in the British Library Acquired since the Year 1906,* Bentley Layton describes FrgPol as "a recension different than the Greek, different also than Balestri's Bohairic version."[43] Yet this important

37. Particular references are included in the text edition (ch. 1) in the register of parallels; see esp. (b) 6–8, (b) 8–10.

38. See AH 3.3.4 (= HE 4.14.3–7), AH 5.33.4 (= HE 3.39.1), the "Letter to Florinus" (HE 5.20.4–8), and the "Letter to Victor" (HE 5.24.11–17).

39. In his letter to Victor, bishop of Rome, Irenaeus discusses a trip by Polycarp to visit Anicetus, bishop of Rome, 154–155 CE; see recently Schoedel, "Polycarp, Martyrdom of," 393, who accepts the report without question, and Dehandschutter, *Martyrium Polycarpi,* 203–204, who discusses problems raised by Irenaeus' report.

40. For further discussion see ch. 4, esp. comments on (a) 11–12, (b) 6–8, 9, (c) 6–8, 11–15, and ch. 5.

41. See Lightfoot, *Apostolic Fathers* 2.1.552–577.

42. Walter Ewing Crum, *Monastery of Epiphanius at Thebes* (2 vols.; New York: Metropolitan Museum of Art, 1926) 1.205.

43. Bentley Layton, *Catalogue of Coptic Literary Manuscripts in the British Library Acquired since the Year 1906* (London: British Library, 1987) 201; see 201–203 for a general

work has remained virtually unknown to the scholarly community and, due to the lack of an edition, unavailable for general use and consideration.

So far as I can determine based on the written record, the literary fragments of the Harris collection were first described by Arthur Des Rivières in a letter to Mr. Harris dated 29 February 1848.[44] Though little is known about Mr. Des Rivières, it is certain that he copied and made French translations of several Coptic works while based in Cairo and/or Alexandria.[45] As a matter of fact, it is Des Rivières' transcripts which enabled ongoing scholarly consideration of various texts within the Harris collection even when the actual fragments of the collection were thought to be lost.[46]

In his letter about the texts within the Harris collection, Des Rivières grants FrgPol pride of place, after making the general statement that "many of these [fragments] are of great interest regarding the history of the Church."[47] His very identification of FrgPol as a work "on the martyrdom of Saint Polycarp, student of Saint John the evangelist" provides some indication of the distinctiveness of FrgPol, since nowhere in the familiar report of Polycarp's martyrdom, MartPol, is the Smyrnaean bishop associated with John.[48]

The Harris collection of Coptic fragments has been associated with some degree of intrigue, including its presumed loss following the bombardment of Alexandria in 1882. Several fragments which were earlier identified as part of the collection are still missing. It appears certain, based on written records, that none of the texts contained on the missing papyrus leaves is concerned with Polycarp.[49]

---

discussion of these fragments and the codex of which they are a part. The Bohairic version referred to is the same as that discussed above (Boh).

44. Published in *Bulletin de l'institut francais d'archéologie orientale* (*BIF*) 5 (1906) 88–91.

45. See Joseph Aumer and Karl Felix Halm, *Catalogus Codicum Manu Scriptorum Bibliothecae Regiae Monacensis III.4: Verzeichniss der orientalischen Handschriften der k. Hof- und Staatsbibliothek in München mit Ausschluss der hebräischen, arabischen und persischen* (Munich: Palm, 1875) 103; see also Layton, *Catalogue of Coptic Literary Manuscripts*, xxxiv, 225–226.

46. For discussion and bibliography see Layton, *Catalogue of Coptic Literary Manuscripts*, xxxiv; also Crum, "Coptic Texts Relating to Dioscorus of Alexandria," *Proceedings of the Society of Biblical Archaeology* 25 (1903) 267.

47. *BIF* 5 (1906) 89.

48. *BIF* 5 (1906) 89; for further discussion see ch. 4, esp. comments on (a) 11–12, (b) 6–8, 9, (c) 6–8, 11–15, (e) 14–21, and ch. 5.

49. For a survey of the modern history of the Harris collection, see Layton, *Catalogue of Coptic Literary Manuscripts*, xxxiii–xliv.

Ancient Production and Preservation of the Harris Fragments

The fragments of the Harris collection are from papyrus codices which were copied in the Sahidic dialect (Sah). As described by Layton, their contents comprise a range of literature: "biblical texts (from both testaments), a Biblical lectionary, and a number of edifying miscellanies containing Acts of Martyrs, lives and encomia of saints and holy persons (many Egyptian), homilies, moralizing epistles, etc."[50] The geographical source of the fragments is not known. Crum's chapter on "Literature" within his important work on the Egyptian monastery of Epiphanius contains the only sustained treatment of the question of the provenance of the collection.[51]

With the goal of describing as nearly as possible those works "read by Theban ascetics about the year 600,"[52] Crum's study centers on a unique find—an ancient catalogue written on an ostracon.[53] Using this catalogue, "actual remains" of literary works, and "chance references occurring in the texts," Crum develops a "combined list" of works available in monastery libraries in seventh-century Thebes.[54] FrgPol is included in that reconstructed list.[55]

Unfortunately, since the core of the reconstructed list is an ancient catalogue whose provenance is itself unknown,[56] the study's conclusions can be accepted only with caution. Nonetheless, until paleographers and codicologists can with confidence confirm, or seriously question, this projected list of works read by Theban ascetics about the year 600, it will provide ten-

50. Ibid., xxxiii.

51. Crum, *Monastery of Epiphanius* 1.196–208.

52. Ibid., 1.196.

53. U. Bouriant, "Notes de voyage, 1: Catalogue de la bibliotheque du couvent d'Amba Helias," *Recueil de travaux relatifs a la philologie et a l'archéologie égyptiennes et assyriennes* 11 (1889) 131–138.

54. Crum, *Monastery of Epiphanius* 1.196–206.

55. Ibid., 1.205.

56. The published report by U. Bouriant indicates that he obtained the ostracon catalogue in December 1888, "through a shopkeeper of Luxor . . . [who] assured me that he had purchased this ostracon from Gournah [at the site of ancient Thebes]." Bouriant goes on to speculate that the limestone fragment must have been brought to Gournah by an inhabitant of Kos (or, Qous) since "the ruins of Qous are extensive and for many years exploited by the Arabs with little impunity" (Bouriant, "Notes de voyage 1," 131).

Bouriant's incorrect translation of the Coptic phrase ⲧⲕⲁⲑⲉⲕⲏ ⲙ̅ⲡⲕⲱⲱⲥ as "The instruction (of the diocese) of Kos" ("Notes de Voyage 1," 134), doubtless led him to associate the catalogue with Kos (or, Qous). Crum, *Monastery of Epiphanius* 1.198 n. 6, recognized that ⲕⲱⲱⲥ is not a place name, but rather the Coptic word for "burial" or "funeral"; see also René-Georges Coquin, "Le catalogue de la bibliothéque du couvent de Saint Elie 'du Rocher,'" *BIF* 75 (1975) 207–239, esp. 207.

tative historical context to the occasion for the copying and maintenance of the fragments of the Harris collection.[57]

Original Location of the Work

The author, date, and provenance of this work on Polycarp are not known. Broadly set, the *termini* for the date of composition can be stated as follows: (1) the work must have been written before the seventh century, which is when the fragments in the Harris collection were, apparently, copied; (2) the work must have been written after the middle of the second century, following Polycarp's martyrdom. The original language of composition is unknown. Among the goals of this work are the consideration of several criteria which allow for some narrowing of these broadly stated *termini.* In my opinion, it is likely that this work was composed in Greek during or after the third century, within the Christian community at Smyrna.[58]

4. Goal and Scope of This Book

Without a critical edition of the Sahidic text on Polycarp found in the Harris fragments, this unique work cannot be studied effectively. The presentation of such a critical edition is found in chapter 1. Following a discussion of editorial method and the physical characteristics of the fragments, the text is edited in literary format. Two registers are included in the critical edition: (1) Parallels to other ancient literature, particularly in works associated with Polycarp or John;[59] (2) Text Critical Notes which make comments, as necessary, about the ink traces on, and physical characteristics of, the papyrus surface; also included here are possible restorations of missing text.[60]

---

57. Layton, *Catalogue of Coptic Literary Manuscripts,* xxiv: "The science of Coptic paleography and codicology is still in its infancy"; see also Layton's essays, "The Recovery of Gnosticism—The Philologist's Task in the Investigation of Nag Hammadi," *Second Century* 1 (1981) 85–99, and "Towards a New Coptic Paleography," *Acts of the Second International Congress of Coptic Study, Rome 22–26 September 1980* (ed. T. Orlandi and F. Wisse; Rome: CIM, 1985) 149–158, esp. 152.

58. For further discussion, see ch. 5.

59. Ancient works are, for the most part, cited in the (Greek, Latin, or Coptic) original; Syriac and Ethiopic texts are cited in English translation. The reader unacquainted with a given ancient language can follow up most references quite readily through published translations.

60. For further explanation of editorial method, including symbols used, see ch. 1.

Chapter 2 provides an English translation of the text. Along with the translation is included a register of Possible Restorations which make available to the English reader the textual restorations suggested within the Text Critical Notes. Those who do not know Coptic but are familiar with Greek and Latin may take almost full advantage of the register of parallels in chapter 1; simply locate the parallels for a given line or lines (the line references in the translation match those of the critical edition). Those who do not know the ancient languages may likewise locate the parallels for a given line or lines and then consult translations of the sources cited.

Chapter 3 is a short essay on the narrative strategy of FrgPol, including an outline of the work. It will orient the reader to the whole of FrgPol, to the degree that that can be known, before a sustained treatment of its parts is taken up in the Commentary. Of particular interest are the methods by which the ancient author depicts Polycarp and John, and the differences of the narrated action in FrgPol as compared to that of MartPol.

The Commentary in chapter 4 is arranged in a conventional format: a given lemma followed by a comment or a series of comments. This format allows for the examination of particular descriptions of Polycarp and John in light of other ancient literature, Christian and pagan, as well as archaeological data. Further, the variations between FrgPol and MartPol are discussed, with reference to both text traditions of MartPol.[61]

The final chapter provides the opportunity to pursue in detail certain central matters which have not received sustained consideration within the Commentary. The isolation of certain characteristics—the particular treatment of John, the particular treatment of Polycarp as a student of John, and the unique understanding of the necessity of Polycarp's martyrdom—provides the opportunity to locate a historical context for the authorship of this work.

FrgPol provides a unique witness to early Christian understandings of Polycarp, the apostle John, and more broadly, matters of apostolicity and martyrdom. The chapters in this book, beginning with the text edition and translation, are meant to build on each other in providing an informed introduction to, and understanding of, this unique work and the literary traditions which it engages.

All translations of ancient literature and of secondary literature in languages other than English are mine unless otherwise noted.[62]

61. Including Boh which, as noted above, is part of Eusebian text tradition.

62. All translations of FrgPol are identical with those provided in the translation in ch. 2; however, in the interest of readability, line breaks are not indicated elsewhere than in ch. 2.

CHAPTER ONE

Text Edition of the Harris Fragments on Polycarp

1. Introduction

The Sahidic text on Polycarp which is edited below is found on four papyrus fragments in the Harris collection of Coptic papyri in the British Library, London: Or.7561, nos. 55, 56, 63, and 64. The fragments have been reconstructed as three separate papyrus leaves in accordance with their presentation in Layton's *Catalogue of Coptic Literary Manuscripts in the British Library Acquired since the Year 1906.*[1] Each papyrus leaf exhibits text on both of its sides, making a total of six pages of text. For ease of reference, I have assigned each page of the reconstructed text a consecutive letter.

Physical Description of the Fragments

The measurements of the papyrus fragments recorded below were made by me at the British Library, Oriental and India Office Collections, in May 1992. Most of the other observations recorded herein were also made at that time. In addition, I have regularly consulted photographs of the frag-

1. Layton, *Catalogue of Coptic Literary Manuscripts*, 201–202, provides the following reconstruction of the order of the fragments: (63v), (63r), (64r + 56v), (64v + 56r), (55v), (55r). Of the significance of the identifications "recto" and "verso," Layton writes: "in the descriptions, the 'recto' of the papyrus (and other) fragments refers merely to the side with British Museum/Library label; this term has no relationship to the true recto side of the fragment as it was anciently found" (lix).

ments produced by the British Library in 1985 and graciously loaned to me by Bentley Layton.

The descriptions below regularly include such observations as "1 standard letter is lacking." A "standard letter" unit = a lacuna sufficient to suit 1 standard letter (ʜ being the standard) plus 1 interliteral space.

1. Page (a) = frag. 63v. 122 x 141 mm (maximum); written area, 117 x 116 mm (maximum); damaged fragment of a much larger manuscript leaf. 13 lines of text are extant; ? lines of text are lacking before the first extant line; ? lines of text are lacking after the last extant line. At the left margin, approx. 3–4 standard letters are lacking in each extant line; at the right margin, 3–5 standard letters are lacking in lines 1–3 and 12–13.

2. Page (b) = frag. 63r. Height and width are the same as page (a); written area is 120 x 122 mm (maximum). 13 lines of text are extant; ? lines of text are lacking before the first extant line; ? lines of text are lacking after the last extant line. At the left margin, 3–5 standard letters are lacking in lines 1–3 and line 13 (traces of the bottoms of letters are visible at line 4; traces of the tops of letters are visible at line 12); at the right margin, approx. 6 standard letters are lacking in each extant line.

3. Page (c) = frags. 64r + 56v. The manuscript leaf of which this page represents one side, is reconstructed from two separately labeled fragments. 24 lines of text are extant, including the last line of the page; ? lines of text are lacking before the first extant line.

For the first 10 lines, page (c) = 64r. 91 x 92 mm (maximum); written area is 89 x 84 mm (maximum). At the left margin, 4 standard letters are lacking in each extant line; at the right margin, 3 standard letters.

For lines 11–24, page (c) = 56v. 179 x 183 mm (maximum); written area, 135 x 150 mm (maximum). At the left margin, 1 standard letter is lacking in lines 11–16, traces of the first letter of the line are visible in lines 17–19; for the last 5 lines the text is complete; at the right margin the text is complete. In the middle of the manuscript page a piece is torn away leaving a fraying hole, affecting lines 19–24.

4. Page (d) = frags. 64v + 56r. This page is the reverse side of the same reconstructed manuscript leaf of which page (c) is a part. 24 lines of text are extant, including last line on page; ? lines of text are lacking before the first extant line.

For the first 10 lines, page (d) = 64v. Height and width are same as the first 10 lines of page (c), 64r; written area, 90 x 84 mm (maximum). At the left margin, approx. 3 standard letters are lacking in each extant line; at the right margin, approx. 4 standard letters.

For lines 11–24, page (d) = 56r. Height and width are the same as lines 11–24 of page (c), 56v; written area, 139 x 148 mm (maximum). At the left margin the text is complete; at the right margin, 1–2 standard letters are lacking in lines 11–18; for lines 19–24 the text is complete. In the middle of the manuscript page a piece is torn away leaving a fraying hole, affecting lines 19–24.

5. Page (e) = frag. 55v. This is the best-preserved single manuscript leaf, 226 x 200 mm (maximum); written area, 190 x 157 mm (maximum). 21 lines of text are extant, including the first line on page; ? lines of text are lacking after the last extant line. Parts of the top of the manuscript leaf are broken off with attendant fraying: at the left margin, 1 standard letter is lacking in line 1 and ambiguous traces of two standard letters are visible in line 2; at the right margin, 1–2 standard letters are lacking in lines 1–3. Also, the bottom of the papyrus leaf is broken and frayed: at the left margin, 2 standard letters are lacking in lines 18–20; the final extant line of text is badly damaged.

6. Page (f) = frag. 55r. Height and width are the same as page (e); written area, 191 x 158 mm (maximum). 21 lines of text are extant, including the first line of the page; ? lines of text are lacking after the last extant line. Parts of the top of the manuscript leaf are broken off with attendant fraying: at the left margin, 2 standard letters are lacking in line 1, and 1 standard letter in lines 2–3; at the right margin, 1 standard letter is lacking, and ambiguous traces of another are visible, in lines 1–2. Also, the bottom of the papyrus leaf is broken and frayed: at the right margin, 2 standard letters are lacking in lines 18–20; the final extant line of text is badly damaged.

Sigla

A. Editorial Signs

[ ]	lacuna in manuscript
[---]	lacuna of unspecified length
[.]	lacuna long enough to suit 1 standard letter (H being the standard) and 1 interliteral space; [..], 2 letters and 2 interliteral spaces, etc., up to 5
[^{6}]	lacuna long enough to suit 6 standard letters and 6 interliteral spaces; [^{7}], 7 letters and 7 interliteral spaces, etc.
	unidentified letter trace

ạ	paleographically ambiguous letter trace
*	raised point in manuscript
ʻ	hook or apostrophe in manuscript
,	dot on line in manuscript
| or ||	new line of manuscript commences (|| every 5th line)
-	Hyphenation added by the modern editor
v	*vacat;* blank space sufficient for 1 standard letter (ʜ) and 1 interliteral space; ^{2v} space for 2 letters and 2 interliteral spaces, etc.

B. Abbreviations

Gk	Greek (language)
pap.	the reading of the papyrus; text of the manuscript
poss.	possibly
Sah	Sahidic (dialect of the Coptic language)
sc.	*scilicet,* namely
superlin.	superlinear stroke
UV	ultraviolet

Format

Following the presentation of each page of text are two registers.

The register of Parallels identifies particular phrases and units of narrated action found in FrgPol and other ancient literature. The words and phrases which most directly parallel the text of FrgPol are underlined for easy identification. For further discussion of particular phrases and units of narrated actions, see chapter 4. For comparison of the narrative structure of FrgPol with that of MartPol, see chapter 3.

The Text Critical Notes include paleographical notes about the state of the manuscript, as well as possible restorations. Only restorations which meet criteria of physical size[2] and grammatical and syntactical compatibility are registered.

2. The proposed restoration must fit the given lacuna. [N.B. The number of letters in the proposed restoration may exceed the number of standard letter units for a given lacuna due to one or both of the following factors: in this manuscript, certain letters consistently occupy less space than the standard letter unit (e.g., ï and o); letters at the end of a line are sometimes crowded (this affects the restoration of lacunas at the ends of lines).]

2. The Fragments

(a) = 63v

[one or more lines lacking; possibly 2 or more pages precede]
[8]ⲧⲉⲣ[....] | [....]ⲥ̣ ⲙ̄ⲡⲉⲛϫⲟⲉ̣ⲓ[ⲥ...]|
[....].ϣⲉ ⲉⲃⲟⲗ ϩ̄ⲛ̄.[....]|

[...].ⲃⲱⲕ ⲉⲃⲟⲗ ϩ̄ⲛ̄ⲧⲟⲓⲕⲟⲩ || [ⲙⲉⲛ]ⲏ̣ ⲧⲏⲣⲥ̄,

ⲉⲧⲣⲉⲡⲟⲩⲁ ⲡⲟⲩ | [ⲁ ⲙ̄ⲙ]ⲟⲟⲩ ϫⲱⲕ ⲉⲃⲟⲗ ⲙ̄ⲡⲉϥ|[ⲇⲣⲟ]ⲙⲟⲥ ϩ̄ⲛ̄ⲛ̄ⲧⲟϣ‘
ⲉⲛⲧⲁⲩ|[ⲧⲟϣ]ⲟⲩ ⲉⲣⲟⲟⲩ*

ⲉⲁⲩϫⲱⲕ| [ⲉⲃⲟⲗ] ⲙ̄ⲡⲧⲁϣⲉⲟⲉⲓϣ ⲛ̄||[ⲧⲙ̄ⲛ̄]ⲧ̄ⲉⲣⲟ̣ ⲛ̄ⲙ̄[ⲡ]ⲏ̣ⲩⲉ
ⲉⲧϩ̄ⲙ̄|[ⲡⲉⲓ̈ⲥ]ⲱ̣ⲛ̄ⲧ̄ ⲧⲏⲣ̄ϥ̄ ⲕⲁⲧⲁⲧⲙⲁⲣ|[ⲧⲩⲣⲓ]ⲁ
ⲙ̄ⲡⲁⲡⲟⲥⲧⲟⲗⲟⲥ̣[..]|

[.....]ⲉⲁⲩϫⲟⲛⲧⲟ̣[..][.][..]|

[one or more lines lacking]

PARALLELS

1–8 ---]ⲧⲉⲣ[to [ⲧⲟϣ]ⲟⲩ ⲉⲣⲟⲟⲩ
---]ter[to [assigned] to them:

Matt 24:14 καὶ κηρυχθήσεται τοῦτο τὸ εὐαγγέλιον τῆς βασιλείας ἐν ὅλῃ τῇ οἰκουμένῃ εἰς μαρτύριον πᾶσιν τοῖς ἔθνεσιν, καὶ τότε ἥξει τὸ τέλος.
Matt 28:19 πορευθέντες οὖν μαθητεύσατε πάντα τὰ ἔθνη . . .
Mark 16:15 καὶ εἶπεν αὐτοῖς (sc. "the eleven") πορευθέντες εἰς τὸν κόσμον ἅπαντα κηρύξατε τὸ εὐαγγέλιον πάσῃ τῇ κτίσει
Luke 24:47 καὶ κηρυχθῆναι ἐπὶ τῷ ὀνόματι αὐτοῦ μετάνοιαν εἰς ἄφεσιν ἁμαρτῶν εἰς πάντα τὰ ἔθνη ἀρξάμενοι ἀπὸ Ἰερουσαλὴμ. ὑμεῖς (sc. "the eleven . . . and those who were with them") μάρτυρες τούτων.
John 17:18 καθὼς ἐμὲ (sc. "Jesus") ἀπέστειλας εἰς τὸν κόσμον κἀγὼ ἀπέστειλα αὐτοὺς (sc. "his disciples") εἰς τὸν κόσμον

1 Clem. 42.1–4 οἱ ἀπόστολοι . . . κατὰ χώρας οὖν καὶ πόλεις κηρύσσοντες καθίσταναν τὰς ἀπαρχὰς αὐτῶν

Kerygma Petri 3a[3] (Clement of Alexandria, *Strom.* VI.5.43) Διὰ τοῦτό φησιν ὁ Πέτρος εἰρηκέναι τὸν κύριον τοῖς ἀποστόλοις . . . μετὰ (δὲ) δώδεκα ἔτη ἐξέλθετε εἰς τὸν κόσμον . . .

Kerygma Petri 3b (Clement of Alexandria, *Strom.* VI.6.48) καὶ ἀποστόλους πιστους ἡγησάμενος εἶναι πέμπω ἐπὶ τὸν κόσμον εὐαγγελίσασθαι τοὺς κατὰ τὴν οἰκουμένην ἀνθρώπους . . .

Epistula Apostolorum 30[4] Go (ⲃⲱⲕ) you and preach to the twelve tribes and preach also to the gentiles . . .

Acts of Thomas 1.1[5] καὶ διείλαμεν (sc. "we apostles") τὰ κλίματα τῆς οἰκουμένης, ὅπως εἷς ἕκαστος ἡμῶν ἐν τῷ κλίματι τῷ λαχόντι αὐτῷ καὶ εἰς τὸ ἔθνος ἐν ᾧ ὁ κύριος αὐτὸν ἀπέστειλεν πορευθῇ

Syriac History of John[6] When these words had been spoken among the blessed assembly of the Apostleship, they parted from one another

3. Chapter numbers as found in Wilhelm Schneemelcher, "The Kerygma Petri," in *New Testament Apocrypha,* vol. 2, *Writings Relating to the Apostles, Apocalypses, and Related Subjects* (ed. Wilhelm Schneemelcher; tr. R. McL. Wilson; Louisville: Westminster/John Knox, 1992) 34–41.

4. Tr. and chapter divisions, C. Detlef G. Müller, "Epistula Apostolorum," in *New Testament Apocrypha,* vol. 1, *Gospels and Related Writings* (ed. Wilhelm Schneemelcher; tr. R. McL. Wilson; Louisville: Westminster/John Knox, 1991) 249–284, 267.

5. For departure statements in other apocryphal acts, see Jean-Daniel Kaestli, "Les scènes d'attribution des champs de mission et de départ de l'apôtres (Eusèbe, HE III,1, 1–3)," *Les actes apocryphes des apôtres: Christianisme et monde païen* (Francois Bovon, et al.; Publications de la Faculté de Théologie de l'Université de Genève 4; Geneva: Labor et Fides, 1981) 249–264, esp. 252–259. Not included therein are: *Acts of Peter and the Twelve* VI,1 5.12–14, "It is necessary for us to spread the word of God in every city harmoniously" (tr. Douglas M. Parrott and R. McL. Wilson, "The Acts of Peter and the Twelve Apostles [VI,1]," in James M. Robinson, ed., *The Nag Hammadi Library in English* [3rd ed.; San Francisco: Harper and Row, 1988] 287–294, 291); and, *The Letter of Peter to Philip*, "Then, when the apostles had come together (133.17–19) . . . the apostles answered and said . . . : 'How did we come to this place?' And: 'In what manner shall we depart [ⲃⲱⲕ]?' (134.18–26). . . . Then the apostles parted from each other" (140.23–24; tr. Frederik Wisse, "The Letter of Peter to Philip [VIII,2]," in Robinson, *The Nag Hammadi Library in English,* 431–437). For the Coptic text of *The Letter of Peter to Philip,* see Frederik Wisse, ed. and tr., "NHC VIII,2: *Letter of Peter to Philip,*" in John H. Sieber, ed., *Nag Hammadi Codex VIII* (NHS, no. 31; Leiden: E. J. Brill, 1991) 234–251. For another occurrence of "depart" (ⲃⲱⲕ) in *The Letter of Peter to Philip,* see 140.19.

6. Tr. W. Wright, "The History of John, the Son of Zebedee, The Apostle and Evangelist," *Apocryphal Acts of the Apostles* (London: Williams and Norgate, 1871) 2.2–60, 4–5; for Syriac text, see 1.4–65, 5.

The *Syriac History of John* is posterior to the *Acts of John* (AJn); perhaps fourth century. For discussion, see Eric Junod and Jean-Daniel Kaestli, *Acta Iohannis* (Corpus Christianorum, in the body . . . Each of them then went to such country and region as he was charged by the grace (of God).

HE 3.1.1 τῶν δὲ ἱερῶν τοῦ σωτῆρος ἡμῶν ἀποστόλων τε καὶ μαθητῶν ἐφ᾽ ἅπασαν κατασπαρέντων τὴν οἰκουμένην

Eusebius, *Commentary on the Psalms*[7] οἵ τοῦ σωτῆρος ἡμῶν μαθηταὶ καὶ ἀπόστολοι, καὶ εὐαγγελισταί, ἥ τε λοιπὴ αὐτοῦ στρατεία . . . κτῆμα ἴδιον ποιησάμενοι,διενειμαντο εἰς ἀλλήλους. . . . [τῶν . . . ἀποστόλων ἕκαστος] τὰ ἐξ ἐθνῶν ἐκληροῦτο σκύλα.

Didascalia Apostolorum 23[8] Cum autem diuidissemus inter nos duodecim uncias saeculi et exiuimus ad gentes ut in omni mundo praedicaremus verbum

8–11 ⲉⲁⲩϫⲱⲕ| [ⲉⲃⲟⲗ] to ⲡⲉⲓ̈ⲥ]ⲱ̣ⲛ̄ⲧ ⲧⲏⲣ̄ϥ
while they com| [pleted] to the whole of [this cr]eation:

Matt 24:14 καὶ κηρυχθήσεται τοῦτο τὸ εὐαγγέλιον τῆς βασιλείας ἐν ὅλῃ τῇ οἰκουμένῃ εἰς μαρτύριον πᾶσιν τοῖς ἔθνεσιν, καὶ τότε ἥξει τὸ τέλος.

Mark 16:15 καὶ εἶπεν αὐτοῖς (sc. "the eleven") πορευθέντες εἰς τὸν κόσμον ἅπαντα κηρύξατε τὸ εὐαγγέλιον πάσῃ τῇ κτίσει.

Luke 9:2 καὶ ἀπέστειλεν αὐτοὺς κηρύσσειν τὴν βασιλείαν τοῦ θεοῦ καὶ ἰᾶσθαι . . .

Luke 24:47 καὶ κηρυχθῆναι ἐπὶ τῷ ὀνόματι αὐτοῦ μετάνοιαν εἰς ἄφεσιν ἁμαρτιῶν εἰς πάντα τὰ ἔθνη ἀρξάμενοι ἀπὸ Ἰερουσαλὴμ. ὑμεῖς (sc. "the eleven . . . and those who were with them") μάρτυρες τούτων.

1 Clem. 42.1–3 οἱ ἀπόστολοι . . . εὐαγγελιζόμενοι τὴν βασιλείαν τοῦ θεοῦ μέλλειν ἔρχεσθαι

AH 4.34.5 suos Apostolos misit [Salvator] in mundum, pure adventum ejus annuntiantes

---

Series Apocryphorum 1–2; Turnhout: Brepols, 1983) 2.707–717; Knut Schäferdiek, "Acts of John," in Schneemelcher, *New Testament Apocrypha*, vol. 2, *Writings Relating to the Apostles*, 161; and Wright, *Apocryphal Acts of the Apostles* 1.ix.

7. *PG* 697c. The "apostles" named in this section are (in order) Paul, Peter, and John.

8. For a second reference in *Didascalia Apostolorum* to the assigning of territories, see ch. 25; for the Syriac version, see Arthur Vööbus, *The Didascalia Apostolorum in Syriac, II: Chapters XI–XXVI* (CSCO 407, Scriptores Syri 179; Louvain: CSCO, 1979) 229; for ch. 25, 240.

Epistula Apostolorum 19[9] and preach concerning the (heavenly) kingdom of my Father[10]

Epistula Apostolorum 42[11] for you have revealed to them . . . the things of the Kingdom of heaven (ⲛ̄ⲧⲙⲛ̄ⲧⲣ̄ⲣⲟ ⲛ̄ⲛ̄ⲡⲏⲩⲉ)

HE 3.24.3 τῆς τῶν οὐρανῶν βασιλείας τὴν γνῶσιν ἐπὶ πᾶσαν κατήγγελλον τὴν οἰκουμένην

For similar descriptions of the preaching of particular apostles, see also Acts 8:12, 19:8, 20:25, 28:23, 28:31, as well as the non-canonical acts.

TEXT CRITICAL NOTES

1–2]ⲧⲉⲣ[....]|[....]ⲥ̣: for ⲥ̣ can also be read ⲉ̣ or ⲟ̣ (bottom right curve plus vertical tail); for similarly shaped omicrons, see (a) 6, (f) 8

poss. ⲛ̄]ⲧⲉⲣ[ⲉⲛⲁⲡⲟ]|[ⲥⲧⲟⲗⲟ]ⲥ̣ for pl. subject see (a) 5, ⲡⲟⲩⲁ ⲡⲟⲩⲁ; for ⲛⲁⲡⲟⲥⲧⲟⲗⲟⲥ see (b) 12; for ⲁⲡⲟⲥⲧⲟⲗⲟⲥ ⲙ̄ⲡϫⲟⲉⲓⲥ see (e)15

2 ⲙ̄ⲡⲉⲛϫⲟⲉⲓ[ⲥ...]: poss. ⲙ̄ⲡⲉⲛϫⲟⲉⲓ[ⲥ ⲥⲟⲟⲩϩ], see Acts 10:27, 15:6; *The Mysteries of St. John and the Holy Virgin* (in E. A. Wallis Budge, *Coptic Texts* [5 vols; 1910–1915; New York: AMS, 1977] vol. 3, 59), ⲁϥⲧⲣⲉⲟⲩⲕⲗⲟⲟⲗⲉ ⲕⲱⲧⲉ ⲉⲛⲉⲭⲱⲣⲁ ⲧⲏⲣⲟⲩ ⲉⲧⲉⲣⲉⲛⲁⲡⲟⲥⲧⲟⲗⲟⲥ ⲛ̄ϩⲏⲧⲟⲩ ⲁⲥⲥⲟⲟⲩϩⲟⲩ ⲉϩⲟⲩⲛ; *The Letter of Peter to Philip* 140.13, ⲁⲩⲱ ⲁⲩⲥⲱⲟⲩϩ ϣⲁⲛⲉ[ⲩ]ⲉⲣⲏⲩ (sc. "Peter and the other apostles"); also *Acts of Andrew and Matthias* 1 πάντες οἱ ἀπόστολοι ἐπὶ τὸ αὐτὸ συναχθέντες καὶ ἐμέριζον ἑαυτοῖς τὰς χώρας

reading of lacuna poss. ends with a dot on line (,); see (b) 12, (d) 21, (f) 3, 8

3 [....].ϣⲉ: poss. [ⲁⲩⲙⲟ]ⲟ̣ϣⲉ

ϩⲛ̄.[....]: for letter trace can be read ⲑ̣, ⲛ̣, or ⲙ̣ (top left horizontal stroke); for ⲑ of this shape see (b) 13

poss. ϩⲛ̄ⲑ̣[ⲓⲗⲏ̄ⲙ], see Luke 24:47

9. This section extant only in Ethiopic.

10. Tr. Müller, "Epistula Apostolorum," 259. Two of the five extant manuscript witnesses to the Ethiopic version contain "heavenly"; Carl Schmidt, ed., *Gespräche Jesu mit Seinen Jüngern nach der Auferstehung: Ein katholisch-apostolisches Sendschreiben des 2. Jahrhunderts* (TU 43; Leipzig: J. C. Hinrichs, 1919) 62.

"The kingdom of the father" is used in *Gos. Thom.* 113 as a synonym for the "the kingdom of heaven" or "the kingdom of God."

11. Tr. Müller, "Epistula Apostolorum," 273.

reading of lacuna poss. ends with a raised point(*)

4 [...].ⲃⲱⲕ: poss. [ⲁⲩⲱ ⲁ]ⲩⲃⲱⲕ; more than three (less than four) standard letters fit in lacuna

10 ⲙⲛ̄]ⲧ̄ⲉⲣⲟ̣: superlin. above ⲧ not extant due to tear in papyrus leaf; for ⲟ̣ can be read ⲉ̣, ⲑ̣, or ⲥ̣

11 [ⲡⲉϊⲥ]ⲱ̣ⲛ̄ⲧ: for ⲱ̣ can be read ⲟ̣ or ϣ̣; for ⲥⲱⲛ̄ⲧ, see Mark 16:15b Sah, ⲛ̄ⲧⲉⲧⲛ̄ⲧⲁϣⲉⲟⲉⲓϣ ⲙ̄ⲡⲉⲩⲁⲅⲅⲉⲗⲓⲟⲛ ⲙ̄ⲡⲥⲱⲛⲧ̄ ⲧⲏⲣϥ̄; for the demonstrative article ⲡⲉϊ, see Ps 73:18 Sah, ⲁⲣⲓⲡⲙⲉⲉⲩⲉ ⲙ̄ⲡⲉϊⲥⲱⲛⲧ̄ ⲛ̄ⲧⲁⲕ

12 ⲙ̄ⲡⲁⲡⲟⲥⲧⲟⲗⲟⲥ̣: for ⲥ̣ can be read ⲟ̣ or ⲑ̣; trace of top of letter remains; surface layer of papyrus fibers broken off at left border of letter trace

13 ⲭⲟⲛⲧⲟ̣: for ⲟ̣ can also be read ⲉ̣, ⲑ̣, or ⲥ̣ (top left curve of letter extant)

Superlin. visible three standard letter spaces from end of line

(b) = 63r

[one or more lines lacking]

[^{5}]ϩⲛ̄[^{12}]| [...]ⲕ̣ⲟⲛ ⲛ̄ⲧⲡⲁⲣⲑ̣[ⲉⲛⲓⲁ...]|[....]ⲉ ⲛⲁϥ ⲉⲡⲙⲁ̣[ⲛ̄.....]|[.].ⲛ̣̄ⲧⲥⲏϥⲉ ⲙ̄ⲛ̄ⲛ[^{6}]|| ⲙ̄ⲛ̄ⲛ̄ⲃⲁⲥⲁⲛⲟⲥ ⲛ̄-ⲛ̄ⲇ̣[ⲓⲕⲁⲥⲧⲏ]|ⲣⲓⲟⲛ $^{*1/2\ v}$

ⲁϥϣⲱϫ̄ⲡ ⲇⲉ̣ [...]|ⲥⲱϥ ⲛ̄ⲟⲩⲙⲁⲑⲏⲧⲏ[ⲥ....]| ⲣⲁⲛ ⲡⲉ ⲡⲟⲗⲩⲕⲁⲣⲡ[ⲟⲥ ⲁⲩⲱ]| ⲁϥⲁⲁϥ ⲛ̄ⲉⲡⲓⲥⲕⲟⲡ[ⲟⲥ ⲉϫⲛ̄]||ⲥⲙⲩⲣⲛⲁ ⲧⲡⲟⲗⲓⲥ..[....]|

ⲛ̄ⲧⲉⲣⲟⲩⲛ̄ⲕⲟⲧ̄ⲕ ⲇⲉ ⲧ[ⲏⲣⲟⲩ]| ⲛ̣̄ϭⲓⲛⲁⲡⲟⲥⲧⲟⲗⲟⲥ, ⲁ[....]|[...]ⲕⲉⲙⲁⲑⲏⲧⲏⲥ ⲉⲙ̣[....]|

[one or more lines lacking; possibly 2 or more pages lacking before (c)]

PARALLELS

6–8a ⲁϥϣⲱϫ̄ⲡ to ⲡⲟⲗⲩⲕⲁⲣⲡ[ⲟⲥ
There remained to Polycar[p:

Boh 62.10–12 ⲫⲁⲓ (sc. Polycarp) ⲉⲧⲁϥϣⲱⲡⲓ ⲙ̄ⲙⲁⲑⲏⲧⲏⲥ ⲛ̄ⲛⲓⲁ̄ⲡⲟⲥⲧⲟⲗⲟⲥ ⲉⲁϥⲙⲟϣⲓ ⲛⲉⲙⲟⲩⲙⲏϣ ⲉⲧⲁⲩⲛⲁⲩ ⲉ̄ⲡϭ̄ⲥ̄

HE 3.36.1 Διέπρεπέν γε μὴν κατὰ τούτους ἐπὶ τῆς Ἀσίας τῶν ἀποστόλων ὁμιλητὴς Πολύκαρπος

HE 4.14.3 = AH 3.3.4 καὶ Πολύκαρπος δὲ οὐ μόνον ὑπὸ ἀποστόλων μαθητευθεὶς καὶ συναναστραφεὶς πολλοῖς τοῖς τὸν κύριον ἑορακόσιν

HE 5.20.6 (Irenaeus, "Letter to Florinus") καὶ τὴν μετὰ Ἰωάννου συναναστροφὴν ὡς ἀπήγγελλεν (sc. Polycarp) καὶ τὴν μετὰ τῶν λοιπῶν τῶν ἑορακότων τὸν κύριον

HE 5.24.16 μετὰ Ἰωάννου τοῦ μαθητοῦ τοῦ κυρίου ἡμῶν καὶ τῶν λοιπῶν ἀποστόλων οἷς (ὁ Πολύκαρπος) συνδιέτριψεν

Vir 17 Joannis apostoli discipulus . . . qui nonnullos apostolorum, et eorum qui viderant Dominum, magistros habuerit et viderit (sc. Polycarp)

ActsIg 3 μαθηταὶ Ἰωάννου (sc. Ignatius and Polycarp)

Acts of John by Prochorus 188.9–12[12] ὁ ἀπόστολος τοῦ χριστοῦ (ὁ Ἰωάννης) . . . καταλιπὼν ἐκεῖσε πρόεδρον Βούκολον καὶ Πολύκαρπον, τοὺς αὐτοῦ μαθητάς . . .

8–10 ⲁⲩⲱ]| ⲁϥⲁⲁϥ to ⲧⲡⲟⲗⲓⲥ..[....]
and] he made him to the [---] city:

Boh 62.12–13 ⲫⲁⲓ ⲉⲧⲁⲩⲧϩⲉⲙⲥⲟϥ ⲛⲉⲡⲓⲥⲕⲟⲡⲟⲥ ϩⲉⲛ ϯⲁ̅ⲥⲓⲁ̅ ⲉ̅ⲭⲉⲛϯⲉⲕⲕⲗⲏⲥⲓⲁ ⲉⲧϩⲉⲛ ⲥⲙⲩⲣⲛⲁ; see also Boh 62.10–12 above

Tertullian, *On the Prescription against the Heretics,* 32.2 Hoc enim modo ecclesiae apostolicae census suos deferunt, sicut Smyrnaeorum ecclesiae Polycarpum ab Iohanne collocatum refert

HE 3.36.1 τῆς κατὰ Σμύρναν ἐκκλησίας πρὸς τῶν αὐτοπτῶν καὶ ὑπηρετῶν τοῦ κυρίου τὴν ἐπισκοπὴν ἐγκεχειρισμένος

HE 4.14.3 = AH 3.3.4 καὶ ὑπό ἀποστόλων κατασταθεὶς εἰς τὴν Ἀσίαν ἐν τῇ ἐν Σμύρνῃ ἐκκλησίᾳ ἐπίσκοπος

Vir 17 ab eo (Ioanno) Smyrnae episcopus ordinatus

VPol 23 οἱ οὖ διάκονοι προσήγαγον πρὸς τὴν διὰ τῶν χειρῶν τῶν ἐπισκόπων κατὰ τὸ ἔθος γινομένην χειροθεσίαν

Acts of John in Rome 14[13] ὁ Ἰωάννης . . . γενόμενος δὲ γηραλέος καὶ μεταλλάσσων ἐπισκοπεύειν τὴν ἐκκλησίαν τῷ Πολυκάρπῳ ἐνεκελεύσατο

11–13 ⲛ̅ⲧⲉⲣⲟⲩⲛ̅ⲕⲟⲧ̅ⲕ̅ ⲇⲉ ⲧ[ⲏⲣⲟⲩ]| ⲛ̣ϭⲓⲛⲁⲡⲟⲥⲧⲟⲗⲟⲥ to ⲕⲉⲙⲁⲑⲏⲧⲏⲥ
After a[ll] the apostles had died to other disciple[s]:

Vir 19 Quadratus apostolorum discipulus

See also above parallels to (b) 6–8, 8–10, esp. *Acts of John by Prochorus* 188.9–12, Vir 17, and *Acts of John in Rome* 14.

---

12. A fifth-century (or later) work; for further discussion see esp. Junod and Kaestli, *Acta Iohannis,* 7–8, 147, 748. References to the Greek text are to page and line in Theodor Zahn, ed., *Acta Joannis* (Erlangen: Andreas Deichert, 1880) 3–165.

13. *Acts of John in Rome* is dated to the "post-Constantinian" era by Junod and Kaestli, *Acta Iohannis,* 857–860, who argue for its dependence on the third book of HE.

TEXT CRITICAL NOTES

1 extended superlin. above ϩⲛ not extant due to broken papyrus leaf

2]ⲕ̣ⲟⲛ: for ⲕ̣ can be read ⲁ̣ or ⲗ̣

ⲡⲁⲣⲑ̣[: for ⲑ̣ can be read ⲉ̣, ⲟ̣, or ⲥ̣

3 ⲙⲁ̣: ⲁ̣ read from small, ambiguous trace

4 superlin. above ⲛ̣ not visible due to broken papyrus leaf

5 ⲛ̄ⲛ̄ⲇ̣[: misplaced papyrus flake is partially covering the letter trace

ⲇ̣[ⲓⲕⲁⲥⲧⲏ]|ⲣⲓⲟⲛ: for ⲛ̄ⲃⲁⲥⲁⲛⲟⲥ ⲙ̄ⲡⲇⲓⲕⲁⲥⲧⲏⲣⲓⲟⲛ see the *Martyrdom of St. Coluthus,* 89r1; for ⲇⲓⲕⲁⲥⲧⲏⲣⲓⲟⲛ see (e) 9, 13, 19

6 ⲇⲉ̣: misplaced papyrus flake is partially covering the letter trace

6–7 [...]|ⲥⲱϥ: poss. [ⲙ̄ⲛ̄ⲛ̄]|ⲥⲱϥ

7–8 ....]|ⲣⲁⲛ: poss. ⲉⲡⲉϥ]|ⲣⲁⲛ

9 ⲉϫⲛ̄]: see Boh 62.12–13 (in register of parallels, above), ⲉ̄ϫⲉⲛ

10 ⲡⲟⲗⲓⲥ..[: poss. read ⲡⲟⲗⲓⲥ[.].[; ambiguous traces (the bottom of a vertical stroke, a curve below the line)

11 superlin. above ⲛ^2 not visible due to tear in papyrus leaf.

12 ⲛ̣̄ϭⲓ: ⲛ̣̄ read from small, ambiguous traces

12–13 ⲁ[....]|[...]: poss. ⲁ[ⲩϭⲱ ⲛ̄]|[ϭⲓⲛ̄]ⲕⲉⲙⲁⲑⲏⲧⲏⲥ

(c) = 64r + 56v

[one or more lines lacking; possibly 2 or more pages lacking after (b)]

[6].ⲛ̄ⲥ̣ⲁⲡⲉϥⲟ̣[..]|[...ⲛⲉ]ⲥ̣ⲛⲏⲩ ⲧⲏⲣⲟⲩ*v

[..]|[...ⲉⲓ]ⲣⲉ ⲛ̄ϩⲉⲛϣⲗⲏⲗ.[..]|[....].ⲙⲟⲩⲛ ⲉⲃⲟⲗ ⲛ̄[...]||
[....]ⲉⲓϣ*1/2v ⲉⲃⲟⲗ ϫⲉⲛ̣̄[...]| [....]ⲁϥϣⲱϫ̄ⲡ̄ ⲙⲁⲩⲁ̣[ⲁϥ
ⲛ̄]|[ⲙ̄ⲙⲁ]ⲑ̣ⲏⲧⲏⲥ ⲛ̄ⲛⲁⲡⲟⲥ̣[ⲧⲟ]|[ⲗⲟⲥ*1/2v]

ⲛⲉϥϣⲟⲟⲡ ⲇⲉ ⲛ̄[...]|[ⲛ̄ⲧⲉ]ⲕⲕⲗⲏⲥⲓⲁ ⲧⲏⲣ̄ⲥ̄
[...]|| [..ⲩ]ϩ̣̄ⲗ̄ⲗⲟ ⲡⲉ ⲉϥϩ̄ⲛ̄ⲁϣⲉ̣ϥ̣[ⲧⲟ]| [ⲛ̄]ⲣⲟⲙⲡ̣ⲉ*1/2v

ⲛⲉϥⲙⲟⲟϣⲉ ⲇⲉ [ϩ̄]ⲛ̄ⲛ̄ⲕⲁⲛⲱⲛ ⲉⲛⲧⲁϥⲧⲥⲁⲃⲟ| [ⲉ]ⲣⲟⲟⲩ
ϫⲓⲛⲧⲉϥⲙ̄ⲛ̄ⲧ̄ⲕⲟⲩⲓ̈| [ⲉ]ⲃⲟⲗ ϩⲓⲧ̄ⲛ̄ⲓ̈ⲱϩⲁⲛⲛⲏⲥ ⲡⲁ||[ⲡ]ⲟⲥⲧⲟⲗⲟⲥ,

ϣⲁⲛⲧ̄ϥ̄ⲡⲱϩ| [ⲉ]ⲧⲉⲓ̈ϩⲏⲗⲓⲕⲓⲁ ⲛ̄ⲧⲉⲓ̈ϭⲟⲧ*

ⲁⲩⲱ| ⲛ̣ⲉⲩϣⲓⲛⲉ ⲛ̄ⲥⲱϥ

ⲉⲛⲁⲩ ⲉⲣⲟϥ| ⲛ̄ϭⲓⲛⲉⲭⲣⲓⲥⲧⲓⲁⲛⲟⲥ ⲧⲏⲣⲟⲩ|
ⲉⲛⲧⲁⲩⲥⲱⲧ̄ⲙ̄ ⲉ̣ⲡⲉϥⲃⲓⲟⲥ,
ⲛ̄||ⲑⲉ ⲛ̄ϩⲉⲛϣⲏⲣⲉ ⲛ̄ⲅⲛⲏⲥⲓⲟⲥ|
ⲉⲩϣⲓⲛⲉ ⲛ̄ⲥⲁⲡ[ⲉ]ⲩⲉⲓⲱⲧ*

ⲡⲉⲓ̈|ϩⲙⲟⲧ ⲇⲉ ⲟⲛ ⲛ[ⲉ]ϥ̣ϣⲟⲟⲡ ⲛⲁϥ| ⲡⲉ
ⲉⲧ̄ⲙ̄ⲧⲣⲉϥ̣[ⲣ̄]ⲡⲱⲃ̄ϣ̄ ⲛ̄ⲣⲱ|ⲙⲉ ⲛⲓⲙ ⲉ[ⲛⲧⲁⲩ]ⲁⲡⲁⲛⲧⲁ ⲉⲣⲟϥ*

PARALLELS

2 ⲛⲉ]ⲥ̣ⲛⲏⲩ ⲧⲏⲣⲟⲩ
all [the] siblings:

Boh 64.6–7[14] ⲛⲓⲥⲛⲏⲟⲩ ⲇⲉ ⲉ̄ⲧⲉⲙⲡⲉϥⲕⲱϯ
HE 4.15.11[15] τῶν ἀδελφῶν
Boh 64.24–25 ⲛ̄ⲧⲉⲛⲓⲥⲛⲏⲟⲩ

---

14. Greek parallels to this passage in Boh do not refer to Polycarp's circle as ἀδελφοί: οἱ πλείους, MPol 5.1; τοῖς ἀμφ' αὐτὸν, HE 4.15.9.

15. The parallel to this passage in MPol (6.1) includes no reference to Polycarp's circle.

3 ⲉⲓ]ⲣⲉ ⲛ̅ϩⲉⲛϣⲗⲏⲗ
ma]ke prayers:

MPol 5.1 νύκτα καὶ ἡμέραν οὐδὲν ἕτερον ποιῶν ἢ προσευχόμενος
HE 4.15.9 νύκτωρ καὶ μεθ' ἡμέραν οὔτι ἕτερον πράττοντα ἢ ταῖς πρὸς τὸν κύριον διακαρτεροῦντα εὐχαῖς
Boh 64.10–11 ⲁⲗⲗⲁ ⲙ̅ⲡⲓⲉϩⲟⲟⲩ ⲛⲉⲙⲡⲓⲉϫⲱⲣϩ ⲛⲁϥⲙⲏⲛ ⲙⲙⲁⲩⲁⲧϥ ⲡⲉ ⲉⲛⲓϣⲗⲏⲗ ⲙ̅ⲡϭ̅ⲥ̅
MPol 5.2 καὶ προσευχόμενος ἐν ὀπτασίᾳ γέγονεν
HE 4.15.10 καὶ δὴ εὐχόμενον, ἐν ὀπτασίᾳ
Boh 64.15–16 ⲁ̅ⲟⲩϩⲟⲣⲁⲙⲁ ϭⲱⲣⲡ ⲛⲁϥ ⲉ̅ⲃⲟⲗ ⲙ̅ⲡⲓⲉϫⲱⲣϩ ⲉϥϣⲗⲏⲗ
MPol 7.3 σταθεὶς προσηύξατο
HE 4.15.14 ἀναστας ηὔχετο
Boh 65.14–15 ⲁϥⲧⲱⲛϥ ⲁϥϣⲗⲏⲗ
MPol 15.1 ἀναπέμψαντος δὲ αὐτοῦ τὸ ἀμὴν καὶ πληρώσαντος τὴν εὐχήν
HE 4.15.36 ἀναπέμψαντος δὲ αὐτοῦ τὸ ἀμὴν καὶ πληρώσαντος τὴν προσευχήν
Boh 70.7–8 ⲉⲧⲁϥⲟⲩⲱⲣⲡ ⲇⲉ ⲉⲡϣⲱⲓ ⲙ̅ⲡⲓⲁ̅ⲙⲏⲛ ⲟⲩⲟϩ ⲉⲧⲁϥϫⲱⲕ ⲉⲃⲟⲗ ⲛ̅ⲧⲉϥⲡⲣⲟⲥⲉⲩⲭⲏ

4 ⲙⲟⲩⲛ ⲉⲃⲟⲗ
perseverance:

Boh 62.14 ⲛⲉ ⲁϥⲱⲥⲕ ⲅⲁⲣ ⲡⲉ ⲟⲩⲟϩ ⲛⲉⲁϥⲉⲣϧⲉⲗⲗⲟ ⲉⲙⲁϣⲱ

See also above parallels to (c) 3, Boh 64.10–11 ⲙⲏⲛ.

7–8 ⲙ̅ⲙⲁ]ⲑ̣ⲏⲧⲏⲥ ⲛ̅ⲛⲁⲡⲟⲥ̣[ⲧⲟ]|[ⲗⲟⲥ]
the di]sciple[s] of the apos[t][les]:

Boh 62.2–3 ⲡⲟⲗⲓⲕⲁⲣⲡⲟⲥ ⲫⲙⲁⲑⲏⲧⲏⲥ ⲛ̅ⲛⲓⲁⲡⲟⲥⲧⲟⲗⲟⲥ
Boh 62.10–11 ⲡⲓⲙⲁⲕⲁⲣⲓⲟⲥ ⲡⲟⲗⲓⲕⲁⲣⲡⲟⲥ ⲫⲁⲓ ⲉⲧⲁϥϣⲱⲡⲓ ⲙ̅ⲙⲁⲑⲏⲧⲏⲥ ⲛ̅ⲛⲓⲁ̅ⲡⲟⲥⲧⲟⲗⲟⲥ

See also above parallels to (b) 11–13.

8–9 ⲛⲉϥϣⲟⲟⲡ ⲇⲉ ⲛ̄[...]|[ⲛ̄ⲧⲉ]ⲕⲕⲗⲏⲥⲓⲁ ⲧⲏⲣ̄ⲥ̄
He was [---] [of the] whole [c]hurch:

Boh 70.28–71.1 ⲫⲁⲓ ⲉⲧⲁϥϣⲱⲡⲓ ⲛ̄ⲥⲁϩ ⲟⲩⲟϩ ⲛⲁⲡⲟⲥⲧⲟⲗⲟⲥ ⲟⲩⲟϩ ⲙ̄ⲡⲣⲟⲫⲏⲧⲏⲥ ⲟⲩⲟϩ ⲛⲉⲡⲓⲥⲕⲟⲡⲟⲥ ⲛ̄ⲧⲉ ϯⲕⲁⲑⲟⲗⲓⲕⲓⲕⲏ[16] ⲛ̄ⲉⲕⲕⲗⲏⲥⲓⲁ ⲧⲏⲣⲥ[17]

10 [..ⲩ]ϩ̄ⲗ̄ⲗⲟ ⲡⲉ
[---] old man:

Boh 62.15 ⲛⲉⲁϥϧⲉⲗⲗⲟ ⲉⲙⲁϣⲱ
MPol 7.2 τὴν ἡλικίαν αὐτοῦ . . . τοιοῦτον πρεσβύτην ἄνδρα
HE 4.15.13 τῷ τῆς ἡλικίας αὐτοῦ παλαιῷ . . ., τοιοῦτον . . . πρεσβύτην
Boh 65.7–10 ⲑⲙⲉⲧⲛⲓϣϯ ⲛ̄ⲧⲉⲧⲉϥϩⲏⲗⲓⲕⲓⲁ . . . ⲟⲩϧⲉⲗⲗⲟ ⲙ̄ⲡⲁⲓⲣⲏϯ
MPol 7.3 = HE 4.15.14 θεοπρεπῆ πρεσβύτην
Boh 65.18–19 ⲙ̄ⲡⲁⲓϧⲉⲗⲗⲟ ⲙ̄ⲡⲁⲓⲣⲏϯ . . . ⲉⲧⲟⲛⲓ ⲙ̄ⲫ̄ϯ̄
HE 4.15.30[18] πρὸ τῆς πολιᾶς
Boh 69.11 ⲡⲉ ϩⲉⲛϯⲙⲉⲧϧⲉⲗⲗⲟ
VPol 17 ἐπεὶ δὲ λοιπὸν ὁσημέραι καὶ ἡλικίᾳ προέκοπτεν, ἥ τε πρόδρομος τοῦ γήρους ἐπήνθει πολιὰ καὶ λευκή τις ὑπὲρ κροτάφων θρὶξ ἤρχετο μειδιᾶν

10–11 ⲉϥϩⲛ̄ⲁϣⲉ̣ϥ[ⲧⲟ]| [ⲛ̄]ⲣⲟⲙⲡⲉ
being one hundred and f[our] years of age:

MPol 9.3 ὀγδοήκοντα καὶ ἓξ ἔτη ἔχω δουλεύων αὐτῷ
HE 4.15.20 ὀγδοήκοντα καὶ ἓξ ἔτη δουλεύω αὐτῷ
Boh 67.3 ⲓ̅ⲥ̅ ⲡ̅ⲉ̅ ⲛⲣⲟⲙⲡⲓ ϣⲁⲫⲟⲟⲩ ϯⲟⲓ ⲛ̄ⲃⲱⲕ ⲙ̄ⲡⲁϭ̄ⲥ̄

16. Suggested reading, ϯⲕⲁⲑⲟⲗⲓⲕⲏ; Balestri and Hyvernat, *Acta Martyrum* II (Textus), 71.

17. Greek parallels to this passage (MPol 16.2; HE 4.15.39) include no equivalent to ⲧⲏⲣⲥ, "all."

18. The parallel to this passage in MPol (13.2) includes no reference to Polycarp's age.

11–15 ⲛⲉϥⲙⲟⲟϣⲉ to ⲡⲁ||[ⲡ]ⲟⲥⲧⲟⲗⲟⲥ
He continued to walk to the a[p]ostle:

Boh 62.15–17 ⲉϥϯⲥⲃⲱ ⲛ̄ⲥⲏⲟⲩ ⲛⲓⲃⲉⲛ ⲉ̄ⲛⲏ ⲉⲧⲁϥϭⲓⲥⲃⲱ ⲉ̄ⲣⲱⲟⲩ ⲉⲃⲟⲗ ϩⲓⲧⲟⲧⲟⲩ ⲛ̄ⲛⲓⲁ̄ⲡⲟⲥⲧⲟⲗⲟⲥ

AH "Prologus Flori Diaconi Lugdunensis I"[19] Hyrenaeus, episcopus civitas Lugdunensis, instructus a Polycaro discipulo Johannis apostoli . . .

HE 4.14.4 = AH 3.3.4 ταῦτα διδάξας ἀεὶ ἃ καὶ παρὰ τῶν ἀποστόλων ἔμαθεν, ἃ καὶ ἡ ἐκκλησία παραδίδωσιν[20]

HE 5.20.6 (Irenaeus, "Letter to Florinus") καὶ τὴν μετὰ Ἰωάννου συναναστροφὴν ὡς ἀπήγγελλεν καὶ τὴν μετὰ τῶν λοιπῶν τῶν ἑορακότων τὸν κύριον, καὶ ὡς ἀπεμνημόνευεν τοὺς λόγους αὐτῶν

MPol postscript (Moscow MS only) Εἰρήναῖος . . . παρ' αὐτοῦ (Πολυκάρπος) ἔμαθεν . . . καὶ τὸν ἐκκλησιαστικὸν κανόνα καὶ καθολικόν, ὡς παρέλαβεν παρὰ τοῦ ἁγίου, καὶ παρέδωκεν

VPol 12 καὶ αὐτὸν (sc. Polycarp) ὑπὸ Κυρίου παιδευθῆναι καὶ ἐν ἐκκλησίᾳ τὸν τῆς κατηχήσεως ποιήσασθαι λόγον. ἐδόθη οὖν ὑπὸ Χριστοῦ τὸ μὲν πρῶτον διδασκαλίας ὀρθῆς ἐκκλησιαστικὸς καθολικὸς κανών

Sozomen, *Church History* 7.19 οἱ δὲ ἐκ τῆς Ἀσίας Ἰωάννῃ τῷ εὐαγγελιστῇ ἀκολουθεῖν ἰσχυρίζοντο

15–16 ϣⲁⲛⲧ̄ϥⲡⲱϩ| [ⲉ]ⲧⲉϊϩⲏⲗⲓⲕⲓⲁ ⲛ̄ⲧⲉϊϭⲟⲧ
until he reached the stature of such a great age:

MPol 9.2 = HE 4.15.18 αἰδέσθητί σου τὴν ἡλικίαν

Boh 66.20 ϣⲓⲡⲓ ϩⲁⲧϩⲏ ⲛ̄ⲧⲉⲕϩⲩⲗⲏⲕⲓⲁ̄

See also above parallels to (c) 10.

19. In W. Wigan Harvey, *Sancti Irenaei, Episcopi Lugdunensis, Libros Quinque Adversus Haereses* (Cambridge: Cambridge University Press, 1857) 1.clxxvii.

20. See similarly HE 4.14.5.

16–19 ⲁⲩⲱ| ⲛ̣ⲉⲩϣⲓⲛⲉ <u>to</u> ⲉ̣ⲡⲉϥⲃⲓⲟⲥ
And all . . . who had heard about his way of life used to seek after him:

VPol 21 ὄχλοι . . . οἱ μὲν εἰδότες, οἱ δὲ <u>ἐπιθυμοῦντες ἐκ τοῦ ἀκούειν περὶ αὐτοῦ τὸν Πολύκαρπον θεάσασθαι</u>

21 ⲡ[ⲉ]ⲩⲉⲓⲱⲧ
th[ei]r father:

MPol 12.2 = HE 4.15.26 <u>ὁ πατὴρ</u> τῶν χριστιανῶν
Boh 68.15–16 ⲉ<u>ⲫⲓⲱⲧ</u> ⲡⲉ ⲛ̄ⲛⲓⲭⲣⲏⲥⲧⲓⲁ̄ⲛⲟⲥ
VPol 27 [Camerius, a deacon, addresses Polycarp] μακάριε πάπα

21–23 ⲡⲉϊ|ϩⲙⲟⲧ ⲇⲉ ⲟⲛ ⲛ[ⲉ]ϥ̣ϣⲟⲟⲡ ⲛⲁϥ| ⲡⲉ
He had this gift:

MPol 7.3 πλήρης ὢν <u>τῆς χάριτος</u> τοῦ θεοῦ
HE 4.15.14 ἔμπλεως <u>τῆς χάριτος</u> ὢν τοῦ κυρίου
Boh 65.15 ⲉϥⲙⲉϩ ⲉⲃⲟⲗϩⲉⲛ <u>ⲡⲓϩⲙⲟⲧ</u> ⲛ̄ⲧⲉⲡϭ̄ⲥ̄

23–24 ⲉⲧⲙ̄ⲧⲣⲉϥ[ⲣ̄]ⲡⲱⲃ̄ϣ ⲛ̄ⲣⲱ|ⲙⲉ ⲛⲓⲙ ⲉ[ⲛⲧⲁⲩ]ⲁⲡⲁⲛⲧⲁ ⲉⲣⲟϥ
that he never [f]orgot any of those w[ho] had come into contact with him:

MPol 8.1 = HE 4.15.15 <u>μνημονεύσας ἁπάντων</u> τῶν καὶ πώποτε <u>συμβεβληκότων αὐτῷ</u>
Boh 65.20–21 <u>ⲁϥⲉⲣⲫⲙⲉⲩⲓ ⲛⲟⲩⲟⲛ ⲛⲓⲃⲉⲛ ⲛⲉⲙⲏⲏ ⲉⲧⲁⲩⲉⲣⲁ̄ⲡⲁⲛⲧⲁⲛ ⲉⲣⲟϥ</u>

TEXT CRITICAL NOTES

1 superlin. above ⲛ not extant due to broken papyrus leaf;
].ⲛ̄ⲥ̣ⲁ: for ⲥ̣ can be read ⲉ̣

ⲡⲉϥⲟ̣: for ⲟ̣ can be read ⲉ̣, ⲑ̣, ⲥ̣ or ϭ̣

1–2 the narrative unit ending with the raised point (*) at line 2 must have included line 1 (in extant pap. all narrative units followed by * are more than one line long)

2 ⲛⲉ]ⲥ̣ⲛⲏⲩ: for ⲥ̣ can also be read ⲉ̣; ⲥⲛⲏⲩ is either the object of a preposition or the actor following ⲛ̄ϭⲓ

ⲧⲏⲣⲟⲩ^{*v}: or ⲧⲏⲣⲟⲩ$^{*1-1/2v}$; for $^{*1-1/2v}$ see (e) 10

3 ⲉⲓ]ⲣⲉ: cf. 1 Tim 2:1 Sah, ⲉⲧⲣⲉⲧⲛ̄ⲉⲓⲣⲉ ⲛ̄ϩⲉⲛⲥⲟⲡⲥ̄ ⲙⲛ̄ϩⲉⲛϣⲗⲏⲗ; Gk, ποιεῖσθαι δεήσεις προσευχὰς

ϣⲗⲏⲗ: second ⲗ partially covered by mislaid papyrus fiber originating above right; the ink trace on the fiber is part of the letter immediately after ϣⲗⲏⲗ, poss. hore

5 ||[....]ⲉⲓϣ: poss. ||[ⲛ̄ⲟⲩⲟ]ⲉⲓϣ; lacuna too small for [ⲟⲩⲟⲩⲟ]ⲉⲓϣ

ⲉⲃⲟⲗ ϫⲉⲛ̣̄[: or ⲙ̣̄; left vertical stroke and superlin. are extant

6 ⲙⲁⲩⲁ̣[ⲁϥ ⲛ̄]|[ⲙ̄ⲙⲁ]ⲑ̣ⲏⲧⲏⲥ: ⲁ̣ read from small, ambiguous trace; a modern library label is partially covering the letter trace

for ⲑ̣ can also be read ⲟ̣

ⲙⲁⲩⲁ̣[ⲁϥ ⲛ̄-], i.e., ⲙⲁⲩⲁ̣[ⲁϥ ϩⲛ̄-]

7–8 ⲁⲡⲟⲥ̣[: for ⲥ̣ can also be read ⲉ̣, ⲑ̣ or ⲟ̣

[ⲗⲟⲥ$^{*1/2v}$]: for raised dot (*) before ⲛⲉ (preterite) + Bipartite + ⲇⲉ see (c) 11

8 ⲛ̄[...]: poss. ⲛ̄[ⲥⲁϩ] or ⲛ̄[ⲉⲓⲱⲧ], lacuna is too small for ⲛ̄[ⲉⲡⲓⲥⲕⲟⲡⲟⲥ]; for ⲥⲁϩ see (d) 4–6 and parallels, for ⲉⲓⲱⲧ (c) 21 and parallels; also poss. ⲛ̄[ⲟⲩⲏⲏⲃ], see VPol 29 ὁ τῶν λεγομένων χριστιανῶν ἱερευς

9–10 [...]|| [..ⲩ] ϩ̣ⲗ̄ⲗⲟ ⲡⲉ: more than three (less than four) standard letters in lacuna at end of line 9; poss. [ⲡⲁï ⲇⲉ]||[ⲛⲉⲩ]ϩ̣ⲗ̄ⲗⲟ ⲡⲉ or [ⲁⲩⲱ]||[ⲛⲉⲩ]-ϩ̣ⲗ̄ⲗⲟ ⲡⲉ

10 ϩ̣ⲗ̄ⲗⲟ: ϩ̣ read from small, ambiguous trace; extended superlin. above ϩⲗ not extant above ϩ due to broken papyrus

ϣⲉ̣: for ⲉ̣ can also be read ⲟ̣ or ⲥ̣

15 ⲡⲱϩ: ϩ confirmed with UV light

16 ϭⲟⲧ*: as at (c) 21, no extra space after the raised point (*)

17 ⲛ̣ⲉⲩ: ⲛ̣ read from small, ambiguous trace

18 ⲭⲣⲓⲥⲧⲓⲁⲛⲟⲥ: spelled ⲭ̣ⲣⲉⲓⲥⲧⲓⲁⲛⲟⲥ at (d) 6

19–24 ink traces surrounding the lacunas read under UV light

19 ⲉ̣ⲡⲉϥ: for ⲉ̣ can also be read ⲑ̣, ⲟ̣ or ⲥ̣

21 ⲉⲓⲱⲧ*: as at (c) 16 no extra space after the raised point

24 ⲉ[ⲛⲧⲁⲩ]: see Boh 65.20–21 (=MPol 8.1; HE 4.15.15), ⲁϥⲉⲣⲡⲙⲉⲩⲓ ⲛⲟⲩⲟⲛ ⲛⲓⲃⲉⲛ ⲛⲉⲙⲏⲏ ⲉⲧⲁⲩⲉⲣⲁ̄ⲡⲁⲛⲧⲁⲛ; ⲉ[ⲛⲧⲁϥ] is paleographically less likely

(d) = 64v + 56r

[one or more lines lacking]

[..ⲧⲉ]ⲕⲕⲗⲏ̣[ⲥⲓⲁ] [6]|[..]ⲟϥ ⲛ̄ϭⲓⲛ̄ⲓ̈ⲟⲩⲇⲁ[ⲓ̈....]|
[.ϩⲏ]ⲣⲱⲇⲏⲥ

ⲉⲩϫⲱ ⲛ̣̄[....]|[..] ⲛ̣̄ⲟⲩⲁ'

ϫⲉⲡⲟⲗⲩ[ⲕⲁⲣⲡⲟⲥ]|| [..]ⲧ̣ⲉⲓ̈ⲡⲟⲗⲓⲥ ⲉⲡⲥⲁ̣[ϩ ⲡⲉ
ⲛ̄]|[ⲛⲉ]ⲭ̣ⲣⲉⲓⲥⲧⲓⲁⲛⲟⲥ*

[....]|[..]ⲕ ⲛ̄ⲟⲩⲟⲛ ⲛⲓⲙ ϣ[...]|[.ⲧⲉ]ϥⲙⲁⲅⲓⲁ*

ⲉϥⲕ[....]| [..].ⲩ ⲉⲧⲙ̄ϯⲫⲟⲣⲟ[ⲥ...]||[.. ⲟ]ⲩⲇⲉ ⲉⲧⲙ̄ϣ̄ⲙ̄ϣ[ⲉ
ⲛ̄ⲛ̄]|ⲛⲟⲩⲧⲉ ⲙ̄ⲡ̄ⲣ̄ⲣⲟ*v

ϩⲏⲣⲱ[ⲇⲏⲥ]| ⲇⲉ ⲛ̄ⲧⲉⲣⲉϥⲥⲱⲧ̄ⲙ̄ ⲉⲛⲁ[ⲓ̈
ⲁϥ]|ϭⲱⲛ̄ⲧ̄ ⲉⲙⲁⲧⲉ*

ⲁⲩⲱ ⲁϥⲕ[ⲉ]|ⲗⲉⲩⲉ ⲉⲧⲣⲉⲩⲛ̄ⲧ̄ϥ̄ ⲛⲁϥ
ϫ̣[ⲉ]||ⲕⲁⲥ ⲉϥⲉⲙⲟⲟⲩⲧ̄ϥ̄ *1/2v

ⲛ̄ⲧ̣[ⲉ]|ⲣⲟⲩⲉⲓⲙⲉ ⲇⲉ ⲛ̄ϭⲓⲛⲉⲥⲛⲏ[ⲩ
ϫⲉ]|ⲥⲉⲕⲱⲧⲉ ⲛ̄ⲥⲱϥ ⲉⲙⲟⲟⲩⲧ̄[ϥ̄.]|

ⲁⲩϥⲓⲧ̄ϥ̄
ⲁⲩϩⲟⲡ̄ϥ̄ ϩ̄ⲛ̄ⲟⲩⲙ[ⲁ]|

ⲛ̄ⲧⲉⲣⲟ,ⲩⲉⲓⲙⲉ ⲇⲉ ⲟⲛ
ϫⲉⲥⲉ̣||ⲕⲱⲧⲉ ⲛ̄ⲥ̣ⲱϥ ⲙⲡⲙⲁ ⲉⲧ̄ⲙ̄|ⲙⲁⲩ,1/2v
ⲁⲩⲡ[ⲟ]ⲟⲛⲉϥ ⲉⲃⲟⲗ ⲛ̄|ⲧⲉⲩϣⲏ ⲛ̄ϭ[ⲓ]ⲛⲉⲥⲛⲏⲩ
ⲁⲩϫⲓⲧ̄ϥ̄| ⲉⲕⲉⲙⲁ*v

[..]. ⲟⲛ ⲁⲩⲉⲓⲙⲉ*|
ⲉⲧⲃⲏⲏⲧⲟ̣[ⲩ ⲛ̄ϭⲓ]ⲛ̄ⲓ̈ⲟⲩⲇⲁⲓ̈*

PARALLELS

4–6 ⲡⲟⲗⲩ[ⲕⲁⲣⲡⲟⲥ] to ⲡⲥⲁ̣[ϩ ⲡⲉ ⲛ̄]|[ⲛⲉ]ⲭ̣ⲣⲉⲓⲥⲧⲓⲁⲛⲟⲥ
Poly[carp] to the teac[her of] [the] Christian[s]:

VPol 28 ὁ τῶν χριστιανῶν διδάσκαλος ὅν λέγουσι Πολύκαρπον
MPol 12.2 οὗτός ἐστιν ὁ τῆς ἀσεβείας διδάσκαλος, ὁ πατὴρ τῶν χριστιανῶν
HE 4.15.26 οὗτός ἐστιν ὁ τῆς Ἀσίας διδάσκαλος, ὁ πατὴρ τῶν Χριστιανῶν
Boh 68.15–16 ⲑⲁⲓ ⲡⲉ ⲡⲥⲁϩ ⲛ̄ⲧⲁⲥⲓⲁ̄ ⲧⲏⲣⲥ ⲉⲫⲓⲱⲧ ⲡⲉ ⲛ̄ⲛⲓⲭⲣⲏⲥⲧⲓⲁ̄ⲛⲟⲥ

8 ⲧⲉ]ϥⲙⲁⲅⲓⲁ
[hi]s magic:

VPol 25 τῶν δι᾿ αὐτοῦ γενομένων μεγαλείων
VPol 28 ἐγένετο δὲ καὶ ἕτερον μεγαλεῖον δι᾿ αὐτοῦ τοιοῦτον

8–11 ⲉϥⲕ[to ⲛ̄]|ⲛⲟⲩⲧⲉ ⲙ̄ⲡ̄ⲣ̄ⲣⲟ
while he [to the] god[s] of the emperor:

MPol 12.2 = HE 4.15.26 Ὁ πολλοὺς διδάσκων μὴ θύειν μηδὲ προσκυνεῖν
Boh 68.16–17 ⲉϥϯⲥⲃⲱ ⲛⲟⲩⲙⲏϣ ⲉϣⲧⲉⲙⲉⲣⲑⲩⲥⲓⲁ̄ ⲟⲩⲟϩ ⲉϣⲧⲉⲙⲟⲩⲱϣⲧ ⲛⲱⲟⲩ

15–18 ⲛ̄ⲧ̣[ⲉ]|ⲣⲟⲩⲉⲓⲙⲉ ⲇⲉ ⲛ̄ϭⲓⲛⲉⲥⲛⲏ[ⲩ to ϩⲛ̄ⲟⲩⲙ[ⲁ]
Aft[e]r the sibli[ngs] knew to somewh[er]e:

MPol 5.1 οἱ δὲ πλείους ἔπειθον αὐτὸν ὑπεξελθεῖν. καὶ ὑπεξῆλθεν εἰς ἀγρίδιον οὐ μακρὰν ἀπέχον ἀπὸ τῆς πόλεως
HE 4.15.9 πεισθέντα γε μὴν ἀντιβολοῦσι τοῖς ἀμφ᾿ αὐτὸν καὶ ὡς ἂν ὑπεξέλθοι παρακαλοῦσι, προελθεῖν εἰς οὐ πόρρω διεστῶτα τῆς πόλεως ἀγρὸν
Boh 64.6–9 ⲛⲓⲥⲛⲏⲟⲩ ⲇⲉ ⲉ̄ⲧⲉⲙⲡⲉϥⲕⲱϯ ⲁⲩϯϩⲟ ⲉⲣⲟϥ ⲉⲑⲣⲉϥϣⲉ ⲉⲃⲟⲗ ϩⲉⲛϯⲡⲟⲗⲓⲥ ⲟⲩⲟϩ ⲉⲧⲁϥⲑⲉⲧⲡⲟⲩϩⲏⲧ ⲁϥϣⲉ ⲉⲃⲟⲗ ⲉ̄ⲟⲩⲕⲟⲓ ⲉⲥⲟⲩⲡ̄ⲟⲩ ⲉⲃⲟⲗ ⲛ̄ϯⲡⲟⲗⲓⲥ

19–23 ⲛ̄ⲧⲉⲣⲟⲩⲉⲓⲙⲉ to ⲉⲕⲉⲙⲁ
After they knew to another place:

MPol 6.1 καὶ ἐπιμενόντων τῶν ζητούντων αὐτὸν μετέβη εἰς ἕτερον ἀγρίδιον

HE 4.15.11 ἐπικειμένων δὴ οὖν σὺν πάσῃ σπουδῇ τῶν ἀναζητούντων αὐτόν, αὖθις ὑπὸ τῆς τῶν ἀδελφῶν διαθέσεως καὶ στοργῆς ἐκβεβιασμένον μεταβῆναί φασιν ἐφ' ἕτερον ἀγρόν

Boh 64.23–25 ⲉⲧⲁⲩⲙⲟⲩⲛ ⲇⲉ ⲉⲃⲟⲗ ⲉⲩⲕⲱϯ ⲛ̄ⲥⲱϥ ϩⲉⲛⲥⲡⲟⲩⲇⲏ ⲛⲓⲃⲉⲛ ⲁⲩϭⲓⲧϥ ⲛ̄ϫⲟⲛⲥ ⲟⲛ ⲉⲃⲟⲗ ϩⲁϯⲇⲓⲁ̄ⲑⲉⲥⲓⲥ ⲛ̄ⲧⲉⲛⲓⲥⲛⲏⲟⲩ ⲉⲑⲃⲉⲡⲟⲩⲙⲉⲓ ⲉϩⲟⲩⲛ ⲉⲣⲟϥ ⲁϥⲟⲩⲱ̄ⲧⲉⲃ ⲉⲡⲓⲙⲁ

TEXT CRITICAL NOTES

1 ⲧⲉ]ⲕⲕⲗⲏ̣[: ⲏ̣ read from small, ambiguous trace

3 ⲉⲩϫⲱ ⲛ̣[....]|: for ⲛ̣̄ can be read ⲛ̣, ⲙ̄ or ⲙ̣; superlin. above ⲛ̣̄ not extant due to broken papyrus leaf

4 [..] ⲛ̣̄ⲟⲩⲁ: for ⲛ̣̄ can be read ⲙ̣̄; traces of superlin. are visible

poss. ⲉⲩϫⲱ ⲛ̣̄[ϩⲉⲛϣⲁ]|[ϫⲉ] ⲛ̣̄ⲟⲩⲁ, cf. Acts 6:11 Sah, ⲉϥϫⲱ ⲛ̄ϩⲉⲛϣⲁϫⲉ ⲛ̄ⲟⲩⲁ; Gk, λαλοῦντος ῥήματα βλάσφημα

5 [..]ⲧ̣ⲉϊⲡⲟⲗⲓⲥ: ⲧ̣ read from small, ambiguous trace; ⲉ confirmed using UV light

poss. [ⲡⲁ]ⲧ̣ⲉϊⲡⲟⲗⲓⲥ; lacuna too small for [ⲡⲣ̄ⲙ]ⲧ̣ⲉϊⲡⲟⲗⲓⲥ;

ⲡⲥⲁ̣[ϩ]: for ⲁ̣ can be read ⲗ̣ or ϫ̣; for ⲥⲁϩ (διδάσκαλος) see above, parallels to (d) 4–6, and Commentary

6 ϫ̣ⲣⲉⲓⲥⲧⲓⲁⲛⲟⲥ: ϫ̣ read from ambiguous letter trace; spelled ϫⲣⲓⲥⲧⲓⲁⲛⲟⲥ at (c) 18

ϫ̣ⲣⲉⲓⲥⲧⲓⲁⲛⲟⲥ*: extra space may follow punctuation mark

6–8 [....]|[..]ⲕ ⲛ̄ⲟⲩⲟⲛ ⲛⲓⲙ ϣ[...]|[.ⲧⲉ]ϥⲙⲁⲅⲓⲁ*: poss. [ⲁⲩⲱ ⲉϥ]|[ⲥⲱ]ⲕ ⲛ̄ⲟⲩⲟⲛ ⲛⲓⲙ ϣ[ⲁⲃⲟⲗ]|[ⲛ̄ⲧⲉ]ϥⲙⲁⲅⲓⲁ*

8–9 ⲉϥⲕ[....]| [..].ⲩ: slightly less than three standard letters can fit in lacuna at line 9

poss. ⲉ̄ⲫⲕ[ⲱⲣϣ]| [ⲉⲣⲟ]ⲟ̣ⲩ

9–10 ⲉⲧ̄ⲙ̄ϯⲫⲟⲣⲟ[ⲥ...]||[.. poss. ⲉⲧ̄ⲙ̄ϯⲫⲟⲣⲟ[ⲥ ⲙ̄ⲡ]||[ⲣ̄ⲣⲟ; cf. Luke 20:22 Sah, ⲉϩⲉⲥⲧⲓ ⲛⲁⲛ ⲉϯⲫⲟⲣⲟⲥ ⲙ̄ⲡⲣ̄ⲣⲟ. See ch. 4, comment on (d) 8–11, Obs. 2

10 ⲟ]ⲩⲇⲉ: see parallels to (d) 8–11, esp. μηδέ, and ch. 4, comment on (d) 8–11, Obs. 2

11 ϩηρω[λhc]: ω faded, confirmed with UV light

15 ⲛ̄ⲧ̣[ⲉ]ⲓⲣⲟⲩ: ⲣ faded, confirmed with UV light

16 ⲥⲛⲏ[ⲩ: signs of erasure evident at NH

19 ⲛ̄ⲧⲉⲣⲟ,ⲩ: arbitrary ink trace, size and placement resemble standard scribal dot on line (,)

ϫⲉⲥ̣ⲉ̣||: for ⲥ̣ can be read ⲑ̣

19–24: ink traces surrounding the lacunas read under UV light

20 ⲛ̄ⲥ̣ⲱϥ: for ⲥ̣ can also be read ⲟ̣

23 ⲙⲁ*v: *at least* one space (v) is vacant before text resumes

[..]. ⲟⲛ: lacuna is too small for [ⲛ̄ⲧⲟ]ϥ ⲟⲛ, poss. [ⲁⲩ]ⲱ̣ ⲟⲛ; see comment.

ⲉⲓⲙⲉ*: arbitrary ink trace, placement similar to standard raised point, but considerably thinner

24 ⲉⲧⲃⲏⲏⲧⲟ̣[ⲩ ⲛ̄ϭⲓ]ⲛ̄ⲓ̈ⲟⲩⲇⲁⲓ̈: for ⲟ̣ can be read ϥ, ⲥ̣, ⲉ̣, or ⲑ̣ (ink trace at top left border of letter); for an omicron of similar shape, see (a) 4, ⲉⲃⲟⲗ

ⲉⲧⲃⲏⲏⲧϥ̣̄ not possible (no superlin. visible above ⲧ; manuscript leaf is complete above ⲧ)

(e) = **55v**

[possibly 2 or more pages lacking after (d)]

[.]ⲩϩⲩⲡⲟⲕⲣⲓⲛⲉ ⲙ̄ⲡⲣⲁⲛ̣[.]|
..ⲧ̄ϥ̄ ⲛ̄ϭⲓⲛⲉⲥⲛⲏⲩ ⲉϩ[ⲣⲁⲓ]| ⲉϫ̄ⲛ̄ⲟⲩⲙⲁ ⲛ̄ϫⲁⲉⲓⲉ*1/2v
ⲛ̄ⲧ[ⲟϥ]| ⲇⲉ ⲛⲉϥϫⲛⲟⲩ ⲙ̄ⲙⲟⲟⲩ ⲡⲉ||
ϫⲉⲉⲧⲃⲉⲟⲩ ⲛ̄ϩⲱⲃ ⲧⲉⲧ̄ⲛ̄|ⲕⲱⲧⲉ ⲛ̄ⲙ̄ⲙⲁϊ ⲕⲁⲧⲁⲙⲁ*|

ⲁⲩⲱ ⲛⲉⲩⲣ̄ϩⲟⲧⲉ ⲡⲉ ⲉⲧⲁⲙⲟϥ|
ϫⲉⲉⲛⲛⲉϥⲕⲱⲗⲩ ⲙ̄ⲙⲟⲟⲩ|
ⲛ̄ϥ̄ⲃⲱⲕ ⲙⲁⲩⲁⲁϥ ⲉⲡⲇⲓⲕⲁ||ⲥⲧⲏⲣⲓⲟⲛ*1–1/2v

ⲛⲉⲁⲩⲥⲱⲧ̄ⲙ̄| ⲅⲁⲣ ⲉⲣⲟϥ ⲡⲉ ⲛ̄ϩⲁϩ ⲛ̄ⲥⲟⲡ,
ⲉϥ|ϫⲱ ⲙⲙⲟⲥ
ϫⲉϩⲁⲡ̄ⲥ̄ ⲉⲧⲣⲁ|ⲙⲟⲩ ϩ̄ⲙ̄ⲡⲇⲓⲕⲁⲥⲧⲏⲣⲓⲟⲛ*
ⲕⲁ|ⲧⲁⲑⲉ ⲉⲛⲧⲁϥⲧⲁⲙⲟⲓ ⲛ̄ϭⲓ̈||ⲡⲁⲡⲟⲥⲧⲟⲗⲟⲥ ⲙ̄ⲡϫⲟⲉⲓⲥ
ⲉϥ|ϫⲱ ⲙ̄ⲙⲟⲥ*
ϫⲉⲉⲡⲉⲓⲇⲏ ⲁⲡϫⲟ|ⲉⲓⲥ ⲭⲁⲣⲓⲍⲉ ⲛⲁϊ
ⲉⲧⲣⲁⲙⲟⲩ|
[ⲉϊ]ϩ̣̄ⲙ̄ⲡⲁϭⲗⲟϭ,
ϩⲁⲡ̄ⲥ̄ ⲉⲣⲟⲕ| [ⲡⲉ]
ⲉⲧⲣⲉⲕⲙⲟⲩ' ϩ̄ⲙ̄ⲡⲇⲓⲕⲁ||[ⲥⲧ]ⲏⲣⲓⲟⲛ*
ϫⲉⲉⲣⲉⲟⲩϣⲱϣ|
[8]ⲙ..[7]|

α-β [two or more lines lacking]
γ [15] [ⲡⲟⲗⲩ-]

PARALLELS

16–18 ⲉⲡⲉⲓⲇⲏ <u>to</u> ϩ̣̄ⲙ̄ⲡⲁϭⲗⲟϭ
Since <u>to</u> on my bed:

AJn 111,115 Ἰωάννης . . . ἀποδύεται τὰ ἱμάτια ἃ ἠμφίεστο καὶ ἐπιβάλλει αὐτὰ ὥσπερ <u>τινὰ στρωμνὴν</u> ἐν τῷ βάθει τοῦ σκάμματος . . . (115) κατεκλίθη <u>ἐπὶ τοῦ σκάμματος ἔνθα τὰ ἱμάτια αὐτοῦ ὑπέστρωσεν</u> . . . <u>παρέδωκε τὸ πνεῦμα</u> χαίρων

AJn (Coptic) 111,115 ⲧⲟⲧⲉ ⲁϥⲕⲁⲁϥ ⲕⲁϩⲏⲩ ⲛ̄ⲛ̄ϩⲟⲓ̈ⲧⲉ ⲉⲧⲧⲟ ϩⲓⲱⲱϥ ⲁϥⲛⲟϫⲟⲩ ⲉⲡⲉⲥⲏⲧ ⲉⲡⲧⲟⲡⲟⲥ ⲛ̄ⲧⲁⲩϭⲱϫⲉ ⲙ̄ⲙⲟϥ ⲉⲡⲉⲥⲏⲧ ⲙ̄ⲡⲉ-ⲥⲙⲟⲧ ⲛ̄ⲟⲩⲙⲁ ⲉϥⲡⲟⲣϣ̄ . . . (115) ⲁϥϥⲟϭϥ̄ ⲉⲡⲉⲥⲏⲧ ⲉⲡϣⲓⲕ ⲛ̄ⲧⲁⲩ-ϣⲁⲕⲧϥ̄ ⲡⲙⲁ ⲉⲧⲉⲛⲉϥϩⲟⲓ̈ⲧⲉ ⲡⲟⲣϣ̄ ⲛ̄ⲏⲏⲧϥ̄

Augustine, *Tractate* 124, 2 "On the Gospel of John": Quem (sc. John) tradunt etiam (quod in quibuscum scripturis quamuis apocryphis reperitur) quando sibi fieri iussit sepulcrum, incolumen fuisse prae-sentem . . . ibi se tamquam in lectulo collocasse, statimque eum esse defunctum

TEXT CRITICAL NOTES

1 [.]| more than one (less than two) standard letters can fit in the lacuna

poss. [ⲁⲩ] or [ⲉⲩ]

ⲣⲁⲛ̣[: for ⲛ̣ can be read ⲙ̣ or ⲏ̣ (vertical stroke at bottom left of letter)

2 ..ⲧ̄ϥ: also possible is . . . ⲧ̄ϥ; ⲧ̄ϥ written over erasure of the letter ⲛ

superlin. above ϫⲛ in the shape of a circumflex, "⌒"

9 ⲇⲓⲕⲁ||ⲥⲧⲏⲣⲓⲟⲛ$^{*1-1/2v}$: unusually wide space after *; for no extra space after ⲇⲓⲕⲁⲥⲧⲏⲣⲓⲟⲛ* see (e) 13, 20

16 ϫⲟ|ⲉⲓⲥ: ⲟ confirmed with UV light

18 of ϩ̄, superlin. is definite, ϩ read from ambiguous traces

19 ⲉⲧⲣⲉⲕⲙⲟⲩ: ⲉ^1 confirmed with UV light

20 ϣⲱϣ: slight ink traces of the tails of both shai's visible

ⲩ: restoration of [ⲡⲟⲗⲩ-] based on the sequence of pages, see (f) 1 and above, Physical Description of the Fragments

(f) = 55r

ⲕ]ⲁ̣ⲣⲡⲟⲥ ϩⲱⲥ ⲉϣϫⲉⲛ̄ⲧⲁⲡ̣[ⲉ]|[ⲡ]ⲣⲏϣ' ⲉⲧϩⲓϫⲱϥ ⲣⲱⲕ̄ϩ

ⲁⲩ[ⲱ]| [ⲛ̄]ⲧⲉⲣⲉϥⲛⲉϩⲥⲉ
ⲁϥϫⲟⲟⲥ ⲉ|ⲛⲉⲥⲛⲏⲩ
ϫⲉϩⲁⲡ̄ⲥ̄ ⲡⲉ ⲉⲧⲣⲉⲩ||ⲣⲟⲕ̄ϩⲧ̄ ⲉïⲟⲛ̄ϩ*1/2v
ⲁⲩⲱ ϯⲣ̄ϣⲡⲏ|ⲣⲉ
ϫⲉⲙ̄ⲡⲟⲩϣⲓⲛⲉ ⲛ̄ⲥⲱï ϣⲁ|ⲡⲟⲟⲩ*v

ⲛⲁï ⲇⲉ ⲛ̄ⲧⲉⲣⲉϥϫⲟ|ⲟⲩ,1/2v
ⲁⲩⲣⲓⲙⲉ ⲛ̄ϭⲓ ⲛⲉⲥⲛⲏⲩ*
ⲉⲩ|ⲥⲟⲟⲩⲛ
ϫⲉⲁϥϩⲱⲛ ⲉϩⲟⲩⲛ ⲉ||ⲧⲣⲉⲩϥⲓⲧ̄ϥ ⲛ̄ⲧⲟⲟⲧⲟⲩ*1/2v

ⲁϥ|ⲧⲁⲣⲕⲟⲟⲩ ⲇⲉ
ⲉⲧⲣⲉⲩⲧⲁⲩⲟ ⲉⲣⲟϥ| ⲛ̄ⲧⲁⲓⲧⲓⲁ*1/2v

ⲁⲩⲱ ⲁⲩϩⲟⲙⲟⲗⲟ|ⲅⲉⲓ*1/2v

ⲧⲟⲧⲉ ⲁϥⲙⲟⲣⲟⲩ
ⲉⲧⲙ̄|ⲧⲣⲉⲩϩⲟⲡ̄ϥ ϫⲓⲛⲙ̄ⲡⲉïⲛⲁⲩ*||

ⲁⲩⲱ ⲁϥϭⲱ
ⲉϥϣⲁϫⲉ ⲛ̄ⲙ̄ⲙⲁⲩ|
ⲉϥⲥⲟⲗⲥ̄ⲗ̄ ⲙ̄ⲙⲟⲟⲩ

ⲉϥϫⲱ ⲙ̄|ⲙⲟⲥ
ϫⲉⲙ̄ⲡ̄ⲣⲟⲩⲱⲗ̄ⲥ̄ ⲛ̄ϩⲏⲧ|
ⲟⲩⲁⲧϭⲟⲙ ⲅⲁⲣ ⲡⲉ
ⲉⲧⲣⲉ̣ⲡ̣[ϫⲟ]|ⲉⲓⲥ ⲕⲱ ⲛ̄ⲥⲱϥ ⲙ̄ⲡⲉϥⲗⲁ̣[ⲟⲥ]||
ⲟⲩⲇ̣ⲉ ⲛ̄ϥⲛⲁⲟⲃ̄ϣϥ̄ ⲁⲛ ⲉⲡ̣[..]|[...ⲛ̄ⲧⲉ]ϥⲕⲗⲏⲣ[ⲟ]ⲛ̣ⲟⲙ̣[ⲓⲁ]|

[one or more lines lacking; possibly one or more pages of text follow]

PARALLELS

1–5 ⲕ]ⲁ̣ⲣⲡⲟⲥ <u>to</u> ⲉⲧⲣⲉⲩ||ⲣⲟⲕ̄ϩⲧ̄ ⲉïⲟⲛ̄ϩ
ca]rp <u>to</u> that I be burned alive:

MPol 5.2 καὶ προσευχόμενος ἐν ὀπτασίᾳ γέγονεν πρὸ τριῶν ἡμερῶν τοῦ συλληφθῆναι αὐτόν, καὶ εἶδεν τὸ προσκεφάλαιον αὐτοῦ ὑπὸ πυρὸς κατακαιόμενον. καὶ στραφεὶς εἶπεν πρὸς τοὺς συνόντας αὐτῷ προφητικῶς δεῖ με ζῶντα καυθῆναι[21]

HE 4.15.10 καὶ δὴ εὐχόμενον, ἐν ὀπτασίᾳ τριῶν πρότερον ἡμερῶν τῆς συλλήψεως νύκτωρ ἰδεῖν τὸ ὑπὸ κεφαλῆς αὐτῷ στρῶμα ἀθρόως οὕτως ὑπὸ πυρὸς φλεχθὲν δεδαπανῆσθαι ἔξυπνον δ' ἐπὶ τούτῳ γενόμενον, εὐθὺς ὑφερμηνεῦσαι τοῖς παροῦσι τὸ φανέν, μόνον οὐχὶ τὸ μέλλον προθεσπίσαντα σαφῶς τε ἀνειπόντα τοῖς ἀμφ' αὐτὸν ὅτι δέοι αὐτὸν διὰ Χριστὸν πυρὶ τὴν ζωὴν μεταλλάξαι

Boh 64.14–22 ϩⲁⲧϩⲏ ⲇⲉ ⲛ̄ⲅ̄ ⲛⲉϩⲟⲟⲩ ⲙ̄ⲡⲁⲧⲟⲩⲧⲁϩⲟϥ ⲁ̄ⲟⲩϩⲟⲣⲁⲙⲁ ϭⲱⲣⲡ ⲛⲁϥ ⲉ̄ⲃⲟⲗ ⲙ̄ⲡⲓⲉϫⲱⲣϩ ⲉϥϣⲗⲏⲗ ⲓⲥϫⲉⲕ ⲛⲁϥⲛⲁⲩ ⲉⲡⲉϥϩⲃⲟⲥ ⲉⲧϩⲓϫⲱϥ ⲉ̄ⲁϥⲣⲱⲕϩ ϩⲓⲟⲩⲥⲟⲡ ⲙⲡⲁⲓⲣⲏϯ ϩⲱⲥ ⲉⲧⲁϥⲣⲱⲕϩ ϩⲓⲧⲉ-ⲛⲟⲩⲭⲣⲱⲙ ⲟⲩⲟϩ ⲉⲧⲁϥⲧⲱⲛϥ ϩⲉⲛⲟⲩⲭⲱⲗⲉⲙ ⲁϥϫⲱ ⲙ̄ⲡⲓϭⲱⲣⲡ ⲉⲃⲟⲗ ⲛⲛⲏ ⲉⲧϩⲁⲧⲟⲧϥ ⲉϥⲉⲣϣⲟⲣⲡ ⲛⲉⲣⲥⲩⲛⲙⲉⲛⲓⲛ ⲛⲱⲟⲩ ⲙ̄ⲫⲏ ⲉⲑⲛⲁϣⲱⲡⲓ ⲙ̄ⲙⲟϥⲟⲩⲟϩ ⲉϥⲧⲁⲙⲟ ⲙⲙⲱⲟⲩ ϩⲉⲛⲟⲩⲧⲁϫⲣⲟ ϫⲉϩⲱϯ ⲡⲉ ⲛ̄ⲧⲉϥϫⲱⲕ ⲙ̄ⲡⲉϥⲃⲓⲟⲥ ⲉⲃⲟⲗ ϩⲓⲧⲉⲛ ⲟⲩⲭⲣⲱⲙ ⲉⲑⲃⲉⲡⲭ̅ⲥ̅

MPol 12.3 δεῖ με ζῶντα καυθῆναι

HE 4.15.28 δεῖ με ζῶντα καῆναι

Boh 68.28 ⲥⲑⲏϣ ⲛⲏⲓ ⲉⲑⲣⲟⲩⲣⲟⲕϩⲧ ⲉⲓⲟⲛϩ

15 ⲁⲩⲱ ⲁϥϭⲱ ⲉϥϣⲁϫⲉ ⲛ̄ⲙ̄ⲙⲁⲩ
And he remained, talking with them:

MPol 5.1 Πολύκαρπος . . . διέτριβεν μετ' ὀλίγων

HE 4.15.9 Πολύκαρπον . . . διατρίβειν τε σὺν ὀλίγοις ἐνταῦθα

Boh 64.9 ⲁϥⲟϩⲓ ⲙⲙⲁⲩ ⲛⲉⲙϩⲁⲛⲕⲉⲭⲱⲟⲩⲛⲓ

18–21 ⲟⲩⲁⲧϭⲟⲙ to ⲛ̄ⲧⲉ]ϥⲕⲗⲏⲣ[ⲟ]ⲛ̣ⲟⲙ̣[ⲓⲁ]
it is impossible to hi]s inher[i]tan[ce]:

---

21. καυθῆναι is found in four extant manuscripts, and is preferred by Dehandschutter, *Martyrium Polycarpi,* 115; the majority of extant manuscripts have καῆναι; see Lightfoot, *Apostolic Fathers* 2.3.371, and Karl Bihlmeyer, ed., *Die apostolischen Väter* (Sammlung ausgewählter kirchen- und dogmengeschichtlicher Quellenschriften; Tübingen: J. C. B. Mohr [Paul Siebeck], 1924) 1.123.

Ps 93:14 (94:14) LXX ὅτι οὐκ ἀπώσεται κύριος τὸν λαὸν αὐτοῦ καὶ τὴν κληρονομίαν αὐτοῦ οὐκ ἐγκαταλείψει

Ps 93:14 (94:14) Sah[22] ⲭⲉⲙ̄ⲡⲭⲟⲉⲓⲥ ⲛⲁⲕⲱ ⲛ̄ⲥⲱϥ ⲁⲛ ⲙ̄ⲡⲉϥⲗⲁⲟⲥ* ⲁⲩⲱ ⲛϥ̄ⲛⲁⲟⲃϣϥ̄ ⲁⲛ ⲉⲧⲉϥⲕⲗⲏⲣⲟⲛⲟⲙⲓⲁ

TEXT CRITICAL NOTES

1 ⲕ]ⲁ̣ⲣⲡⲟⲥ: ⲁ̣ read from ambiguous trace touching ⲣ; for ⲁ and ⲣ as a ligature, see (b) 2, (f) 11

ⲛ̄ⲧⲁⲡ̣[ⲉ]: superlin. read from ambiguous traces above the left and right vertical strokes of ⲛ; part of manuscript leaf missing above ⲛ

ⲡ̣ read from small, ambiguous trace

2 ⲡⲱⲕ̄ϩ ⲁⲩ[ⲱ]: ⲕ̄, ϩ̄, and ⲁ confirmed with UV light; ⲩ read from small, ambiguous trace

3 ⲭⲟⲟⲥ: ⲥ confirmed with UV light

9 ⲉϩⲟⲩⲛ: left, right, and top borders of ⲟ are straight lines; for ⲟ with straight borders, see note to (d) 23 above

18 ⲉⲧⲣⲉ̣: for ⲉ̣ can be read ⲑ, ⲟ̣ or ⲥ̣

18–19 ⲡ̣[ⲭⲟ]|ⲉⲓⲥ: ⲡ̣ read from small, ambiguous trace

20 ⲟⲩⲁ̣ⲉ ⲛ̣̄ϥ̣ⲛⲁⲟⲃ̄ϣϥ̄: ⲁ̣ faded, traces of left upward stroke visible

ⲛ̣̄ faded; for ⲛ̣̄ can be read ⲙ̄; superlin. read from ambiguous traces above the letter trace

ϥ̣̄ faded; superlin. read from ambiguous traces above the letter trace

ⲉⲡ̣[: ⲡ̣ read from small, ambiguous trace

21 ⲕⲗⲏⲣ[ⲟ]ⲛ̣ⲟⲙ̣[ⲓⲁ]: for ⲛ̣ can also be read ϥ; ⲙ̣ read from small, ambiguous trace

22. As in E. A. Wallis Budge, *The Earliest Known Coptic Psalter* (London: Kegan Paul, Trench, Truebner, 1898) 101b; for a variant text, see Carl Wessely, *Griechische und Koptische Texte theologischen Inhalts* (Studien zur Paleographie und Papyruskunde 9; Amsterdam: Hakkert, 1966) 1.46, no. K9850.2, in which there is no ⲙ̄ preceding ⲡⲭⲟⲉⲓⲥ.

CHAPTER TWO

Translation

1. Introduction

Objectives

This translation has as its primary goal to translate the text as it is found on the papyrus fragments in the Harris collection. Secondarily it is intended to accomplish the very closely related task of translating the untitled work on Polycarp which is witnessed by this text. Therefore, the concern to present a concise translation of the text is, for the most part, favored over considerations for offering a more fluid, stylistic translation into the vernacular. Consequently, pronouns are translated literally, including the masculine pronoun referring to "the [Lo]rd" as found on page (f). Line breaks in the manuscript are indicated in the translation.

Possible Restorations

The translated restorations correspond to those restorations which are presented as "possible" in the Text Critical Notes in chapter 1, where supporting evidence is cited. Only restorations which meet criteria of physical size (i.e., they must fit the given lacuna) as well as grammatical and syntactic compatibility are presented in the Text Edition.[1]

Sigla

[---]	text missing owing to physical damage (i.e., a lacuna)[2]
| or ||	new line of manuscript commences (|| every fifth line)
5	line number of the manuscript

1. For further discussion, see ch. 1, Introduction.
2. For more precise information on the size of a given lacuna, see ch. 1.

2. Translation

(a) = 63v

[one or more lines lacking; possibly 2 or more pages precede]

[---]ter[---]||[---]s of our Lor[d ---]| [---]ed out from [---]|, [---] went out in the whole|| inha[bite]d world so that each on|[e of t]hem might complete his| [co]urse within the regions which were| [assigned] to them, while they com|[pleted] the preaching about|| [the kin]gdom of [h]eaven throughout| the whole of [this cr]eation, according to the testi|[mon]y of the apostle [---]|

[---]while they bega[n ---]|

[one or more lines lacking]

POSSIBLE RESTORATIONS

1–2]ter[---]||[---]: af]ter [the apo]|[stle]s
2 Lor[d ---]: Lor[d had gathered]
3a [---]ed: [they travell]ed
3b from [---]: from [Jerusalem]
4 [---] went: [and they] went

(b) = 63r

[one or more lines lacking]

[---] in [---]|| [---]ic[3] [---] of virg[inity ---]|| [---]to him instead [of ---]||[---] of the sword and the [---]s|| and the tortures of the [lawcou]|rts.

There remained [---]|ter him a discipl[e ---]| name was Polycar[p, and]| he made him[4] bisho[p over]|| Smyrna, the [---] city|.

After a[ll] the apostles| had died[5] [---]| other disciple[s][6] to [---]|

[one or more lines lacking; possibly 2 or more pages lacking before (c)]

POSSIBLE RESTORATIONS

6–7 [---]|ter: [af]|ter him
7–8 discipl[e ---]| name: discipl[e whose]| name
12–13 [---]| other disciple[s]: [the] other disciples [remain]ed; lit., "they remained, namely the other disciple[s]"

3. A borrowed Greek word whose ending (-[ι]κον) indicates that it is an adjective, presumably modifying an inanimate entity.
4. Polycarp.
5. Lit., "After they a[ll] had died,| namely the apostles [---]|"; for "died," lit., "fallen asleep."
6. Or, "disciple."

(c) = 64r + 56v

[one or more lines lacking; possibly 2 or more pages lacking after (b)]

[---] his[7] [---]|[---] all [the] siblings.[8] [---]| [--- ma]ke prayers [---]|[---] perseverance[9] [---]|| [---] because [---]| [---] he alo[ne] remained| [among the di]sciple[s] of the apos[t]|[les].

He was [---]| [of the] whole [c]hurch [---]|| [---] old man, being one hundred and f[our]| years of age. He continued to walk[10]| [i]n the canons which he had learned| during his youth| from John the a||[p]ostle, until he reached| the stature of a very great age.|

And all the Christians| who had heard about his way of life| used to seek after him to see him, li||ke genuine children| seeking after th[ei]r father.[11]

Moreover, he| had this gift|, that he never [f]orgot an|y w[ho] had come into contact with him.

POSSIBLE RESTORATIONS

4–5 perseverance [---]|| [---]: perseverance [---]|| [--- a ti]me

8 He was [---]: He was [teacher]; or, He was [father]; also possible, He was [priest]

9–10 [---]|| [---] old man: [and he was]|| [an] old man

---

7. Or, "after his."

8. For an argument, based on social-historical and literary context, for the use of "siblings" as opposed to the arguably more literal "brothers," see ch. 4, comment on (c) 2. For the purpose of conciseness I have felt it unadvisable to expand a one-word label into a phrase such as "sisters and brothers."

9. Or, as part of an adverbial phrase, "continually."

10. Lit., "walked" (=Greek imperfect).

11. Lit., "they used to seek after him to see him,| namely all the Christians| who had heard about his way of life."

(d) = 64v + 56r

[one or more lines lacking]

[--- the c]hur[ch ---]| [---] the Jew[s ---][12]| [--- He]rod, saying| slanderous [---][---]: "Poly[carp]||, [---] this city, [is] the teac[her of]| [the] Christian[s]; [---]|[---] everyone [---]| [hi]s magic; while he [---]|[---] them neither to give tribu[te ---]||[--- n]or to worshi[p the]| god[s] of the emperor."

Hero[d]|, after he had heard these thin[gs, was]| very angry. And he o[r]|dered that he[13] be brought to him i[n]|| order that he might kill him.[14]

Aft[e]|r the sibli[ngs] knew[15] [that]| he[16] was being sought after in order to be killed|, they took him and they hid him somewh[er]e|. After they knew again that he|| was being sought in that pl|ace, the siblings tr[a]nsferred him by| night[17] and took him| to another place.

[---] once again the Jews[18] knew| about th[em].

POSSIBLE RESTORATIONS

3–4 slanderous [---]|[---]: slanderous [wor]|[ds]
4–5 Polycarp||, [---] this city: Polycarp||, [a person of] this city

---

12. Lit., "namely the Jew[s]" (the subject of a preceding verb).
13. Polycarp.
14. Polycarp.
15. Lit., "After they knew, namely the sibli[ngs]."
16. Polycarp.
17. Lit., "they tr[a]nsferred him by night, namely the siblings."
18. Lit., "they knew about th[em], [namely] the Jews."

6–8 [---]|[---] everyone [---]| [hi]s magic: [even while he is]| u[tterly] [begu]iling everyone [with]| [hi]s magic

8–9 while he [---]|[---] them: while he [persu]|[ades] them

9–10 neither to give tribu[te ---]|| [--- n]or: neither to give tribu[te to the]|| [emperor n]or

23 [---] once again the Jews knew: [And] once again the Jews knew

(e) = 55v

[possibly 2 or more pages lacking after (d)]

[---]they assume[d][19] the name[20][---]| [---]him, the siblings,[21]| to a deserted place.

As for hi[m]||, he was asking them||, "Why are you[22]| going around with me from place to place?"| And they were afraid to tell him| lest he forbid them| and go alone to the law||court. For they had heard| him say many times|: "It is necessary that I| die by[23] the lawcourt, in the man|ner that the apostle of the Lord|| told me[24]| when he said, 'Since the Lo|rd granted to me that I die| on my bed, it is necessary that you[25]| die by the law||[co]urt, so that an equilibrium might|[---]|."

[two or more lines lacking]|

[---] [Poly-]

19. Or, "they feigned"; or, present tense: "assume," "feign."
20. Or (rare), "the condition of."
21. Lit., "namely the siblings" (the subject of a preceding verb, possibly also the subject of "assume[d]").
22. "You," pl.
23. I.e., "by agency of."
24. Lit., "in the manner that he told me, namely the apostle of the Lord."
25. "You," sing.

(f) = **55r**

ca]rp, as if the| bedspread over him were burning.

And| [w]hen he woke he said to| the siblings, "It is necessary that|| I be burned alive; and I marv|el that they have not sought after me as of| today."

After he had said these things|, the siblings cried[26]| knowing that it would be soon|| that he would be taken from them. He| made them swear that they would tell him| the reason;[27] and they confes|sed. Then he bound them not to| hide him, beginning from this hour||.

And he remained, talking with them| and consoling them, saying|: "Do not be discouraged|, for it is impossible for the [Lo]|rd to abandon his peo[ple]||, neither will he forget the [---]| [--- of hi]s inheritan[ce]|."[28]

[one or more lines lacking; possibly one or more pages of text follow]

26. Lit., "they cried, namely the siblings."

27. I.e., "the reason" for their crying. The Greek loanword αἰτία may also mean: "cause," "indictment," or "motive."

28. For the purpose of conciseness, I have translated the pronouns literally.

CHAPTER THREE

Apostolicity and Martyrdom

An Introduction to the Narrative Strategy of the Text

1. Missing Title and Contents

The title of this work on Polycarp will probably never be known. The only extant witness to the text are papyrus leaves from an ancient codex which contains several other works as well. All the extant papyrus fragments from that codex have been catalogued as a "Miscellany (Acts of Martyrs)."[1] There is one work from the ancient codex for which a title is extant: "The Memorials (ὑπομνήματα) of James the Persian."[2] Did (all) other works in that codex bear the same title, "memorials"? Even if that could be confirmed, it would not necessarily indicate an original or earlier title under which the work might have been known. What this work on Polycarp might have been titled, how it might have circulated before its inclusion in a particular codex of collected works, or for what purpose it might have been written, cannot be discovered from the extant manuscript itself.[3]

Besides the missing title, neither the beginning nor the end of the text are extant. On both internal and external evidence,[4] one may assume that the first line of page (a) lies very near the beginning of the work; perhaps

1. Layton, *Catalogue of Coptic Literary Manuscripts*, 201.
2. Ibid., 202.
3. For possible social-historical and literary context, see esp. ch. 5.
4. See ch. 4, comment on (a) 1–8.

within a few lines. Further one may assume that the narrative continued well beyond the final lines of page (f), wherein Polycarp is awaiting arrest. A full text would likely include descriptions of his arrest, trial, execution, and perhaps other items.

2. Narrative Structure

Of the six pages which have survived, the first half, pages (a)–(c), are concerned with material which might be considered introductory or pre-narrative. Included in these pages are significant descriptions of John's activity and Polycarp's relationship with that apostle. On page (d), the narration of a continuous sequence of events begins.

The following is a summary in outline form of the content of the work:

I. Polycarp's apostolic credentials (via John)
   A. Account of the division of the world among the apostles for the purposes of missionary preaching
   B. Description of the ministry of the apostle John
      1. John as virgin
      2. John's reprieve from a death by martyrdom
   C. Introduction of Polycarp
      1. Disciple of John
      2. Bishop ordained by John
   D. General statement about the death of the apostles
   E. Polycarp as the sole remaining "disciple of the apostles"
      1. Polycarp is exceedingly old (104 years)
      2. Polycarp lived according to the "canons" he learned from John
      3. News of Polycarp's ministry spread and drew followers to him
      4. Polycarp never forgot any of those with whom he had come into contact

II. Polycarp's martyrdom (via John's divine reprieve)
   A. "The Jews" are in discussion with a government official
      1. A list of "slanderous" charges is presented
      2. The official is angered and orders Polycarp's execution
      3. The search for Polycarp begins
   B. Polycarp's community hears about the search
      1. The community hides Polycarp
      2. The community transfers Polycarp to a more secure place

   3. The community and Polycarp are together in a "deserted place"
C. Polycarp questions the community
   1. The community members are "afraid" to answer, for fear that:
      a. Polycarp will forbid them to move him again
      b. Polycarp will "go alone to the lawcourt"
   2. The community remembers what Polycarp said "many times":
      a. "It is necessary" that Polycarp be martyred in lieu of John
D. Polycarp has a vision and interprets it
   1. Polycarp confirms the "necessity" of his martyrdom
   2. The community members cry
   3. The community confesses that it has been hiding Polycarp
   4. The community is "bound" to cease from hiding Polycarp "from this hour"
E. Polycarp "consoles" the community
   1. Polycarp recites Ps. 93:14 (LXX)

3. Part One: Polycarp's Apostolic Credentials (via John)

The preliminary description of Polycarp indicates that the scope of this work is broader than one might expect from a martyrdom or acts of a martyr. More specifically, its scope is broader than that of MartPol, whose interest is bounded by a particular local action against a group of Christians. At the same time, it bears little resemblance to VPol: there is no sustained narrative of an event or series of events from Polycarp's ministry before the consideration of his last days, and no recounting (or even mention) of the hero's exhortations on ethical behavior or of the performing of miracles, both of which are characteristic of VPol and the genre of saint's lives generally.[5]

Preceding any discussion of Polycarp is a report about the division of the world among the apostles for their missionary enterprise. This recounting of the apostles' departure is typical of, though not limited to, the apocryphal acts of the apostles, where it often appears at the beginning of the work.[6] The presence of this departure narrative as introductory material to a work on Polycarp, who is not one of the apostles, is in itself quite note-

5. For a discussion of martyrdoms, lives, and other genres, see ch. 4, comment on (a) 1–8, Obs. 6.

6. See ch. 4, comment on (a) 1–8, esp. Obs. 4.

worthy. Following the departure narrative is a discussion of John's career, including his "virginity" and reprieve from a martyr's death. Polycarp's direct association with John is then recorded, along with the description of Polycarp as the sole remaining "disciple of the apostles."

There can be no doubt that the author has intended to portray the hero Polycarp as "apostolic."[7] The portrait is multifaceted. Polycarp is apostolic: (1) by direct association, having been taught and ordained by John; (2) by chronology, owing to his great age and status as the only remaining student of an apostle; (3) by demeanor, living according to the "canons" he learned from John.

Does the author assume or promote more than "apostolic" status for Polycarp? Yes. This is a work whose fictive world is introduced to the reader through the narrative of the assignment of the regions of the world for missionary preaching, a motif associated with the apostles and literary acts of the apostles. Further, as the narrative unfolds, Polycarp's martyrdom is presented as a surrogate for that of the apostle John; since John has not suffered a martyr's death, Polycarp must.[8] Polycarp is the central figure of a work which begins with a classic account of the ministry of the apostles and which records a martyr death that was itself allotted for an apostle. To the extent that the author's purpose is—or, at least, includes—presenting Polycarp's martyrdom as a surrogate for John's (lack of a) martyrdom, the preliminary descriptions of John and Polycarp are vital to the plot, preparing the reader for the major plot development: Polycarp's martyrdom is to be accounted for as that of the apostle John.

Specifically, the first part of the work provides a vantage point from which to develop a unique understanding of Polycarp: his major act, i.e., his martyrdom, *is* an apostle's martyrdom. Such an authorial strategy is unique within ancient Christian literature. No other ancient Christian document, so far as I am aware, makes such an assertion about Polycarp, or any other individual who is not recognized as an apostle.

There are other descriptions, besides those which serve to develop the notion of Polycarp's martyrdom as being equivalent to an apostle's, which

7. For a discussion of the adjective "apostolic," see L.-M. Dewailly, *Envoyés du père: Mission et apostolicité* (Paris: Éditions de l'Orante, 1960) 46–113, esp. 50: "It designated a person or a thing in direct contact with the apostles"; for the adjective "apostolic" (ἀποστολικός) as applied to Polycarp, see MartPol (MPol 16.2 = HE 4.15.39 = Boh 70.28–71.1) and HE 3.36.10; for the possibility that Boh 70.28–71.1 includes a description of Polycarp as "apostle," see ch. 4, comment on (e) 14–21, Obs. 3.

8. See ch. 4, comment on (e) 14–21; for further discussion, see ch. 5.

connect the introductory material with the narrative of events. For example, the preliminary portrayal of the community leader Polycarp as one pursued by followers who are "like genuine (γνήσιος) children seeking after th[ei]r father," is built on several motifs familiar within panegyrics and biographies of philosophers written in the imperial period.[9] In turn, the narrated action includes many descriptions reminiscent of the portrayal of persecuted teachers within popular philosophical literature: for example, the "slanderous" charge of "magic" and the hero awaiting execution surrounded by a cadre of his followers.[10]

Though it is likely that the length of the narrative of events, were it extant in its entirety, would far exceed that of the preliminary description, this work appears to be more than a martyrdom with a few preliminary, introductory remarks. The distinct parts of the work, as is evidenced even in their fragmentary state, make up an integral and integrated whole.

4. Part Two: Polycarp's Martyrdom (via John's Divine Reprieve)

This work likely contained a complete account of Polycarp's martyrdom. Unfortunately, the extant text breaks off as Polycarp, surrounded by his followers, is awaiting arrest. Among the passages recorded in the register of parallels in chapter 1 are all particular episodes and descriptions which FrgPol shares with MartPol. When the narrated action of the two accounts are compared, one finds that particular episodes and descriptions found in both FrgPol and MartPol often occur in different locations within the overall narrative structure. It is important to consider elements shared by both FrgPol and MartPol, as well as elements unique to FrgPol and lacking in MartPol.

Of less scholarly value is a consideration of elements unique to MartPol and lacking from FrgPol. Since only part of FrgPol is extant it is inconclusive, and therefore less helpful and potentially misleading, to render any judgment based on the observation of items contained in MartPol not found in the extant text of FrgPol.

That said, it may be worthwhile to note the apparent lack in FrgPol of a given episode or detail from the narrative line running through the move-

9. For further discussion, see ch. 4, comment on (c) 16–24.

10. For further discussion of "slanderous" charges, see ch. 4, comment on (d) 3–4; for a discussion of the use of "magic," see comment on (d) 8; for a discussion of scenes of consolation and waiting, see comment on (f) 7–15.

ments of Polycarp before his arrest (that is, through the point in the narrated action at which the extant text of FrgPol breaks off). Among the items which can tentatively be considered to be lacking from FrgPol are: (1) any mention of the execution of other Christians within the same local persecution—compare (d) 1–15 with MPol 2.2–3.2 and HE 4.15.4–6; (2) a description of the first hiding place—compare the stark description, "somewhere" (d) 18, with "little farm" in MPol 5.1 or "farm" in HE 4.15.9; (3) any indication of the location of the first hiding place, such as "outside of" or "not far from" the city (as in MPol 5.1 and HE 4.15.9, respectively); (4) any exhortation directed to the reader (as in MPol 1.2 and 4 and, to a lesser extent, HE 4.15.8); and (5) direct mention of the motif of *imitatio Christi* (as in MPol 1.1).

Among the episodes and descriptions shared by MartPol and FrgPol is one which is actually found in Part One of FrgPol. Consideration of that will be followed by discussion of items found in Part Two of FrgPol.

A. In FrgPol the narrator states that Polycarp "never [f]orgot any of those w[ho] had come into contact with him" ([c] 23–24). Within MartPol, a parallel statement occurs in a summary of the content of the prayer which Polycarp speaks upon his arrest (MPol 8.1 = HE 4.15.15). Since the last extant lines of FrgPol depict Polycarp awaiting his arrest, one cannot know whether a similar description occurs in that work at the point of Polycarp's arrest.

What is certain, however, is that FrgPol includes the parallel sentence as one of several descriptions used to develop a portrait of Polycarp in the first part of the work. It follows the statement, familiar in contemporary literary depictions of teachers, that followers sought after him "like genuine children seeking after th[ei]r father" ([c] 17–21).[11] In comparison with MartPol, both (1) general context[12] and (2) immediate context[13] are different.

B. Within FrgPol, the account of Polycarp's martyrdom begins with a discussion between "the Jews" and a certain "Herod" ([d] 4–5).[14] At (d) 5–11, a set of charges against Polycarp is presented which contains three basic elements: Polycarp (1) is "the teac[her of] [the] Christians"; (2) is associated with "magic"; and (3) urges his followers "neither to give tribu[te ---] [--- n]or to worshi[p the] god[s] of the emperor."

11. For further discussion, see ch. 4, comment on (c) 16–24.
12. Narrated action in MartPol versus preliminary description in FrgPol.
13. Prayer in MartPol versus attraction to the community leader in FrgPol.
14. For consideration of the identity of this Herod, see ch. 4, comment on (d) 2–3.

Within MartPol a set of charges sharing, in part, two of these three elements (nos. 1 and 3) is recorded *following* Polycarp's trial, not preceding his arrest.[15] Therein it is called out by "the crowd of gentiles and Jews" who are in "the stadium"—the location, in MartPol, of Polycarp's trial.[16]

The occurrence in FrgPol of a formal set of charges at or near the beginning of the account of the last days is significant for several reasons. In FrgPol the search and eventual trial of Polycarp are not initiated by mob action.[17] There is a clear list of charges and one collective accuser, "the Jews."[18] Further, Polycarp's trial and execution are treated as a closed set of independent or isolable events; unlike MartPol, there is apparently no mention of, and definitely no narrative reliance on, a preceding trial of fellow Christians which escalates into the action against Polycarp.

C. Like MartPol, FrgPol records the movement of Polycarp to two separate hiding places ([d] 15–23). Unlike MartPol, FrgPol includes no consideration of the state of Polycarp's mind or any repartee between him and his circle before the first move (nor is there any text missing at this point in the narrative).[19] Further, unlike MartPol, there is no description of Polycarp's demeanor, nor any narrative action recorded, at the first hiding place (nor is there any text missing at this point in the narrative).[20] By way of contrast, while MartPol contains neither a description of Polycarp's demeanor nor a record of any action at the second hiding place prior to the arrival of the government forces, FrgPol contains extended descriptions of dialogue and action at the second hiding place.

The relationship of FrgPol and MartPol on the matter of the hiding of Polycarp and the activities/state of mind recorded, might be charted as follows:

---

15. See MPol 12.2 and HE 4.15.26; for further discussion, see ch. 4, comments on (d) 4–6, 8–11.

16. It should be noted that in MartPol the search for Polycarp is prompted by the demand of "the crowd": "Take away the atheists. Let Polycarp be searched for" (MPol 3.2 = HE 4.15.6). Implicit in the crowd's words is the charge of "atheism"; for further discussion of that, and other charges against Christians, see Robert Wilken, *The Christians as the Romans Saw Them* (New Haven: Yale University Press, 1984), esp. ch. 3; and G. E. M. de Ste Croix, "Why Were the Early Christians Persecuted," *Past and Present* 26 (1963) 6–38, 27 (1964) 28–33, and A. N. Sherwin-White, "Why Were the Early Christians Persecuted: An Amendment," *Past and Present* 27 (1964) 23–27.

17. Compare MartPol (MPol 3.2, HE 4.15.6).

18. For discussion of "the Jews," see ch. 4, comment on (d) 2–3, esp. Obs. 4–9.

19. Compare MPol 5.1, HE 4.15.9.

20. Compare MPol 5.1–2, HE 4.15.9–10.

	*Prior to first move
MartPol:	Narrates activities/state of mind
FrgPol:	Does not narrate activities/state of mind
	*At first hiding place
MartPol:	Narrates activities/state of mind
FrgPol:	Does not narrate activities/state of mind
	*At second hiding place
MartPol:	Does not narrate activities/state of mind prior to the arrival of government forces
FrgPol:	Narrates activities/state of mind[21]

D. The episode of Polycarp's dream and subsequent interpretation is shared by both MartPol and FrgPol. In MartPol it occurs at the first hiding place, while in FrgPol it does not occur until Polycarp is at the second hiding place ([f] 1–7). Therein it is part of a complex of narrated events and dialogue which serves to indicate Polycarp's state of mind and lack of awareness of his community's action on his behalf.

After arriving at the second hiding place, Polycarp asks the community, "Why are you going around with me from place to place?" ([e] 5–6). The choice of verb within Polycarp's question, "going around," stands in contrast to that used by the voice of the narrator, who has already told the reader that Polycarp's circle "took him" to the first hiding place and "tr[a]nsferred him" to the second ([d] 18, 21). Furthermore, it is recorded that the community members are "afraid" to answer the question posed by Polycarp, "lest he forbid them and go alone to the lawcourt" ([e] 7–10). The message to the reader is clear: Polycarp does not recognize that his community is moving him around for purposes of fleeing the authorities.

The dream sequence in FrgPol appears to parallel that of MartPol fairly closely. However, the subsequent interpretation includes an additional sentence not found in MartPol: "and I marvel that they have not sought after me as of today."[22] Of course, within the narrative line of MartPol

21. Up to the point in the narrative at which FrgPol breaks off, there has been no arrival of government forces. One cannot simply assume that such an event would be narrated in the full text of FrgPol (were it available).

22. For a discussion of the use of the Coptic preposition ϣⲁ ("until"), see ch. 4, comment on (f) 5–7.

such a statement would make no sense, since Polycarp had "heard" that he was being sought out before his circle's first attempt to hide him (MPol 5.1, HE 4.15.9).

In addition, unlike MartPol the interpretation of the vision in FrgPol is followed by dialogue between Polycarp and his circle. The interpretation elicits an emotional response from the community—they know what their beloved teacher does not know; Polycarp is indeed being sought after by government forces—which leads, in turn, to a discussion in which Polycarp learns of his followers' (neatly masked) efforts to hide him. Once Polycarp had become aware that he was being sought, he "bound them not to hide him" any longer.

Within this work, the narrated action of Polycarp's dream and interpretation, followed by the community response, is central to Polycarp's understanding of his immediate plight and of the community's action in hiding him. Unlike the Polycarp of MartPol, this Polycarp is not "persuaded" to flee; rather, he is duped for a time. Once he becomes aware that a search is on, he orders the community no longer to move him and remains where he is.[23]

In sum, FrgPol and MartPol contain many similar descriptions and episodes. However, by way of paraphrasing Yogi Berra, Jr., their similarities are different. Maintaining a keen awareness of these differences is important.

As for the "expansions" into the narrated action which are found in Part Two of FrgPol (as compared to MartPol), the descriptions in Part One serve to orient the reader to these. For example, regarding items such as the particular set of charges and the particular descriptions of community consolation narrated in Part Two, the inclusion in Part One of conventional motifs found in literary portrayals of teachers have already provided the reader a context for understanding. Further, having been reminded in Part One of John's "virginity" and lack of a martyr's death, the reader is provided with a broader hagiographical framework within which to place the recollection of the community that Polycarp had said "many times" that his martyrdom was necessitated by the reprieve granted to John. Finally, where the accounts of other martyrdoms at the top of MartPol provide the context for elevating Polycarp as "the only one remembered by all," whose action puts an end to a local persecution as though "having sealed it,"[24] the recollection of the division of the world among the apostles at the top of FrgPol

23. Compare MPol 5.1, HE 4.15.9; see also MPol 6.1 and HE 4.15.11.
24. MPol 19.1 = HE 4.15.45; MPol 1.1 = HE 4.15.3.

provides the greater context for portraying Polycarp as one who accomplishes an apostle's martyrdom.

The narrative strategy of FrgPol is unfolded deliberately and artfully. Even in its fragmentary state this ancient work provides clear evidence of the care and skill with which it has been composed.

CHAPTER FOUR

Commentary

1. Introduction

No commentary is exhaustive, nor should it mean to be. This commentary has as its primary objectives the observing and describing of literary and social phenomena indicated in and by the text, with the goal of understanding this unique work. Secondarily, I hope that many of the comments contribute more broadly to our understanding of the literary traditions regarding both Polycarp and the apostle John; the commentary does on occasion speak directly to one or both of those matters. The "observing and describing" undertaken herein means to be "historical," that is, governed by the conventions of historiography in the service of locating phenomena which might reasonably be considered to have been available to those who produced and were among the first to experience—through reading and/or hearing—this work. Comments range from the observation of a particular grammatical or lexical phenomenon to broad considerations of a theological development or a literary motif.

The commentary is arranged according to conventional format; the citation of a given section of text is followed by the comments on that text. The lengthier comments are organized into a series of "observations" (abbr. "Obs.").

Quotations are taken from the full translation found in chapter 2, though the indications of line breaks have been removed. For an explanation of the editorial signs used, see Sigla at the beginning of chapter 2.

2. Commentary

(a) 1–8 [---]ter[---][---]s of our Lor[d ---] [---]ed out from [---], [---] went out in the whole inha[bite]d world so that each on[e of t]hem might complete his [co]urse within the regions which were [assigned] to them

Obs. 1. The whole of lines 1–11 recount the legend of the division of the world among the apostles for the purpose of missionary preaching.[1] At least one summary statement that the apostles went out into the regions of the world following the earthly ministry of Jesus is extant in late first-century literature.[2] In one of the classic scholarly essays on the subject, Richard Lipsius states that "the legends of the activity of the apostles in the various lands of the earth are struck up already in the Second Century."[3] The conclusion of Adolf von Harnack, that "apostolic mission reports" were circulating by approximately the end of the second century or beginning of the third century, has generally been accepted.[4]

By way of clarifying the content of these early "apostolic mission reports," Eric Junod writes, "the most ancient [reports] never give a complete list of the apostles with the region of the mission of each."[5] Further, Junod notes that there are five particular apostles who appear in an early mission report and about whom the earliest acts of the apostles were written: Thomas, Andrew, John, Peter, and Paul.[6]

---

1. Besides the works cited below, see Walter Bauer, "Accounts [of the Apostles in Early Christian Tradition]," in *New Testament Apocrypha,* vol. 2, *Writings Relating to the Apostles, Apocalypses, and Related Subjects* (ed. Edgar Hennecke and Wilhelm Schneemelcher, tr. R. McL. Wilson; Philadelphia: Westminster Press, 1965) 35–74, esp. 45, and more recently, Wolfgang A. Bienert, "The Picture of the Apostle in Early Christian Tradition," in Schneemelcher, *New Testament Apocrypha,* vol. 2, *Writings Relating to the Apostles,* 5–27, esp. 18–27.

2. *1 Clem.* 42.1–4; for text, see ch. 1, register of parallels, (a) 1–8; see also therein citations from the canonical Gospels in which Jesus commands the "apostles" or "disciples" to "go out."

3. Richard Lipsius, "Die Legende von der Aposteltheilung," *Die apokryphen Apostelgeschichten und Apostellegenden* (Braunschweig: C. A. Schwetschke und Sohn, 1883) 1.11.

4. Adolf von Harnack, *Der kirchengeschichtliche Ertrag der exegetischen Arbeiten des Origenes zum Hexateuch und Richterbuch* (TU 42.3; Leipzig: J. C. Hinrichs, 1918) 16.

5. Eric Junod, "Origène, Eusèbe et la tradition sur la répartition des champs de mission des apôtres," in *Les actes apocryphes des apôtres* (Francois Bovon et al.; Publications de la Faculté de Théologie de l'Université de Genève; Geneva: Labor et Fides, 1981) 243.

6. Ibid., 248 (similarly 233), commenting on the report of Origen recorded by Eusebius (HE 3.1).

Obs. 2. As stated by Jean-Daniel Kaestli, "no one, ancient and coherent tradition regarding the division of the mission fields [among the apostles] is found."[7] After observing the broad range of elements and motifs which are extant within the ancient literature, one might consider such items as: (A) initiative—is it Christ's (through a vision), the apostles' collectively, or Peter's? (B) is a full list of the apostles and their respective regions included? and (C) does Peter accompany the individual apostle to his allotted region?[8] In the early non-canonical acts,[9] the apostles act as a group (with no stated impetus from Christ or Peter), a complete list of apostles and their allotted territories is not included, and there is no report of Peter accompanying the individual apostle.

Given the extent of the lacunas within and surrounding page (a), it is impossible to be sure how each of the three elements outlined above might have been treated in FrgPol. What can be stated with certainty is that, given the extant text, there is no reason that the tradition as narrated in FrgPol must be placed any later than the second or third century. That is, the contents of the text contain elements all of which are recognizable within the early strata of mission reports.

Obs. 3. Within those apocryphal acts which include an account of the division of the world, that account does not always occur at the beginning of the work.[10] Does the departure narrative as contained in FrgPol mark the beginning of this work? One cannot be certain. However, since the main character, Polycarp, is introduced at (b) 5–6, well after the departure narrative, and since a summary statement about the character and ministry of the central secondary figure, John, begins on page (a) sometime after the departure narrative, it is unlikely that any narrative content pre-

---

7. See Jean-Daniel Kaestli, "Les scènes d'attribution des champs de mission et de départ de l'apôtre dans les actes apocryphes," in Bovon et al., *Les actes apocryphes des apôtres,* 264.

8. See Kaestli, "Les scenes d'attribution," throughout.

9. As typified by the *Acts of Thomas.*

10. See esp. *Acts of Philip* 8; see also *Acts of Peter* 5, "God was already preparing Peter for what was to come, now that the twelve years in Jerusalem which the Lord Christ had enjoined on him were completed" (tr. Wilhelm Schneemelcher, "The Acts of Peter," in Schneemelcher, *New Testament Apocrypha,* vol. 2, *Writings Relating to the Apostles,* 290), and *Kerygma Petri* 3a, "For that reason Peter records that the Lord had said to the disciples . . . And after 12 years go ye out into the world" (tr. Schneemelcher, "The Kerygma Petri," 39).

In the *Acts of Peter and the Twelve,* the disciples set out together in one boat (VI.1.1) and later announce, "It is necessary for us to spread the word of God in every city harmoniously" (VI.5.12–14); see ch. 1, n. 5.

cedes (a) 1–11.[11] If the departure narrative of FrgPol lies at the beginning of the work, which is probable based on internal evidence and which is the case in the early *Acts of Thomas*,[12] then the beginning of the full text of FrgPol occurred just one or several lines before the first line of extant text.

Obs. 4. The beginning of the *Acts of John* (AJn) is not extant. Of the early acts of the apostles, *Acts of Thomas* includes a summary statement of the division of the world at the top of the work; *Acts of Peter* and *Acts of Paul* do not; the beginning of the *Acts of Andrew* is not extant. Among related literature associated with the apostle John, both the *Syriac History of John* and the *Acts of John by Prochorus* include such a statement at the top of the work.

Since it includes a summary statement about the division of the world which, at least in its extant form, is consistent with the early literature, and since it displays a close association with traditions about the apostle John, the reading of FrgPol may be used as evidence to support the argument that a statement about the division of the world was present at the beginning of AJn.[13]

Obs. 5. In the entry on Polycarp in the slavonic *Menology* of Dimitrius of Rostov, it is noted that Polycarp joins the apostles in their world mission. That claim is not made in FrgPol or, to my knowledge, in any extant works from the early or late antique periods.

Nevertheless, such a claim is not wholly foreign to extant, early Christian discussion which might relate indirectly to Polycarp. The following description of those "possessing the first rank in the succession from the Apostles" occurs at HE 3.37.1, immediately following an extended reference to Polycarp's depiction of the martyr Ignatius (HE 3.36.13–15):

> And others besides them were well known at this time, possessing the first rank in the succession from the apostles. These, being pious disciples of such great ones, in every place built upon the foundations of the churches laid by the apostles, increasing even more the preaching

11. Though (a) 11, "the apostle," may signal previous text in which that character is introduced; for discussion of the identity of "the apostle," see below comment on (a) 11–12.

12. See below, Obs. 4.

13. For an argument against the likelihood of a summary statement about the division of the world being present at the beginning of the *Acts of John*, see Kaestli, "Les scènes d'attribution," 262; Lipsius, *Die apokryphen Apostelgeschichten und Apostellegenden* 1.13, suggests that AJn began with such a statement; for further discussion, see below, comment on (b) 2–6, Obs. 8.

and spreading the saving seed of the kingdom of heaven into the whole inhabited world.

The reference to a definable and describable group of "disciples" of "apostles" and to the missionary preaching of the apostles are notable parallels to the early, extant lines of FrgPol. One wonders whether Eusebius, his source(s), and, more broadly, early Christians familiar with Polycarp would have included Polycarp among those described in a report such as that found in Eusebius.[14]

Obs. 6. The presence of a summary statement about the division of the world among the apostles, as introductory matter, raises the question of the genre of this work. Does the departure narrative signal the genre "acts" of an apostle?

Among those works of early Christian literature which include a summary statement on the division of the world one finds various genres represented: gospel, letter or epistle, heresiology, commentary, church history, and acts of the apostles. Further, as noted in Obs. 4 above, many acts do not begin with such a summary statement. So, to conclude that this work means to present itself as—or means to mimic—literary acts of the apostles would be premature or misleading.

Nonetheless, it is apparent from the subsequent content of FrgPol that it does not present itself as a gospel, a letter or epistle, a heresiological work, a biblical commentary, or a church history. Are there any genres or kinds of ancient Christian literature other than that of the acts of an apostle for which FrgPol might be considered a candidate?

The genre "Life" or *Vita* fails as a possibility if one takes it to be characteristic of that genre that "while the saints die a martyr's death, this event, far from being the central narrative interest of the story, comprises but one element in a complex tale."[15] Though the extant text of FrgPol indicates that its author is concerned with more than a simple recounting of the martyr's death,[16] "the central narrative interest" is that of Polycarp's last days.[17]

It has recently been suggested that "the title 'Martyrdom of' (*passiones* or *martyria*) is given to Christian accounts whose focus is upon descrip-

14. For further discussion of the designation "disciple of the apostles," see comments on (b) 6–8.

15. Alison Goddard Elliot, *Roads to Paradise: Reading the Lives of the Early Saints* (Hanover: University Press of New England, 1987) 21.

16. See above, ch. 3.

17. See the transition from page (c) to page (d) and following.

tions (purportedly of eyewitnesses or contemporaries) of the last events and heroic sufferings of martyrs."[18] Though it does appear that the "focus" or narrative interest of FrgPol is on Polycarp's "last events,"[19] the departure narrative and other material on pages (a)–(c) present serious intrusions into the "martyrdom" genre.[20]

Given the very close relationship with the apostle John which is developed in FrgPol, especially surrounding the martyr's death,[21] it is likely that the departure narrative is meant to present the reader with at least a motif (division of the world), if not a genre (acts), which is associated directly with the apostles.

Obs. 7. The restoration of the text in the lacunas of page (a) is complicated by the variety of detail within the tradition on the division of the world among the apostles. For example, a possible restoration for (a) 3 is "Jerusalem,"[22] a reading which is consistent with relevant passages in the NT[23] as well as later tradition. However, a specific location within or around Jerusalem may have been identified. In works associated with John, the *Syriac History of John* includes the "upper room" as the setting in which the apostles gather for the division of the world, while the *Mysteries of St. John and the Holy Virgin* identifies the Mount of Olives as the setting.

Obs. 8. In Sah, "region" and "assigned" are cognates, an association not readily made in an English translation. A similar pair of cognates available to the Greek stylist would be χώρα and χωρίζω, though I find no extant Greek parallel which employs these.

(a) 8–11 while they com[pleted] the preaching about [the kin]gdom of [h]eaven throughout the whole of [this cr]eation

Obs. 1. The departure narrative in FrgPol contains both (A) a statement regarding the division of the world into assigned territories, and (B) a description of the content of the apostles' preaching. The second ele-

---

18. Bisbee, *Pre-Decian Acts of Martyrs and Commentarii,* 5.

19. Given such an understanding, (a)–(c) are introductory to the action that begins on (d); the emphasis on "lawcourt" at (e) 10, 13, 19, and possibly (b) 5 may indicate to the reader such a "focus on last events and heroic sufferings."

20. See, for example, the corpus of texts in Herbert Musurillo, *The Acts of the Christian Martyrs* (Oxford: Clarendon Press, 1972).

21. See below, esp. comment on (b) 2–6, (e) 14–21; also ch. 3, ch. 5.

22. As suggested in the text critical notes; see above, ch. 1.

23. Esp. Luke 24:47; see also ch. 1, parallels to (a) 1–8.

ment, a description of the content of the apostles' preaching, is not commonly found in reports of the division of the world from the second and third century. For example, it is not found in either HE 3.1 or *Acts of Thomas* 1. However, it is present in texts that predate these.

1 Clem. 42.3–4 includes both elements: "they went out announcing the good news that the kingdom of God was coming, preaching throughout the regions and cities." Several NT passages, notably Mark 16:15, include both elements: "And he said to them, 'Go into all the world and proclaim the good news to the whole creation.'"[24]

The vocabulary and content of the departure narrative in FrgPol are consistent with the earliest (first- and second-century) records of the apostolic division of the world.

Obs. 2. The syntax of the Sah phrase is ambiguous due to the relative pronoun, "which."[25] A literal translation would be "while they com[pleted] the preaching of [the kin]gdom of [h]eaven which is in all of [this cr]eation." Is it "the preaching" (about the kingdom of heaven) or "[the kin]gdom of [h]eaven," "which is in all of [this cr]eation"?

Obs. 3. Given the strength of the parallels presented,[26] and the tradition of the division of the world for the apostolic preaching, the former is to be favored as the probable meaning of the text: it is "the preaching," accomplished by the apostles, "which is in all of [this cr]eation." Such is the understanding presented in the translation given in chapter 2. The somewhat unusual use of "creation" in this context can be explained by the influence of Mark 16:15.[27]

---

24. NRSV; see similarly, Matt 24:14, Luke 24:47; see also ch. 1, parallels to (a) 1–8 and (a) 8–11.

25. Bare ⲉⲧ.

26. See ch. 1, register of parallels.

27. "In the whole creation" (Gk, πάσῃ τῇ κτίσει; Sah, ⲙ̄ⲡⲥⲱⲛⲧ̄ ⲧⲏⲣϥ̄). The apparent presence of the demonstrative pronoun "this" before "creation" does not find a parallel in Mark 16:15. However, the pronoun "this" (Gk, ἄυτη; Sah, ⲡⲉï) is coupled with "creation" in Ps 73:18 (LXX): "Remember this creation of yours."

If this phrase in (a) 8–11 does indicate the influence of Mark 16:15, the occurrence is noteworthy, since many of the earliest manuscript witnesses to the second Gospel do not include the so-called "longer ending" of Mark, 16:9–20. According to Kurt Aland and Barbara Aland, *Text of the New Testament: An Introduction to the Critical Editions and the Theory and Practice of Modern Textual Criticism* (tr. Erroll F. Rhodes; Grand Rapids: William B. Eerdmans, 1987) 287:

> in Codex Vaticinus . . . as well as in Codex Sinaiticus . . . the Gospel of Mark ends at Mark 16:8, as it did also in numerous other manuscripts according to the statements

Obs. 4. What of the less likely possibility, that it is "[the kin]gdom of [h]eaven which is in all of [this cr]eation"? Such a notion may be found within early documents associated with the apostles generally, and with the apostle John specifically.

A) The book of *Revelation* includes such statements as "the kingdom of the world has become the kingdom of our Lord and of his Messiah."[28] As recorded by Eusebius, Dionysius of Alexandria states that he does not agree with the assertion in Rev that "the kingdom of Christ will be on earth."[29] Here the grammatical tense and, presumedly, the state of affairs being commented on are in the future.

In Gaius' criticism of Rev, as recorded also by Eusebius (HE 3.28.2), the time element is less clear. Not the indicative but the infinitive is used in summarizing the teaching which Gaius finds disagreeable: "that after the resurrection the kingdom of Christ be earthly." Since the adverbial phrase "after the resurrection" is itself ambiguous, one cannot know for certain whether Gaius assumes this earthly "kingdom" to be a future event. If the adverbial phrase, "after the resurrection," points back to the resurrection of Christ which has already occurred, then presumedly, "the kingdom" might be understood to be (already) "on earth." If, as is more probable, the phrase points to a future resurrection of believers,[30] then this earthly "kingdom" is necessarily a future occurrence.

---

of Eusebius of Caeserea and Jerome. The same is true for the Sinaitic Syriac sy^s, the Old Latin manuscript k of the fourth/fifth century, and at least one Sahidic manuscript of the fifth century. . . .

On the other hand, according to *Biblia Patristica* 1.318–319 and 3.285, Mark 16:15 is cited by such early Christian writers as Clement of Alexandria, Origen, and Tertullian, as well as in several non-canonical or apocryphal works, including the *Epistula Apostolorum* (for the possible influence of Mark 16:15 in the latter, see *Epistula Apostolorum* 30; in Müller, "Epistula Apostolorum," 267 [translation], 282 [notes], and Schmidt, *Gespräche Jesu*, 94–95). Perhaps more pertinent, as stated by Werner Georg Kümmel, *Introduction to the New Testament* (rev. ed.; tr. Howard Clark Kee; Nashville: Abingdon Press, 1984) 100, the longer ending is "known to Tatian and Irenaeus (who knows it as the end of Mark)." Irenaeus, of course, hails from Smyrna and claims to have been Polycarp's student; his knowledge of Mark 16: 9–20 may indicate the presence of that manuscript tradition in Smyrna from as early as the time of Polycarp.

28. Rev 11:15b (NRSV); see also Rev 12:9–10, 14:6.

29. HE 3.28.5, 7.25.3. Dionysius attributes Rev to Cerinthus, stating that the book is falsely circulating under John's name (HE 7.25.1–2; similarly Gaius, 3.28.1–2); for a discussion of the association of Cerinthus with the Montanism and chiliasm of Phrygia and Asia Minor, see Benjamin G. Wright, "Cerinthus *apud* Hippolytus," *SecCent* 4 (1984) 103–115, esp. 112–113.

30. Apparently the meaning which Dionysius, writing *after* Gaius, understood.

Though unlikely, it is possible that the reading of FrgPol is alluding to a tradition associated with Rev that the heavenly "kingdom" would be or perhaps, already is, "on the earth."

B) The following summary statement occurs within the *Syriac History of John:* "And when the apostles had travelled about in the countries, and had planted the cross, and it had spread over the four quarters of the world. . . ."[31] The mission of the apostles is equated with the planting of "the cross."

Since "cross" and "kingdom" are closely associated in certain early Christian texts,[32] the statement in the *Syriac History* might be understood as a parallel to the reading of FrgPol. Though unlikely,[33] it is possible that the reading of FrgPol is alluding to a tradition in which "the kingdom of heaven" is considered to be "in the world" *as a result of* the apostolic mission.[34]

C) *Gos. Thom.* 113 presents the following dialogue between Jesus and "his disciples":

> His disciples said to him, "When will the kingdom come?" "It will not come by watching for it. It will not be said, 'Behold, here' or 'Behold, there.' Rather, the kingdom of the Father is spread out upon the earth, and people do not see it."[35]

The last sentence as preserved in Coptic emphasizes the adverbial element, "upon the earth," through the use of the second tense. There appears to be no ambiguity here: it is "upon the earth" that the "kingdom of the Father" is now, already "spread out." Fueled in part by the Jesus Seminar's interest in reconstructing the sayings of the historical Jesus, recent scholarly discussion on *Gos. Thom.* 113 and (possibly) related texts has

---

31. W. Wright, *Apocryphal Acts of the Apostles: Edited from Syriac Manuscripts in the British Museum and Other Libraries* (London: Williams and Norgate, 1871) 2.58; for the Syriac text, see 1.63.

32. For example, Barn. 8.5: "the kingdom of Jesus is on the cross"; see the discussion below regarding *Martyrdom of Peter* 9.

33. See above, Obs. 3.

34. See also above, comment on (a) 1–8, Obs. 5, for HE 3.37.1.

35. John S. Kloppenborg, Marvin W. Meyer, Stephen Patterson, Michael G. Steinhauser, *Q - Thomas Reader* (Sonoma: Polebridge Press, 1990) 154; includes translation (as cited above) and Coptic text. For a critical edition with translation, see Bentley Layton, ed., Thomas O. Lambdin, tr., "The Gospel According to Thomas," *Nag Hammadi Codex II, 2–7, together with XIII.2, Brit. Lib. Or. 4962(1), and P.Oxy. 1, 654, 655* (NHS 20; Leiden: E. J. Brill, 1989) 52–93.

sought to delineate a "cluster of sayings" of Jesus which indicate "that God's imperial rule had arrived."[36] Though unlikely, it is possible that the reading of FrgPol remembers a Christian—or, at least, a Jesus—tradition in which "the kingdom" is reckoned to have already arrived.

Regardless of the relationship of *Gos. Thom.* 113 with the other kingdom sayings of Jesus, consideration of the use of the verb "spread out" in the context of other early Christian literature might shed light on (a) 8–11. Metaphysical discussions associating Christ or "the cross" with the ordering principle of the universe that is "spread out," "hung," or "extended" are familiar in early Christian literature. In the *First Apology* 60, for example, Justin equates "the cross" with the crosswise arrangement of the universe as described in Plato's *Timaeus,* thereby recognizing "the word" (i.e., Christ) as the ordering principle.[37] Within the traditions associated with John, AJn 97–101 presents a vision from "the Lord" in which John learns that it is "this Cross then, which has made all things stable . . . and separated off what is transitory[38] and inferior."[39]

But how does one move from "cross" or "Christ" to "kingdom"? *Martyrdom of Peter* 9 presents an answer.[40] In his final speech, made while suspended (upside down) on the cross, Peter uses his own predicament to launch a metaphysical discussion about "the first man" who "being drawn down . . . cast his first beginning down to earth" and "established the whole of this cosmic system, being hung up. . . ."[41] The speech closes with the appeal to "recognize the Kingdom."[42]

---

36. Robert W. Funk, Roy W. Hoover, and the Jesus Seminar, *The Five Gospels: The Search for the Authentic Words of Jesus* (New York: Macmillan, 1993) 531–532. A consideration of the particulars of the debate regarding the meaning of *Gos. Thom.* 113 and (possibly) related texts cannot be undertaken here. For recent discussion besides *The Five Gospels,* see Stephen Patterson, *The Gospel of Thomas and Jesus* (Sonoma: Polebridge Press, 1993) 72; for further discussion and bibliography, see Jacques-E. Ménard, *L'Évangile selon Thomas* (NHS 5; Leiden: E. J. Brill, 1975) 209, and *L'Évangile selon Philippe: Introduction, texte-traduction, commentaire* (Paris: Letouzy and Ané, 1967) 168–170; also Ernst Haenchen, *Die Botschaft des Thomas-Evangelium* (Theologische Bibliothek Töpelmann 6; Berlin: Alfred Töpelmann, 1961).

37. See similarly the cosmology of Ptolemy (the Valentinian) as recounted in AH, esp. 1.2.4, 1.3.5.

38. Lit., "generated."

39. Tr. Schäferdiek, "The Acts of John," 185.

40. *Martyrdom of Peter* 9 = *Acts of Peter with Simon* 38.

41. Tr. Schneemelcher, "The Acts of Peter," in Schneemelcher, *New Testament Apocrypha,* vol. 2, *Writings Relating to the Apostles,* 315.

42. In the *Gospel of Philip,* the "Son," who is present on earth, is equated with both "Father" and "Kingdom"; sentences 81 and 96 in Ménard, *L'Évangile selon Philippe;* see also above, Obs. 4B on the *Syriac History of John.*

Against the backdrop of extant second-century Christian descriptions about the significance of Christ for the ordering of the universe, the phrase "[the kin]gdom of [h]eaven which is in all of [this cr]eation" might be understood as a summary of the content of the apostolic preaching. Though unlikely,[43] it is possible that the reading of FrgPol is alluding to a cosmological tradition in which "the kingdom of heaven" is considered to be "in the world."

(a) **11–12** according to the testi[mon]y of the apostle

Obs. 1. The identity of "the apostle" cannot be known with certainty given the fragmentary nature of the text at this point. Has "the apostle" already been introduced by name (previous to the first line of extant text)? Is it simply assumed that the reader will know the identity of "the apostle" given the association with (A) Polycarp, or (B) the report of division of the world among the apostles? There are several factors to be considered.

Obs. 2. Internal evidence indicates that "the apostle" is John. John is named as Polycarp's teacher at (c) 11–15. Also within the extant text are two extended references to John's life and ministry—one beginning after (a) 13 and continuing to (b) 11, the other, (e) 13–21. Both link Polycarp's ministry and martyrdom very closely to John. One can be reasonably certain that John is "the apostle" here.

Obs. 3. A simple garnering of evidence from other literature associated with Polycarp might suggest Paul as a more likely candidate for "the apostle" who has influenced Polycarp.

A) In Pol. *Phil.* the only apostle named is Paul (four times).[44] "The apostles" are referred to twice, once alone (Pol. *Phil.* 6), once as "Paul and the rest of the apostles" (Pol. *Phil.* 9.1). Pauline quotations and allusions predominate.[45] As for the language of Johannine literature, it can be identified in, at most, three phrases within the letter.[46] Given these data, is it even possible to consider a John in Polycarp's past?

---

43. See above, Obs. 3.

44. Chs. 3, 9, 11 (twice).

45. See esp. C. M. Nielsen, "Polycarp and Marcion: A Note," *TS* 74 (1986) 297–299; for further discussion and bibliography, see Schoedel, "Polycarp of Smyrna and Ignatius of Antioch," esp. 276–285.

46. Lightfoot, *Apostolic Fathers* 2.3.321–350, 522–523, cites for Pol. *Phil.* 7, 1 John 3:8 and 4:2ff; for Pol. *Phil.* 12, John 15:16.

Martin Hengel, who argues for "unmistakable" Johannine influence only at Pol. *Phil.* 7, finds it significant that therein Polycarp "addresses a 'dogmatic problem.'" Therefore, for Hengel this one instance of Polycarp's allusion to Johannine material is particularly telling: the warning in Pol. *Phil.* 7 "sounds not so much like a scriptural quotation as like a well-tried battle-cry which comes from the Johannine school, though we may of course assume that Polycarp knew the letters (and the Gospel)." Hengel concludes: "above all in the polemic Polycarp seems to have remained . . . a disciple of John."[47] R. Alan Culpepper, citing the earlier work of Raymond Brown, likewise finds a "distinct echo" of Johannine material in Pol. *Phil.* 7 and posits a tradition of Johannine usage "from Papias to Polycarp and then to Irenaeus."[48] If there is no evidence of direct association with someone named John, there is, at least, evidence of distinct usage of Johannine literature and, perhaps, identity with a Johannine school or tradition.

On the other hand, many scholars have downplayed or even dismissed Polycarp's identification with John or a Johannine school. Most recently M.-É. Boismard, who, not unlike Hengel, identifies "one sole allusion" to Johannine material, writes: "This is truly little for such a one who would have been a disciple of John!"[49] In his own recent consideration of the matter, Helmut Koester suffers no consideration of Johannine influence: "Polycarp is a church leader in the tradition of Paul, to whom he referred explicitly, and whose tradition he interpreted . . . it is certain that [Polycarp] did not know the Gospel of John."[50] (Curiously, Koester does not mention the Johannine epistles). In two classic studies, that of von Loewenich regarding Johannine literature, and that of von Campenhausen on Polycarp's letter, the findings are similar to that of Boismard, if not Koester.[51]

47. Martin Hengel, *The Johannine Question* (tr. John Bowden; London: SCM Press, 1989) 15–16.

48. Culpepper, *John, the Son of Zebedee*, 92.

49. Boismard, *Le Martyre de Jean*, 67.

50. Helmut Koester, "Ephesos in Early Christian Literature" (in idem, ed., *Ephesos: Metropolis of Asia* [Harvard Theological Studies 41; Valley Forge: Trinity Press International, 1995]) 135.

51. W. von Loewenich, *Das Johannes Verständnis im zweiten Jahrhundert* (Beihefte zur Zeitschrift für die neutestamentliche Wissenschaft und die Kunde der älteren Kirche 13; Giessen: Alfred Töpelmann, 1932) 25, comments that even if Polycarp's use of 1 John is "by design," there remains no question that "for him, the apostle is Paul." Hans Frhr. von Campenhausen, *Polykarp von Smyrna und die Pastoralbriefe* (Sitzungsberichte der Heidelberger Akademie der Wissenschaften, Philosophisch-historische Klasse, no. 2; Heidelberg: Carl

There is an important consideration which has, by and large, been lacking in the scholarly literature devoted to this matter: in Pol. *Phil.* Polycarp is writing to a community founded by Paul. For purposes of comparison one would like to have extant a letter from Polycarp to a Johannine—or, at least, a non-Pauline—community. The Johannine scholar Rudolf Schnackenberg speaks to this point: "the silence of the Bishop of Smyrna in his letter to the Philippians must not be overstressed, especially as he wished to honour St. Paul, on account of the recipients."[52]

B) Consideration of MartPol arguably offers no candidate for the role of "the apostle" in Polycarp's life. No apostle is named and, as is shown in Dehandschutter's recent studies, the influence of various biblical and apostolic writings may be evident, including possible allusions to both Johannine literature and the Pauline letters. However, it should be noted that both Hengel and von Loewenich, who disagree on the matter of Johannine influence in Pol. *Phil.*, have argued for significant Johannine influence in MartPol.[53]

C) In VPol, Paul is twice referred to as "the apostle," and Polycarp is linked with Paul through the bishops Strateas and Bucolos. John is absent. With the exception of a reference to Peter at the close of the work, no other apostle besides Paul is considered.[54]

D) According to the MPion 2, the martyr Pionius, a presbyter at Smyrna during Decius' reign, was arrested on the anniversary of Polycarp's martyr-

---

Winter, 1951) 42–43, writes, "For purposes of comparison, the Johannine literature generally does not come into question."

52. Rudolf Schnackenberg, *The Gospel according to John,* vol. 1 (tr. Kevin Smyth; 1968; New York: Crossroad, 1990) 79.

53. See two works by Dehandschutter: "The Martyrium Polycarpi: A Century of Research," 503–507, and *Martyrium Polycarpi: Een literair-kritische Studie,* 233–258. In neither discussion does Dehandschutter reach a conclusion in favor of the influence of any one apostle over another, or of the local influence of an apostle or apostles over that of a written text.

Hengel, *The Johannine Question,* 5, asserts that "in the *Martyrdom of Polycarp* we find some allusions to the Johannine passion narrative which prove that its usage in Smyrna was a matter of course between 160 (150?) and 170 CE"; earlier, Loewenich, *Das Johannes Verständnis,* 23–24, argued for MartPol's direct dependence on the passion account in the Fourth Gospel for various descriptions of Polycarp's martyrdom. Even if one accepts that MartPol displays dependence on the Fourth Gospel, one may remain cautious regarding Hengel's assertion that "its usage was a matter of course between 160 (150?) and 170"; see Campenhausen, *Bearbeitungen und Interpolationen des Polykarpmartyriums,* 12 and throughout, for the influence of a later "'gospel' redactor" upon the text of MartPol.

54. See VPol 1–3, 31.

dom. Further, MPol 22 includes a postscript by Pionius in which his loyalty to Polycarp's memory is striking.[55] In MPion 14, "the apostle" is Paul.

Obs. 4. The immediate context of the departure narrative in FrgPol raises another possibility for the identity of "the apostle." Peter figures prominently in many recountings of the apostolic division of the world.[56] For example, even at the beginning of the *Syriac History of John* in which John, of course, is the prominent character, it is only after Peter's speech that the apostles agree, *en masse*, to engage in their missionary activity. Could "the apostle" be Peter?

Obs. 5. Within second-century literature, such as AJn and the works of Ptolemy, Heracleon, and Theodotus, John is referred to as "the apostle."[57] In the *Epistula Apostolorum* 2, John holds the prominent position as the first-named of the apostles.[58]

Obs. 6. John is cast as the disciple who is privy to special discussions with, and visions of, Jesus in both canonical and non-canonical literature. Within the Gospels, John is one of a handful of disciples who is granted a "privileged witness" of such events as the Transfiguration.[59] Further, according to the narrative about transfiguration found in AJn 90–91, John and Jesus engage in their own private conversation on the mountaintop, while in AJn 98 John is chosen as the "one . . . to hear" about the mystery of the cross.

In at least two works, the narrator indicates that John has occasion to share his special knowledge with his colleagues. At the close of *The Secret*

55. See recently Fox, *Pagans and Christians* 472–473, 483–484; also Lightfoot, *Apostolic Fathers* 2.1.638–645, and 2.3.427–431.

56. See above, comments on (a) 1–8, Obs. 1, and Kaestli, "Les scènes d'attribution," esp. 260.

57. "The apostle of Christ," AJn 57; for John as "the apostle" in Ptolemy, *Letter to Flora*, and the writings of Heracleon and Theodotus, see Hengel, *The Johannine Question*, 8–9, and Culpepper, *John, the Son of Zebedee*, 116–117; for all citations of John as "the apostle" in the Excerpts of Theodotus, see M. R. Hillmer, "The Gospel of John in the Second Century" (Th.D. diss., Harvard Divinity School, 1966). In *The Johannine Question*, esp. 2–5, 7–9, 146 n. 44, Hengel argues for "a special tradition from Asia Minor" in which John is *not* called "the apostle"; in so doing, Hengel ignores AJn and diminishes the importance of such passages as AH 1.9.2.

58. For a recent statement regarding the "origin" of the "Epistula Apostolorum" in "about the middle of the 2nd century," see Müller, "Epistula Apostolorum," 251; similarly Culpepper, *John, the Son of Zebedee*, 119.

59. As noted by Boismard, *Le Martyre de Jean*, 73; cf. Matt 17:1–8, Mark 9:2–8, Luke 9:28–36.

Book according to John it is reported that John "came to his fellow disciples and began to tell them about the things the savior had told him."[60] In the *Mysteries of St. John and the Holy Virgin* the gathering of the apostles at Jerusalem is the setting for John's heavenly journey, which ends with his eventual return to earth for a final meeting with the apostles before "each one departed to his own country."[61]

Could "the testi[mon]y of the apostle" be a particular message associated with John or, more specifically, a special revelation from (the resurrected) Jesus to John?

Obs. 7. The direct association of Polycarp with John is found in various Christian writings, in particular from two prominent writers of the late second century, Tertullian and Irenaeus, the latter of whom claims to have been taught by Polycarp.[62]

Based on both internal and external evidence, "the apostle" is most likely John.

(b) 2–6 [---]ic [---] of virg[inity ---][---] to him instead [of ---] [---] of the sword and the [---]s and the tortures of the [lawcou]rts.

Obs. 1. Virginity is an important characteristic of John's hagiographical biography,[63] and more generally of literature associated with John.

Within AJn 113, John's final prayer celebrates and remembers his virginity. This section of the prayer begins with an address to God: "you who

60. Berol, 77 (NHC II.32.4), as found in W. Till and H.-M. Schenke, *Die gnostischen Schriften des koptischen Papyrus Berolinensis* 8502 (2d ed.; TU 60; Berlin: Academie, 1972) 194.

61. For the text, see ch. 1, register of parallels, (a) 1–8; see also the *Muratorian Canon* 10–34 on John, esp. 10–16:

> When his fellow disciples and bishops urged him he said: "what will be revealed to each one let us relate to one another." In the same night it was revealed to Andrew, [one] of the apostles, that, while all were to go over [it], John in his own name should write everything down. [tr. Harry Y. Gamble, *The New Testament Canon: Its Making and Meaning* (Philadelphia: Fortress Press, 1985) 93]

62. See ch. 1, register of parallels, (b) 6–8 and (b) 8–10; for discussion, see ch. 5.

63. See Eric Junod, "La virginité de l'apôtre Jean: recherche sur les origines scripturaires et patristiques de cette tradition," in *Lectures anciennes de la Bible* (Cahiers de Biblia Patristica, no. 1; Strasbourg: Centre d'Analyse et de Documentation Patristiques, 1987) 113–135; see also below, ch. 5.2.

have guarded me until this hour for yourself, pure and untouched from intercourse with a woman." John then recalls Jesus' series of interventions in order to prevent John from marrying, culminating with the third incident: "the third time I wished to marry, you prevented me immediately, saying to me . . ., 'John, if you were not mine, I would have allowed you to marry.'" Following these recollections, John thanks God, "who contained me from the foul madness associated with flesh, took me from a bitter death, appointed me for you [sc. God] only." Between two motifs already familiar within the prayer, John's virginity and his special status vis-à-vis God,[64] is included the short phrase "[you] took me from a bitter death." It is that phrase, or more generally the tradition which it engages, which lies behind the assertion of (e) 16–20.

In his description of the "second Epistle of John," Clement of Alexandria notes that it is "written to virgins."[65] Culpepper suggests that later church tradition which identifies the intended addressee of John's first letter as "the Parthians" rests on "a corruption of an earlier superscription which read either "the Epistle of John to the Virgins" . . . or "The Epistle of John the Virgin."[66]

***Obs.* 2.** Within FrgPol, the discussion of John's ministry which follows the report of the division of the world among the apostles includes the statement that John received the "[---]ic [---] of virg[inity]" "instead [of]" the bitter death of the martyr who is subject to "the sword" and various "tortures" which are meted out by the "[lawcou]rts." The tradition about the peaceful death of John is alluded to again in FrgPol at (e) 16–20, wherein John's charge to Polycarp begins: "Since the Lord granted to me that I die on my bed. . . ."[67] The portrayal of John in FrgPol is consistent with the descriptions contained in AJn.

***Obs.* 3.** In its discussion of the feast day of the "Translation of John" (December 30), the *Synaxarium Alexandrinum* records that "on account of his virginity and purity, [John] was not killed by the sword, as were the rest of the disciples."[68]

64. I.e., "for himself," "mine," "appointed for me."

65. ANF 2.576.

66. Culpepper, *John, the Son of Zebedee,* 169, citing the similarity of the Greek παρθένος, "virgin," with the place name.

67. In AJn, upon finishing his prayer, John lies down inside the trench/grave, in which he had previously "spread out his clothes like a mattress" (AJn 111, 114). For further discussion, see below, comment on (e) 14–21.

68. Tr. Forget, *Synaxarium Alexandrinum* 1.308.

Obs. 4. In our text "sword" is stated as one of the means of punishment meted out by the "[lawcour]ts." The famous sophist Polemo, a contemporary of Polycarp, established a school in Smyrna and curried much royal favor for his adopted city. He too associates justice with the "sword," declaring the following about certain heinous criminals, including "those who commit sacrilege": "a judge who possesses a sword is required for them."[69]

Obs. 5. Many descriptions of the different tortures which were meted out in the amphitheater, prison, and courtroom are extant in both pagan and Christian literature.[70] Within its discussion of those Christians who were executed with Polycarp, MartPol includes descriptions of various tortures. In a summary statement MPol records: "Likewise, those condemned to the wild beasts endured terrible punishments, being stretched over shells and punished with various other tortures."[71] The missing text of FrgPol presumably includes items such as "wild beasts" (θηρία) or "punishments" (κόλασις).

Obs. 6. In the Eusebian account of MartPol, the same noun for "lawcourt" is used in the statement that Quintus "rushed to the lawcourt" (HE 4.15.8). The narrative about Germanicus and Quintus—a positive and negative model, respectively, for the would-be martyr—follows the description of "all kinds of punishments and tortures" which the "other martyrs" endured.[72]

Obs. 7. A phrase similar to that found in FrgPol, "in the lawcourts," occurs in discussions of torture within both Hellenistic biography

---

69. Philostratus, *Lives of the Sophists,* 532; "judge" (δικαστής) and "lawcourt" (δικαστήριον) share the same root in Greek.

70. For a general discussion of the methods used, with reference to the extant literature, see Craig Steven Wansink, *Chained in Christ: The Experience and Rhetoric of Paul's Imprisonments* (JSNTS 130; Sheffield: Sheffield Academic Press, 1996) esp. 46–55; within the NT, Hebrews 11:35–37 identifies various means of torture and execution.

71. MPol 2.4; see similarly HE 4.15.4 and Boh 62.27–63.3; the same (Greek and Coptic) noun "torture" as used in FrgPol (b) 5 is included in both the MPol and HE passages, while Boh employs the cognate verb form. The same (Greek and Coptic) noun "sword" as used in FrgPol (b) 4 appears in Boh 70.23 to describe the instrument with which the executioner pierces and kills Polycarp; MPol 16.1 and HE 4.15.38 use a different term for that instrument.

72. HE 4.15.4; "tortures" is the same noun used in FrgPol. MPol 4 does not mention "the lawcourt" in its description of Quintus; MPol 2.2–3 includes verbal and nominal cognates of "torture" in describing the experience of the martyrs. For further discussion of "lawcourt," see comments on (e) 2–13, Obs. 3.

and Coptic martyrdoms. In the *Martyrdom of St. Victor the General,* for example, the emperor asks, "do you think that there is no punishment or torture in the lawcourt?"[73] In his *Lives of the Philosophers* 461, Eunapius explains that the renowned, eclectic philosopher Iamblichus became interested in the realia of torture while working on a biography of Alypius. In the biography Iamblichus "shows the magnitude of the punishments and sufferings in the lawcourts."

***Obs.* 8.** As discussed above,[74] the beginning of AJn is not extant. In his consideration of departure narratives in the non-canonical acts, Jean-Daniel Kaestli suggests that given the significance placed on John's virginity within the final prayer of AJn, that work may have begun with an incident or set of incidents associating John with virginity rather than with a recounting of the legend of the division of the world among the apostles.[75]

It must be observed, however, that in AJn John's final prayer begins with an address recalling the mission of the apostles to the world: "O you who elected us to be an apostolate to the nations, O God who sent us into the inhabited world" (AJn 112). Might the preliminary missing chapters of AJn, like the final prayer found therein, have contained both a recounting of the division of the world and a narrative about the virginity of John?

The text of FrgPol, for example, includes as prefatory material both of these elements: a statement about the division of the world, followed by a discussion of John's status as a virgin. Given the close association which FrgPol displays with the traditions about the apostle, FrgPol might be used as evidence to support an argument that the beginning of AJn contained both a statement about the division of the world and a narrative about John's virginity.

(b) 6–8 There remained [---]ter him a discipl[e ---] name was Polycar[p

***Obs.* 1.** In second-century literature about John, he is cast as one who has "disciples." The voice of the narrator in AJn 92 refers to "all of us

73. Budge, *Coptic Texts* 4.11; Budge's own translation, *Coptic Texts* 4.264, is misleading in its use of "prison-house" for δικαστήριον. See similarly, *Martyrdom of Coluthus* 89 R i: "The governor said to him, 'The tortures of the lawcourt are many.'"

74. See comment on (a) 1–8, Obs. 4.

75. Kaestli, "Les scènes d'attribution," 262–263; see also Junod and Kaestli, *Acta Iohannis* 1.76–86, and Culpepper, *John, Son of Zebedee,* 190–191.

who are his disciples." In the *Hypotyposeis,* Clement narrates that John was "urged on by his pupils" to write his Gospel.[76]

Obs. 2. The figure of John is central to the depiction of Polycarp within FrgPol. Polycarp is John's "discipl[e]," he is appointed bishop by John, (b) 8–10, his career is defined by "the canons" associated with John, (c) 11–15, and his martyr-death is inextricably tied to John, (e) 13–21. The extant text of FrgPol records no contact of Polycarp with any apostles other than John. Irenaeus, who records Polycarp's association with "John,"[77] also mentions that Polycarp had come into contact with other "apostles" and witnesses of the Lord;[78] for example, he writes that Polycarp had been "taught by apostles."[79] Does the fact that Polycarp is described as John's disciple exclude the possibility, for the author of FrgPol, that Polycarp had contact with other apostles and eyewitnesses?[80]

(b) 9 he made him bisho[p

Obs. 1. The inscription of Pol. *Phil.* records that it is a letter from "Polycarp and the presbyters who are with him." Nowhere does Polycarp refer to himself as "bishop."

Obs. 2. That Polycarp was known as "bishop" is evident in early sources.[81] Within his letters, Ignatius twice refers to Polycarp, his contemporary, as a "bishop."[82] Within MartPol, Polycarp is referred to as a "bishop," while VPol records his ordination.[83]

---

76. As recorded in HE 6.14.7; the word translated "pupil" (γνώριμος) is different than that translated "disciple" herein. For a different account of the urging of John to write, see *Muratorian Canon* 10–16, as quoted in a note above, comment on (a) 11–12, Obs. 6.

77. For further discussion, see ch. 5.

78. In AH 3.3.4 (= HE 4.14.3), AH 5.33.4 (= HE 3.39.1), the "Letter to Florinus" (HE 5.20.4– 8), and the "Letter to Victor" (HE 5.24.11–17); for texts, see ch. 1, register of parallels.

79. See Hengel, *The Johannine Question,* 15: "Irenaeus stresses . . . that Polycarp knew John of Ephesus . . . [yet] even for Irenaeus, Polycarp is no 'exclusive' disciple of John."

80. Jerome, Vir 17, reports that Polycarp, "disciple of the apostle John," "had for a teacher and saw some of the apostles and those who had seen the Lord"; for the text, see ch. 1, register of parallels.

81. See Schoedel, *Polycarp, Martyrdom of Polycarp, Fragments of Papias,* 7.

82. Ign. *Magn.* 15, *Polycarp,* inscr.; see also Ign. *Smyrn.* 12.2.

83. MPol 16.2 = HE 4.15.39; MPol 23; for texts, see ch. 1, register of parallels. See also VPol 3.

Obs. 3. An alternate tradition, in which there is no record of Polycarp being listed among the early bishops of Smyrna, is preserved in the *Apostolic Constitutions*.[84]

Obs. 4. After reporting that Polycarp had been instructed by the apostles and had been in the company of other eyewitnesses of the Lord,[85] Irenaeus states that Polycarp "was also installed as bishop in the church at Smyrna by the apostles who were in Asia."[86] Several sentences later he records Polycarp's association with John.[87] Tertullian, writing after Irenaeus, states that "Polycarp was established at the Church of Smyrna by John just as, at Rome, Clement was ordained by Peter."[88] It has been suggested that in this passage, Tertullian "spins out the remark by Irenaeus in a tendentious way."[89]

Does FrgPol, in remembering a Polycarp ordained by John, "spin out" the tradition reported by Irenaeus for its own purposes?[90]

Obs. 5. There is a tradition, evident in the second century, that John had practiced ordination in Asia Minor. Besides the statements by Tertullian,[91] Clement of Alexandria records that "the Apostle John," after serving his term of exile on Patmos, settled in Ephesus, "and used also to go, when called on, to the neighboring districts of the gentiles, in some places ordaining (καθίστημι) bishops, in others uniting whole churches, and in others appointing (κληρόω) a given individual pointed out by the

84. "At Smyrna, Ariston is first, after whom is Strateas, the son of Lois, and thirdly, Ariston," 7.46.8; Streeter, *The Primitive Church*, 95–96, asserts that this list "pre-dates Irenaeus" and "goes back to an early tradition."

85. See above, comment on (b) 6–8, Obs. 2.

86. AH 3.3.4 (= HE 4.14.3); in his own comments earlier in HE, Eusebius likewise records Polycarp's truck with the apostles, but on the matter of ordination does not include "the apostles," writing instead that Polycarp "had been appointed to the episcopate of the Church at Smyrna by the eyewitnesses and attendants of the Lord" (HE 3.36.1); for the texts, see ch. 1, register of parallels.

87. AH 3.3.4 (= HE 4.14.6).

88. *On the Prescription against the Heretics* 32.2.

89. Hengel, *The Johannine Question,* 153 n. 90. Certainly it is consistent with Tertullian's agenda to recognize an apostle at the foundation of important local Christian communities; for commentary on the origin of the churches in the cities named in Rev 1–2, see *Adv. Marc.* 4.5.2: "We have also the churches fostered by John . . . [which], tracing their line of bishops to its beginning, stand on John as their founder."

90. For further discussion, see ch. 5.

91. As commented on in Obs. 4, above.

Spirit."[92] When, in discussing John, the *Muratorian Canon* mentions "his own bishops,"[93] might it be referring to bishops ordained by John?[94]

(b) 10 Smyrna, the [---] city.

Obs. 1. Ancient literature about Polycarp, including Ignatius' letters to Smyrna and to Polycarp, is consistent in placing him in Smyrna. Pol. *Phil.* does not contain any reference to the city.

Obs. 2. The missing text most likely modifies the noun "city."[95] There were a number of impressive epithets used by the ancients to describe Smyrna.[96]

(b) 13 other disciple[s]

The "other disciple[s]" are presumably "disciples of the apostles" other than Polycarp, who has already been described as "a discipl[e]" of John.[97] Like Polycarp, these "other disciple[s]" would be ones who had survived their teachers and carried on the traditions in which they were trained.[98]

For discussion of the category "disciple of the apostles," see below comment on (c) 6–8, Obs. 3.

---

92. Clement, *Quis Dives Salvetur,* as recorded in HE 3.23.6.

93. *Muratorian Canon* 10; for translation of *Muratorian Canon* 10–16, see above comment on (a) 11–12, Obs. 6.

94. For further discussion, see ch. 5.

95. The lacuna falls at the end of the Coptic sentence, after "the city"; possibly an ⲛ-attributive construction followed. The size of the lacuna and the extant traces following it do not accomodate ⲉⲧ-.

96. For "beautiful" (κάλλος) and "most beautiful," see, respectively, MPion 4.2 and *Life of Apollonius of Tyana* 4.7; VPol 30 employs the cognate "very beautiful" (περικαλλής). Aelius Aristides, esp. Orat. 17–21 (in Charles A. Behr, tr., *P. Aelius Aristides: The Complete Works,* vol. 2: *Orations XVII–LIII* [Leiden: E. J. Brill, 1981]), sings the praises of—and labels—Smyrna variously; see also Strabo, *Geography* 14.1.37 (646). For examples of municipal and imperial titles, such as are inscribed on coins, steles, and buildings, see T. R. S. Broughton, "Roman Asia" (in Tenney Frank, ed., *An Economic Survey of Ancient Rome* [orig. pub. 1938; New York: Octagon Books, 1975] vol. 4) 742; see further GIBM 3.153–155 and *CIG,* nos. 3199, 3202–3205; also *Jh* 53 (1981–1982) 90. For further discussion see Broughton, "Roman Asia," 750–752; Cadoux, *Ancient Smyrna,* esp. 291–294; David Magie, *Roman Rule in Asia Minor: To the End of the Third Century after Christ* (Princeton: Princeton University Press, 1950) esp. 635–637, 684–685; and below, ch. 5.

97. (b) 7.

98. (b) 11–13, (c) 11–16.

(c) 2 all [the] siblings

Obs. 1. A simpler translation of the Greek term ἀδελφός might be "brothers"; however, within Hellenistic literature generally, and Christian literature specifically, the term is used for members of a group without any assumption as to gender.[99] For example, in the Coptic *Martyrdom of Shenoufe and His Brethren,* one of the "brethren" is "a woman . . . Sophia."[100] In the *Acts of John by Prochorus,* John addresses that group which has previously been identified with the Greek term ἀδελφός (160.9) as follows: "my sons and daughters" (161.3–4).[101] In earlier literature associated with Smyrna and Polycarp, the *Martyrs of Lyons and Vienne* employs the term repeatedly to refer to groups of Christians which include women,[102] while MPion reports that one of Pionius' circle was a woman named Sabina.[103]

Obs. 2. "The siblings" is consistently used within FrgPol to indicate Polycarp's circle of attendants.[104] No other term is used in FrgPol to refer to this group.

Obs. 3. Within the narrative of MartPol several descriptions are used to indicate Polycarp's attendants, such as, "those around him,"[105] "the whole,"[106] "a few,"[107] "those present,"[108] "those with him,"[109] and "the siblings."[110] The only instance of "the siblings" as a designation for Polycarp's circle within the Greek versions is recorded in the Eusebian

99. See BAGD 15b–16b.
100. Sophia is introduced into the text at 106 R i.
101. As explained in ch. 1, n. 12, the references given are to page and line numbers in Zahn's edition (*Acta Joannis*). There is, to my knowledge, no English translation available, though Culpepper, *John, Son of Zebedee,* 206–222, includes a helpful and somewhat detailed narrative summary.
102. Recorded in HE 5.1.3–5.2.8; see esp. 5.1.32, 5.2.8.
103. Introduced into the text at MPion 2.
104. See also (d) 16, 22; (e) 2; (f) 4, 8.
105. HE 4.15.9 and 4.15.10.
106. MPol 5.1.
107. MPol 5.1 = HE 4.15.9.
108. HE 4.15.10.
109. MPol 5.2.
110. HE 4.15.11=Boh 64.25.

tradition of MartPol.[111] Boh uses "the siblings" in the same place in the narrative as does HE, as well as in one other instance.[112]

(c) 3–5 [--- ma]ke prayers [---][---] perseverance [---][---] because [---]

Obs. 1. The extant text is very incomplete in this section. At least three elements correspond to a particular section of MartPol:[113] (1) prayers, (2) perseverance, and (3) a sentence-ending subordinate clause introduced by "for" or "because." Two other elements may correspond: (4) the reference to the circle around Polycarp in line 2,[114] and (5) the reference to a period of time.[115] Though several elements correspond, the context here is not that of MartPol: the arrival of Polycarp at his first hiding place.[116]

Obs. 2. In his letter to Polycarp, Ignatius urges his colleague to "allow time for continuous prayer" (Ign. *Pol.* 1.3.). Prayer figures prominently also in the portrait of Polycarp within MartPol. After first reporting that "Polycarp prayed constantly, night and day," MartPol describes three specific occasions of prayer.[117]

VPol 27 suggests a Polycarp who is more inclined to use the night hours "to study the Scriptures" than to pray. A certain deacon tells Polycarp: "you

111. MPol simply does not use "the siblings" within the narrative to indicate Polycarp's attendants. However outside the narrative, in the remarks at the conclusion of the letter, there are references to "our sibling Marcianus" and "the distant siblings."

112. Compare "those around him" (HE 4.15.9) with "the siblings who are around him" (Boh 64.6–7).

113. MPol 5.1 = HE 4.15.9 = Boh 64.3–14, wherein Polycarp has just arrived at his first hiding place.

114. For discussion of the use of "sibling(s)" among the versions of MartPol, see above comment on (c) 2.

115. See ch. 1, Text Critical Notes, and ch. 2, Possible Restorations, for a possible restoration in the lacuna following "perseverance." MartPol (similarly Boh) includes a reference to "night and day," while Rufinus has "night" only, the latter suggesting an allusion to Luke 6:12.

116. For comparison of the structure of FrgPol with that of MartPol, see ch. 3.

117. See ch. 1, register of parallels for (c) 3, and below comment on (c) 21–24, Obs. 1; for further discussion of prayer in MartPol, see Frederick W. Weidmann, "Polycarp's Final Prayer (*Martyrdom of Polycarp* 14)," in Mark Kiley, ed., *Prayer from Alexander to Constantine: A Critical Anthology* (New York: Routledge, 1997) 285–290, and Dehandschutter, "The Martyrium Polycarpi: A Century of Research," esp. 507–508.

are always studying the Scriptures and therefore awake, you have not even slept." However, later in VPol two incidents involving Polycarp at "prayer" are recorded.[118]

(c) 6–8 he alo[ne] remained [among the di]sciple[s] of the apos[t][les]

Obs. 1. In a classic scholarly essay on "Apostles and Disciples of the Apostles in Asia Minor," Theodor Zahn states that "these disciples of the apostles had completely died out by about 145 [CE]."[119] The exception is Polycarp who, according to Zahn, outlived the other "disciples of the apostles" by ten years.[120]

Obs. 2. Irenaeus describes Polycarp as one "whom we also saw in our youth" and who "was always teaching these things which he learned from the apostles."[121] Therefore Irenaeus writes from the point of view of one who is a step removed from direct contact with "the apostles"; that is, he claims to have had contact with someone who had been taught by "the apostles."

The narrator of FrgPol can mark time, it appears, based on the collective passing of two important categories of persons: "the apostles," (b) 11, and "[the di]sciple[s] of the apos[t][les]," (c) 7–8.[122] As such, FrgPol is narrated from the point of view of one who is removed from direct contact with "the apostles" at least to the degree of Irenaeus.

Obs. 3. Among second-century Christian writers, recognition was accorded those who had themselves been taught by the apostles. For example, in the *Stromata* Clement of Alexandria writes of the "blessed and truly praiseworthy individuals" from whom he was privileged to learn: "But they were preserving the true tradition of the blessed teaching directly

118. VPol 30 and 31–32.

119. Theodor Zahn, *Apostel und Apostelschüler in der Provinz Asien* (*Forschungen zur Geschichte des Neutestamentlichen Kanons und der altchristlichen Literatur,* vol. 6; Leipzig: A. Deichert, 1900) 38.

120. Ibid., 275.

121. AH 3.3.4 (= HE 4.14.4).

122. For similar recognition of the passing of the era in which the followers of the apostles were influential, see AH 5.33.4 (= HE 3.39.1). Irenaeus, who had been taught by Polycarp when a child and was flourishing in the 180s, refers to Papias (fl. 130) as "the hearer of John," "a companion of Polycarp," and a "*man of the old time*"; italicized phrase trans. by Hengel, *The Johannine Question,* 159 n. 123; for further discussion of Irenaeus' accounts, see below, Obs. 3, and ch. 5.

from Peter, James, John, and Paul, the holy apostles; child receiving it from father. . . ."[123] As recorded also by Clement in the *Stromata,* the reason that Basilides' followers are able "to boast" of their teacher's relationship with a certain Glaucias is, no doubt, the latter's direct association with Peter.[124]

For Irenaeus in AH, the collective label, "disciples of the apostles," may represent a distinct, fixed group.[125] He refers both to "a presbyter" who is "a disciple of the apostles" (4.32.1) and to "presbyters" (5.5.1) who are "disciples of the apostles."[126] One of Irenaeus' primary concerns in these passages, as throughout AH,[127] is to indicate the succession of individuals and teachings from the apostles through his teacher(s) and, finally, to himself.[128]

According to Zahn, Irenaeus portrays Polycarp as "a model for the whole class of disciples of the apostles."[129] The same might be said of FrgPol's portrayal of Polycarp. First, given its use of "disciples"[130] and "[di]sciple of the apos[t][les]," FrgPol, like AH, conveys the sense of a distinct group. Secondly, the Polycarp presented by FrgPol, given both his association with John and his own career, appears to hold impeccable credentials as a member of that group. Further, Polycarp survives all the others within his group, making him—for a time—the sole survivor of that group and the only direct witness to the tradition he represents.

---

123. *Strom.* 1.11 (= HE 5.11.3–6).

124. *Strom.* 7.17.

125. Zahn, *Apostel und Apostelshüler,* 69.

126. For a discussion of the relationship of the label "presbyter(s)" to "disciple(s) of the apostle," see Zahn, *Apostel und Apostelschüler,* esp. 65–69, and John Chapman, *John the Presbyter and the Fourth Gospel* (Oxford: Clarendon Press, 1911) esp. 13–19.

127. And not unlike Clement of Alexandria and the Basilideans in the passages cited above.

128. Zahn, *Apostel und Apostelschüler,* 67, likens Irenaeus' approach to "the symbol of a canal . . . through which the apostolic tradition has flowed to him"; for Irenaeus as an early, perhaps the earliest, proponent of "apostolic succession," see Zahn, *Apostel und Apostelschüler,* 27, and Arnold Ehrhardt, *The Apostolic Succession in the First Two Centuries of the Church* (London: Lutterworth Press, 1953), esp. 109; for a general discussion of the concept of "apostolic succession," which represents a series of issues related to, but distinct from, the particular matter under discussion herein, see Dewailly, *Envoyés du père,* 46–113.

For "the presbyter" as denoting different individuals in different passages within AH, see comments by Harvey, *Sancti Irenaei, Episcopi Lugdunensis, Libros Quinque adversus Haereses,* 2.254 n. 5, and Chapman, *John the Presbyter,* 13–16.

129. Zahn, *Apostel und Apostelschüler,* 73, commenting on AH 3.3.4 (= HE 5.20.4); see similarly Hengel, *The Johannine Question,* 15, who writes that for Irenaeus, John is "an authority from the very early period which reaches right back to the time of the eyewitness and apostles."

130. (b) 13, following "apostles"; see above, comment to (b) 13.

Obs. 4. In the preface of Boh, within a section (62.10–17) which closely follows Irenaeus' remarks as recorded in AH 3.3.4 (=HE 4.14.3–4), it is reported that Polycarp "was a disciple of the apostles."[131]

(c) 8 He was [---] [of the] whole [c]hurch

As suggested in the textual apparatus within both chapters 1 and 2, the text in the lacuna is probably a title.[132] Several possibilities are presented above.

(c) **10–11** [---] old man, being one hundred and f[our] years of age.

Obs. 1. The parallels in MartPol mention "eighty-six years." During his trial, Polycarp says, "I have served [Christ] for eighty-six years" (MPol 9.3; HE 4.15.20). As summarized by J. B. Lightfoot over a century ago, the question is "whether Polycarp means that he was a Christian from his birth and was now 86 years old, or that it was 86 years since he became a Christian,"[133] perhaps through baptism. That question has continued to exert primary influence in scholarly consideration of this passage.[134]

Obs. 2. Since the text of FrgPol breaks off while Polycarp is awaiting arrest, it is impossible to know, firstly, whether the full narrative recounted the trial scene, and secondly, whether Polycarp makes the same—or a similar—statement regarding his eighty-six years. What appears certain is that within FrgPol Polycarp was martyred at the age of one hundred and four. For FrgPol the soon-to-be-martyred Polycarp cannot have been eighty-six years old.

---

131. Boh 62.10–11; compare HE 4.14.3: "But Polycarp also had not only been taught by the apostles and had conversed with many who had seen the Lord. . . ."

132. For the Coptic construction, ϣⲟⲟⲡ ⲛ̄-, see Ariel Shisha-Halevy, *Coptic Grammatical Categories: Structural Studies in the Syntax of Shenoutean Sahidic* (AnOr 53; Rome: Pontificium Institutum Biblicum, 1986) 39–40.

133. Lightfoot, *Apostolic Fathers* 2.3.379 n. 8.

134. In his short comment in *Polycarp, Martyrdom of Polycarp, Fragments of Papias,* 65, Schoedel concludes (citing P. Nautin, *Lettres et écrivains chrétiens des IIe et IIIe siècles* [*Patristica,* vol. 2; Paris, 1961] 72 n. 1): "It means . . . 'I have always served Christ and I am not going to cease doing so at the age of eighty-six.'" According to Adolf von Harnack, *Geschichte der altchristlichen Litteratur bis Eusebius,* part 2, *Die Chronologie,* vol. 1 (Leipzig: J. C. Hinrichs, 1897) 342, "the most obvious sense of Polycarp's own words is, 'I have been a Christian since birth, and am 86 years old'"; Zahn, *Apostel und Apostelschüler,* 96, counts Polycarp's "eighty-six" years from the time when "he was baptized as a youngster, at 10–14 years of age."

Obs. 3. If the figure one hundred and four, as it appears in FrgPol, is consistent with Polycarp's statement that he had "served [Christ] for eighty-six years," then he would have had to have begun that service at the age of eighteen or nineteen. According to VPol 3, Polycarp was a "little child" (παιδάριον) at the time of his adoption by the Christian, Callisto. Certainly the term "little child" cannot refer to an eighteen-year-old. No other statement of the age at which Polycarp became a Christian survives. Where might the figure one hundred and four have come from, and what might it indicate?

Papylus' confession in the Greek recension of the *Martyrdom of Carpus, Papylus, and Agathonice* 34 suggests a possible solution.[135] To the proconsul's question, "Are you going to sacrifice, or what are you going to say?" Papylus replies: "I have served God since my youth" (νεότης). Both the text and context of this dramatic sentence bear a resemblance to Polycarp's statement about his eighty-six years. It may not be coincidental that just as Papylus reckons his career of service from (some point in) his "youth," so VPol 11 preserves a tradition in which it is recorded that Polycarp was "enrolled . . . in the order of deacons" when he had reached "young adulthood" (ὁ νέος τῆς ἡλικίας). Indeed, "youth" and cognate terms may have been used with a kind of technical meaning among some early Christians, not least among them Polycarp himself.[136]

During the Classical and Hellenistic periods, the term "youth" was used, with some fluidity, to refer to someone who was eighteen years of age or more, somewhat akin to the American-English "young adult" or, when

---

135. See Musurillo, *Acts of the Christian Martyrs*, xv–xvi, 22–37. Though the *Martyrdom of Carpus, Papylus, and Agathonice* does not stand in the Polycarp tradition in the manner of MPion, it is associated with both MPion and MartPol from an early date (at least mid-late third century) and may be dependent to some degree on MartPol; see Dehandschutter, "The Martyrium Polycarpi: A Century of Research," 501, and HE 4.15.46–48.

136. Besides the literature already cited, see *1 Clem.* 63.3 in which the term is used to describe certain "faithful and prudent ones who have lived among us from youth to old age irreproachably." In Pol. *Phil.* 5.3, within a discussion of the role of deacons and presbyters, Polycarp exhorts "young ones" to hold to certain guidelines of appropriate behavior ("virgins" are also addressed). Is Polycarp using "young ones" (νεώτεροι) in a technical sense to refer to a particular group, with particular functions, within his community (contra Schoedel, *Polycarp, Martyrdom of Polycarp, and Fragments of Papias*, 21)?

In the story which appears at the end of Clement of Alexandria's *Quis Dives Salvetur*, and which is recounted by Eusebius in HE 3.23, the apostle John takes interest in a particular youngster living in a city nearby Ephesus (which Chronicon Paschale identifies as Smyrna). After having strayed, the "youth" (νεανίσκος) is "restored to the church" by John (HE 3.23.5–19).

referring specifically to a male, "young man." The age of eighteen itself was used to mark the entry into adulthood.[137]

Perhaps Polycarp's eighty-six years are to be reckoned neither from his birth nor, if he was baptized as a youngster, from his baptism into a Christian community. Reckoning his own career of service to be from his "youth," in a manner consistent with other early Christians, and perhaps more precisely from the generally acknowledged age of maturity (i.e., eighteen), the one-hundred-and-four-year-old Polycarp would have been engaged in Christian service for eighty-six or eighty-seven years. The record of Polycarp's age in FrgPol may be a gloss on Polycarp's statement in MartPol. If independent of the statement about eighty-six years, the age reference in FrgPol preserves either a piece of realia (i.e., the actual age of Polycarp when he was killed), or a unique tradition about the great age of the bishop.

(c) 11–15 He continued to walk [i]n the canons which he had learned during his youth from John the a[p]ostle

Obs. 1. The Coptic verb for "walk" (ⲙⲟⲟϣⲉ), like its Greek counterpart (περιπατέω), is used figuratively in Hellenistic literature, including both Pauline and Johannine writings, with regard to "the walk of life."[138] Polycarp himself uses the Greek verb in precisely this manner in Pol. *Phil.* 5.1 ("We ought to walk worthily of [God's] commandment and glory") and Pol. *Phil.* 5.3 ("Wherefore it is necessary . . . that the virgins walk in a blameless and pure conscience").

Obs. 2. The use of "canons" is similar to that found in traditions about both John and Polycarp. Within the literature on Polycarp, the extended postscript included at the end of the Moscow manuscript of MPol includes a report from Irenaeus that he was taught the "canons" of his faith by Polycarp.[139] In AJn 57 John is approached by a stranger who requests that the apostle pray for him. The narrative continues: "after instructing him and giving him canons, [John] sent him away."

137. See pertinent articles in *OCD*, 3rd ed.: "Age," 38a–b, "Education, Greek," 506a–509a, esp. 508b, "Epheboi," 527a-b; also ἔφηβος, and νεότης and cognates, in LSJ. See also Philostratus, *Life of Apollonius of Tyana* 2.30: "18 years . . . the measure of maturity."

138. BAGD 649.

139. For the text, see ch. 1, register of parallels, (c) 11–15.

Obs. 3. The Coptic verb translated "learned" (ⲧⲥⲁⲃⲟ) has as its basic meaning "to teach," with the passive meaning "be taught." It does not appear here in the passive voice. Rather, its particular usage appears to be an ingressive one, bearing the meaning "to become taught" or "to learn."[140]

Obs. 4. FrgPol portrays Polycarp as one standing within a tradition of teaching which is received from John and, apparently, passed along by Polycarp to his students. Such a description is consistent with that found within the writings of Irenaeus and later authors.[141]

Obs. 5. Pionius' self-description in MPion 4.7 appears consistent with the description of his hero Polycarp in this passage: "and I struggle not to change the things which I first learned and later taught."

Obs. 6. At the close of the *Acts of John by Prochorus,* 160.9–10, John addresses his followers: "Children, hold fast to the traditions which you received from me. . . ." Both the addressees, "children," and the content of the message are consistent with descriptions in FrgPol.

(c) 16–21 And all the Christians who had heard about his way of life used to seek after him to see him, like genuine children seeking after th[ei]r father.

Obs. 1. This description of crowds who come "seeking after" Polycarp is unique within the Polycarp tradition.[142] It is a motif in the philosophical school tradition. Philostratus, *Lives of the Sophists,* records that the young "flocked to Athens because of their desire for [Herodes'] words."[143] Soon after, in a description à propos to the situation of Poly-

140. I am indebted to Prof. Stephen Emmel, Institut Ägyptologie/Koptologie, Münster, for consulting with me about this particular usage. In a personal correspondence, he cites Athanasius, *Ep. Fest.* 39, as "an unambiguous example" of this Coptic verb employed with an ingressive meaning: "ⲛ̄ⲧⲁϥⲧⲥⲁⲃⲟ ⲅⲁⲣ ⲁⲛ ϩⲓⲧⲛ̄ⲕⲉⲟⲩⲁ ⲉⲣ̄ⲥⲁϩ, 'For it was not from someone else that he [Jesus] learned to be a teacher.'"

141. Though see Irenaeus as quoted above, comment on (c) 6–8, Obs. 2, and Hengel, *The Johannine Question,* 15: "even for Irenaeus, Polycarp is no 'exclusive' disciple of John"; also 82, for a description of Polycarp as "a patriarch who formed a tradition." For references to primary material, see ch. 1, register of parallels to (c) 11–15; for further discussion, see Zahn, *Apostel und Apostelschüler,* esp. 66–67.

142. Though see below, comment on (c) 21–24, Obs. 2.

143. *Lives of the Sophists* 562; see also 520, 571; see also Philostratus, *Life of Apollonius of Tyana* 7.40, as quoted below, Obs. 3E, and similarly Eunapius, *Lives* 458, 482.

carp's followers, Philostratus reports that these seekers and all Athenians mourned Herodes' loss like "children bereft of an excellent father."[144]

***Obs.* 2.** The descriptions in FrgPol, and in the MartPol parallels to (c) 16–19 and 23–24, suggest that Polycarp is consistently remembered as one who was generally available to, and cognizant of, others. Within the philosophical tradition, availability to students and others is an important component of the profile of the teacher. Dio Chrysostom, a younger contemporary of Polycarp, writes that "[Socrates] made himself accessible to all who wished to approach and converse with him."[145] In FrgPol these descriptions of crowds "seeking after" Polycarp and his openness to them immediately follow comments on Polycarp's training, status, and manner of life.[146]

***Obs.* 3.** The descriptions "genuine children" and "father" strongly suggest the teacher-student relationship and draw on various traditions with which Polycarp and his hagiographers would likely have been conversant. The latter, "father," is familiar within the literature on Polycarp and will be considered in Obs. 4. The former, "genuine children," as used with regard to Polycarp's followers, is unique to FrgPol.

A) Within the Pastoral Epistles, both Timothy and Titus are addressed as Paul's "genuine child."[147] Elsewhere, Paul's rhetoric draws on the same metaphor: "my beloved children . . . you do not have many fathers . . . I became your father" (1 Cor 4:14–15).[148]

B) Within 1 John, "little children" is used repeatedly (seven times) as a form of address. Similarly, the Fourth Gospel records a saying of Jesus in which the disciples are addressed as "little children" (John 13:33). Once among the extant Pauline letters are the addressees referred to as "little children" (Gal 4:19).

---

144. *Lives of the Sophists* 566.

145. *Dio Chrysostom* 54.3; see also Plato, *Crito* 44E–45E.

146. See also below, Obs. 4.

147. 1 Tim 1:2, Titus 1:4. In light of this close parallel, it is worth noting that similarities between Polycarp's rhetoric in Pol. *Phil.* and the Pastoral Epistles has long been recognized; see Harrison, *Polycarp's Two Epistles to the Philippians,* 241–255. Campenhausen, *Polykarp von Smyrna und die Pastoralbriefe,* 49–50, 51, treats seriously the notion of Polycarp's authorship of the Pastorals: "If the Pastoral Epistles were not written by Polycarp of Smyrna, they must have arisen in his proximity and, so to speak, under his eyes . . . but it would surely be simpler to make Polycarp himself the author."

148. NRSV; for another citation from Paul, see Obs. 3B.

C) Within the early martyr literature, the *Martyrdom of Carpus, Papylus and Agathonice* 32 employs the metaphor. When asked if he has any children, Papylus responds "Yes," and continues, "in every province and city are my children in God." In MPion the hero twice refers to his "Christian siblings" as "little children."[149]

D) In AJn 27–28 a follower of John is referred to as "child,"[150] while in AJn 45 John comforts his community with the words, "I will not leave you until I have weaned you, like children from their wetnurse's milk."[151]

E) Within the philosophical school tradition writers draw heavily on familial language, often describing the student or other interested listener as "child."[152] In his discussion of the philosopher Lucius, Philostratus mentions three youngsters whom the philosopher nurtured and thought of "as [his] genuine [children]" due to their "love of learning."[153] In a similar vein, Philostratus writes of the prison-mates of Apollonius of Tyana: "And when the prisoners in the free prison saw him again, they all flocked round him . . . for they entertained the same affectionate longing for Apollonius as children do for a parent. . . ."[154]

---

149. "Christian siblings" is the term used by the narrator. The first use of "little children" in MPion 12 occurs within a quotation from Paul (Gal 4:19). Given the question of Pauline and Johannine influences within the literature associated with Polycarp—see esp. above, comment on (a) 11–12—one would value knowing whether Pionius or his hagiographers were familiar with this term only through its one Pauline usage, or through its Johannine usage as well.

150. See below, Obs. 4B.

151. Regarding the matter of kinship language, it is worth noting that the term "wetnurse" (τρόφος) could also be used in reference to the biological mother. Paul employs the same metaphor in 1 Thess 2:7.

152. For discussion and bibliography see Benjamin Fiore, *Function of Personal Example in the Socratic and Pastoral Epistles* (AnBib 105; Rome: Biblical Institute Press, 1986); Peter Brown, "The Rise and Function of the Holy Man in Late Antiquity," *JRS* 61 (1971) 80–101, in Peter Brown, *Society and the Holy in Late Antiquity* (Berkeley: University of California Press, 1982) 103–152, 149–150; Henri Crouzel, ed., *Grégoire le Thaumaturge: Remerciement a Origène suivi de la lettre d'Origène a Grégoire* (SC 148; Paris: Éditions du Cerf, 1969) 175 n. 11; Martin Dibelius and Hans Conzelman, *Pastoral Epistles* (tr. Philip Buttolph and Adela Yarbro; Hermeneia; Philadelphia: Fortress Press, 1972) 13; Bentley Layton, ed., *The Gnostic Treatise on Resurrection from Nag Hammadi* (HDR 12; Missoula: Scholars Press, 1979) 38; Abraham J. Malherbe, "Gentle as a Nurse: The Cynic Background of 1 Thess ii," *NovT* 12 (1970) 203–217.

153. *Lives of the Sophists* 558; see also *Lives* 576 regarding Alexander, who upon his (natural) father's death "began studying as the most genuine [child] of Favorinus"; similarly Eunapius, *Lives* 459.

154. *Life of Apollonius of Tyana* 7.40, tr. F. C. Conybeare (LCL; London: William Heinemann, 1912) 2.261.

Obs. 4. Polycarp is referred to as "father" in MartPol and VPol as well as FrgPol.[155] It may well be the case that the usage in MartPol (MPol 12.2=HE 4.15.26) is the earliest extant reference to a bishop being called "father."[156]

A) The equation of "teacher" with "parent" or "father" is standard within the Greek philosophical tradition. Within Philostratus' *Lives of the Sophists,* the metaphor is first used by the same Herodes discussed in Obs. 1. It is reported that he "regarded [Socrates] as his teacher and father."[157] In turn, Herodes' student Polemo refers to Herodes as "father."[158]

In *Apology* 97, Apuleius, a contemporary of Polycarp, recalls that his close associate Pontianus "called me his parent, his master, his instructor." In Plato's *Phaedo*, the (first-person) voice of the narrator reports, "we felt that [Socrates] was like a father to us and that when bereft of him we should pass the rest of our lives as orphans."[159]

B) As Christian literature developed, the metaphor assumed more clearly the academic connotation of the philosophical tradition. It is only in the Pastorals, for example, that the same Paul who calls his addressee "genuine child"[160] refers to himself as a "teacher."[161] In AJn, wherein "the Lord" appears to John as a "teacher" (97) and John himself is called "the teacher" (37), the reciprocal terms "father" and "child" are used in a conversation between John and one of his followers (AJn 27–28).[162]

Within other ancient literature about John, the early tradition about the troublesome teenager in Smyrna recounted by Clement of Alexandria,

---

155. See ch. 1, register of parallels, (c) 21. See also *Synaxarium Alexandrinum* as quoted in comment on (f) 7–15, Obs. 2D, below.

156. Guido Bosio, "Policarpo," *Biblioteca Sanctorum* (Filippo Caraffa, ed.; Rome: Instituto Giovanni XX11 della Pontificia Universita Lateranense, 1968) 987.

157. *Lives of the Sophists* 490.

158. Ibid., 537; see also 566, 587, 617.

159. Plato, *Phaedo* 116A; tr. Harold North Fowler, *Plato: Euthyphro, Apology, Crito, Phaedo, Phaedrus* (LCL, Plato, 1; Cambridge: Harvard University Press, 1971; orig. pub., 1914) 395.

160. See above, Obs. 2A.

161. 1 Tim 2:7, 2 Tim 1:11.

162. Gregory Thaumaturgos considers himself and his colleagues to be "true sons" of their teacher, Origen, who is "truly our Father"; in *Oration and Panegyric to Origen* 16. Earlier, Clement of Alexandria wrote that each student is a "son" to the teacher (*Strom.* 1.2.1).

MPion has likewise been influenced by the philosophical school tradition. Pionius is "the teacher" of the "cult or sect" (θρησκείαν ἤ αἵρεσιν) which he calls "catholic," ch. 19; see also MPion 17 for a reference to Socrates as one who previously suffered a similar ordeal to that of Pionius.

and preserved by Eusebius, contains the following question, as put by John to his charge: "Child, why are you fleeing me, your own father?" (HE 3.33.17). In the *Acts of John by Prochorus* 161.2, John is called "father" by his followers, whom he refers to as "children" (160.9, 161.2), as well as "my sons and daughters" (161.3–4).

C) In VPol 10 the apprenticeship of Polycarp under Bucolos, bishop of Smyrna,[163] is recounted as follows:

> Therefore Bucolos, the bishop who preceded [Polycarp], loved him and made much of him from his childhood. Being enthusiastic, he had great hopes for him, just as the fathers of excellent sons rejoice in having prudent successors. [Polycarp] responded to Bucolos as one who loves his parent.

Later in the narrative, Polycarp is called "father" by one of his deacons.[164]

Like Herodes in Philostratus' *Lives,* Polycarp in VPol finds himself to be in a particular line of succession in which he eventually attains the status "father."[165]

Obs. 5. In *The Johannine Question,*[166] Martin Hengel includes a discussion of ancient literature in which one finds "the designation of 'pupils' as παῖδες [lit., "children"] and the bearers of tradition as 'old men' (γερόντων ἀνδρῶν)." It has already been observed that FrgPol participates in that tradition in which the teacher-student relationship was described in terms of parent-child. Note that herein the description of Polycarp as an "old man," (c) 10, immediately precedes his depiction as one who bore the tradition ("the canons") with integrity, (c) 11–15, and as one whom followers seek out and relate to as "father." The reference to Polycarp's age in (c) 10 arguably participates directly and consistently in the portrayal of Polycarp as teacher and bearer of tradition.

---

163. The extant text of FrgPol does not include consideration of Bucolos. For a different description of the relationship of Polycarp to Bucolos, see *Acts of John by Prochorus* 188.9–12, as cited in ch. 1, register of parallels, (b) 6–8, wherein both are referred to as "[John's] disciples."

164. VPol 27; see also ch. 1, register of parallels, (c) 21.

165. The term "successors" (διαδόξοι) as used in VPol 10 is jargon for the successor to a teacher. As a technical term, it is part of the philosophical school tradition at least since the time of Sotion of Alexandria (c. 200 BCE). The classic scholarly work on the ancient doxographical tradition is Hermann Diels, *Doxographi Graeci* (Berlin: Walter de Gruyter, 1929; orig. pub., 1879). This is now being updated by J. Mansfield and D. T. Runia, *Aetiana: The Method and Intellectual Context of a Doxographer* (Leiden: E. J. Brill, 1997–).

166. Hengel, *The Johannine Question,* 28–29, with 164 n. 18.

(c) 21–24 Moreover, he had this gift, that he never [f]orgot any w[ho] had come into contact with him.

Obs. 1. This sentence in FrgPol includes two motifs reminiscent of MartPol's description of Polycarp at prayer just prior to being taken away by his captors. Firstly, MartPol records that Polycarp is "filled with grace" before he prays. The Coptic noun ϩⲙⲟⲧ, like its Greek counterpart χάρις, can mean either (or both) "grace" or "gift." Secondly, during the prayer, Polycarp "remembered all who had ever encountered him, both small and great, noteworthy and unnoted, and the catholic church throughout the world."[167]

Obs. 2. VPol presents a very different characterization of Polycarp than do FrgPol and MartPol:

> And of those also who came to see him and desired his conversation, he was wont to shun and avoid, if he possibly could, the garrulous and foolish talkers, on the plea that he was intent on some important business *and had not noticed the person who met him*. . . . Such was his behavior towards those from whom no benefit could be got.[168]

(d) 2–3 the Jew[s ---] [--- He]rod, saying

Obs. 1. Though the extant text is quite fragmentary at this point, it is certain, according to the principles of Coptic grammar, that "the Jew[s]" are the actors (i.e., subject) within this sentence.

Obs. 2. The name "Herod" appears here for the first time in FrgPol.[169] No title is given with Herod's name. It is possible that this character is introduced into the narrative along with a title within the missing lines of text preceding (d) 1.

This "Herod" is presumably the same who is referred to as the *eirenarch* or "chief of police" in MartPol.[170] In proconsular Asia "the duties of the *eirenarch* included . . . the arrest and interrogation of bandits . . . [and]

167. MPol 7.3–8.1 = HE 4.15.14–15 = Boh 65.20–23; see ch. 1, register of parallels, (c) 21–23 and (c) 23–24.

168. VPol 7; tr. Lightfoot, *Apostolic Fathers* 2.3.491, emphasis mine.

169. The name appears one other time, (d) 11, also without a title.

170. MPol 6.2 and MPol 8.2 = HE 4.15.15; at MPol 17.2 = HE 4.15.41, Herod is named without a title.

under his command was a body of troopers called *diogmitae*, who made the actual arrests."[171] The actions of Herod in FrgPol appear to be consistent with those of an *eirenarch*.

Obs. 3. The charges which precede and prompt the search for Polycarp in FrgPol are very similar to those which follow the arrest—and result from the trial of—Polycarp in MartPol.[172] Their placement within the narrated action of FrgPol is significant given contemporary Roman law.

In his well-known response to the inquiry of Pliny, governor of Bithynia-Pontus in northwestern Asia Minor, the emperor Trajan writes regarding "persons charged with being Christians" that "*these people must not be hunted out*."[173] Nonetheless, in MartPol[174] it is recorded that in the absence of any formal charges having been brought or recognized, "all the crowd . . . shouted, 'Away with the atheists; Let Polycarp be sought for,'" and a search was undertaken. That search as described in MartPol is apparently "contrary to the rescript of Trajan."[175]

The narrated action within FrgPol presents a different situation than that of MartPol. Before the search for Polycarp begins, clear charges are levied. The search for Polycarp in FrgPol would apparently not contradict Trajan's guidelines. Further, the events described in FrgPol appear to be in keeping with the rescript of the emperor Hadrian as preserved at the conclusion of the *First Apology* of Justin. On the matter of accusations brought against Christians, Hadrian, according to the record preserved by Justin, states: "if, therefore, someone brings charges and shows the individual has acted contrary to the laws, a legitimate trial can be had."[176]

Obs. 4. According to FrgPol, it is "the Jew[s]" who make the allegations, while in MartPol it is "the whole crowd of gentiles and Jews living in Smyrna" that calls out the charges.[177]

171. Magie, *Roman Rule in Asia Minor*, 647.

172. For discussion regarding the placement of the charges within the narrative of FrgPol, see ch. 3.

173. Pliny, *Ep.* 97.1–2, tr. Betty Radice, *Pliny: Letters and Panegyricus* (LCL; Cambridge: Harvard University Press, 1969) 2.291; emphasis mine.

174. MPol 3.2 = HE 4.15.6 = Boh 63.16–19; text of Boh adds the comment, "atheists *who are Christians*," emphasis mine.

175. Schoedel, *Polycarp, Martyrdom of Polycarp, Fragments of Papias*, 57.

176. *1 Apol.* 68.10; for further consideration of Hadrian's rescript, see below, comment on (d) 3–4, Obs. 4.

177. MPol 12.2 = HE 4.15.26 = Boh 68.12–13. For the charges, see ch. 1, register of parallels, (d) 4–6, 8–11.

***Obs.* 5.** According to FrgPol, "the Jew[s]" make the allegations directly to Herod.

A) In MartPol there is no direct contact between "the Jews" and Herod. However, after Polycarp has been killed, it is reported in MartPol that "the Jews" are able to pressure a certain Nicetas into asking the governor (ὁ ἡγεμών) that the corpse be withheld from Polycarp's Christian followers (MPol 17.2, HE 4.15.41, Boh 71.17–18). This Nicetas is "the father of Herod" (MPol 17.2 = HE 4.15.41 = Boh 71.13) who, along with Herod, rides out of town to meet the recently arrested Polycarp (MPol 8.2 = HE 4.15.15 = Boh 65.26–27).

B) Accounts of "the Jews" making charges against Christians are extant within early martyr literature, including MPion. In a speech, the imprisoned Pionius lists charges which "you have heard that the Jews say" against Jesus (MPion 13). In the *Martyrdom of Conon* 6 the governor himself reports that he has "learned accurately from the Jews" about Christianity. Tertullian, who writes often about martyrdom, refers to synagogues as "sources of persecution" (*Scorpiace* 10). Several episodes in the New Testament book of Acts, along with the well-known Passion narratives in the canonical Gospels, include narrative descriptions of Jewish individuals or groups bringing charges against Jesus or an individual or group of Christians.

***Obs.* 6.** Following (d) 2, "the Jews" appear once more within FrgPol, (d) 24.[178] It cannot be known how many times "the Jews" might have appeared in the complete text.

In MartPol, "the Jews" are mentioned in connection with four incidents. Two have been mentioned above: (1) their influence over Nicetas, and (2) their presence in the crowd which calls out the charges against Polycarp. The two further occurrences are: (3) following the report that "a crowd" had gathered to prepare the fire for Polycarp's execution, the voice of the narrator states, "and the Jews were especially eager [to help], as is their custom" (MPol 13.1=HE 4.15.29, Boh 69.3); and (4) it is reported that the centurion sets out Polycarp's bones and burns them after seeing "the contentiousness of the Jews" (MPol 18.1 = HE 4.15.43, Boh 72.1–3).

***Obs.* 7.** Consistent with MartPol, pejorative statements regarding "the Jews" occur in both VPol and MPion. VPol 28 associates "the Jews" with fire as follows:

---

178. See below, comment on (d) 23–24, Obs. 2.

> the Jews . . . always present themselves uninvited at a fire: for they assert that conflagrations cannot possibly be stopped in any other way but by their presence. This is an artifice of theirs to plunder the property in the houses.[179]

Within the same speech mentioned in Obs. 5B above, Pionius warns his hearers,

> Do not become with ["the Jews"] rulers of Sodom and people of Gomorrha, whose hands are tainted with blood. We did not slay our prophets nor did we betray Christ and crucify him.[180]

Obs. 8. Besides the more clearly pejorative descriptions, the extant literature does provide suggestive, if somewhat ambiguous, data regarding "the Jews" and their identification in and with Smyrna. Through the particular use of the cognate verbs παροικέω (sojourn) and κατοικέω (dwell, reside), the voice of the narrator in MartPol provides an understanding of "the Jews" as ones aligned with "the [non-Christian] gentiles," while the Christian community remains unaligned. Compare (1) "God's community which *sojourns* at Smyrna" (MPol inscr. = HE 4.15.3), with (2) "The whole crowd of gentiles and Jews *residing* in Smyrna" (MPol 12.2 = HE 4.15.26). As in MartPol, so in FrgPol, "the Jews" appear active and engaged.

Jewish literature from roughly the same period presents a very different picture. Though it is more likely indicative of a sentiment associated with the Jewish community in mid-second-century Egypt (where it is presumed to have been written) than with that of Polycarp's Smyrna, the *Sibylline Oracles*, book 5, does in fact contain harsh statements about Smyrna reflective of "the alienation of the Jewish community from its environment."[181] There is no indication in FrgPol of such a sentiment among "the Jew[s]."

179. Tr. Lightfoot, *Apostolic Fathers* 2.3.508.

180. MPion 13, tr. Musurillo, *Acts of the Christian Martyrs,* 153.

181. John J. Collins, "Sibylline Oracles," in James H. Charlesworth, ed., *The Old Testament Pseudepigrapha, vol. 1, Apocalyptic Literature and Testaments* (Garden City, N.Y.: Doubleday, 1983) 392. The statements are: "Smyrna will one day weep . . . She who was once revered and famous will perish" (lines 122–123), and "Smyrna also will come, bewailing its musician . . . and she herself will truly perish" (lines 306–307), tr. Collins, 396, 400. The phrase, "its musician," is an allusion to Homer, who is likewise remembered in MPion 4.2.

***Obs.* 9.** It is worthy of note that neither Polycarp in Pol. *Phil.*, nor Ignatius in his letter to Polycarp, make any mention of "the Jews." In the letter to the Smyrnaeans, in which "the Jews" do appear, Ignatius writes of the "Lord Jesus Christ" who is crucified "under Pontius Pilate and Herod the tetrarch . . . for his saints and faithful people, whether among Jews or among Gentiles" (Ign. *Smyrn.* 1.2).[182] The anti-Jewish sentiment within the Polycarp traditions are not based on extant writings by Polycarp or extant works written to Polycarp or Polycarp's community.

(d) **3–4** saying slanderous [---]

***Obs.* 1.** The Sah word ⲟⲩⲁ, found in FrgPol as part of the adjectival construction which is translated "slanderous," is used in the Sah NT to translate a narrow range of Greek verbs. For example, within the compound infinitive ϫⲓ-ⲟⲩⲁ it translates both "revile" (κακολογέω, Acts 19:19) and "slander" (δυσφημέω, 1 Cor 4:12–14), while in a noun construction it translates "blasphemy" (βλασφημία, Rev 2:9).

***Obs.* 2.** Rev 2:9 associates "blasphemy" with those at Smyrna "who say, 'We are Jews.'" The Greek term "blasphemy," like its Sah counterpart, has a range of meaning. For example, in the Pastorals it is used in the context of slandering an individual.[183] Similarly Rev 2:9 understands the "blasphemy" of "the Jews" to be "slander" against the Smyrnaean(s) who are addressed in Rev 2:9–11.

As discussed in the comments on (d) 2–3 above, esp. Obs. 6–9, beginning with MartPol one can trace an ongoing anti-Jewish sentiment in—or at least, associated with—Smyrna. Does FrgPol provide evidence of a Smyrnaean tradition stemming from Rev 2:9–11, or a similar tradition, which specifically associates "the Jews" with "slander"?

***Obs.* 3.** "Slander" against the philosopher-hero is a recurring motif in the philosophical tradition. For example, in his *Apology* against

182. Tr. Lightfoot, *Apostolic Fathers* 2.2.567. If Ignatius' letters to Polycarp and to his Smyrnaean church are authentic, then these two letters along with Pol. *Phil.* represent the earliest stratum of literature associated with Polycarp. For a case against the genuineness of Ignatius' personal relationship with, and letters to, Polycarp and his Smyrnaean church, see Rius-Camps, *Four Authentic Letters of Ignatius, the Martyr,* esp. 81–139; recently Schoedel, "Polycarp of Smyrna and Ignatius of Antioch," 291–292, writes of Rius-Camps' "highly original view": "it remains doubtful that [it] . . . has been proved."

183. Titus 3:2; similarly 1 Tim 6:4.

the charge of practicing magic, the second-century philosopher Apuleius speaks repeatedly about the *maledicta* of his accusers.[184] Another of Polycarp's contemporaries, Adrian, also faced the charge of practicing magic. For Philostratus, Adrian's was just another case in which ignorant opponents had "slandered" a philosopher.[185] Not surprisingly, according to Plato Socrates had likewise been slandered.[186]

In a telling variation on the motif of slander against philosophers, Justin, whose career as a Christian teacher in Rome is concurrent with Polycarp's leadership among Christians at Smyrna, writes of the slanders he was privy to during his association with a Platonist school: "For even as I was myself rejoicing in the teachings of Plato, I would hear the Christians being slandered" (2 *Apol.* 12.1).

Obs. 4. In the rescript of Hadrian on the matter of bringing charges against Christians,[187] the emperor states that his interest is in assuring that "neither may [would-be accusers] promote confusion nor may occasion be given for the vicious tactics associated with slanderers."[188] By labeling the charges levied against Polycarp as "slanderous," FrgPol may be associating them directly with those accusations which are, according to Hadrian's rescript, "vicious" and unacceptable.[189]

(d) 4–6 Poly[carp], [---] this city, [is] the teac[her of] [the] Christian[s]

Obs. 1. Beginning with line 4, the text of FrgPol includes several charges which are made against Polycarp. With the exception of the mention of magical activity, (d) 6–8, the charges recorded in (d) 4–11 closely

---

184. For discussion, see below, comment on (d) 8, Obs. 4A.

185. *Lives of the Sophists* 590; similarly 523. The term for "slander" preferred by Philostratus is διαβάλλω, which is also used by Plato in recounting Socrates' trial. In Clement of Alexandria, *Ecl.* 30, διαβολή and βλασφημία are closely associated.

186. "As a slanderer [the accuser] goes into court, knowing such slanders to be well accepted by the people," *Euthyphro* 3B.

187. Discussed above, (d) 2–3, Obs. 3.

188. In Justin, *1 Apol.* 68.7.

189. Hadrian also condemns those accusations which are "mere shouts" (μόναις βοαῖς; in Justin, *1 Apol.* 68.8); Karl Bayer, ed., *Justin, Philosoph und Märtyrer: Die Erste Apologie* (Munich: Kösel, 1966) 142, assumes that this section, like Hadrian's earlier comments, is against "slander" (Nachrede). In MartPol, the search for Polycarp commences after "all the crowd . . . *shouted*" against Polycarp (MPol 3.2, ἐπεβόησεν; HE 4.15.6, ἐπιβοᾶν).

parallel those recorded in MartPol (MPol 12.2 = HE 4.15.26 = Boh 68.15–17).

Obs. 2. According to the familiar narrative of MartPol, the charges are "called out" by the crowd at the close of Polycarp's trial. In FrgPol the charges are levied directly to Herod by "the Jew[s]" before Polycarp has been arrested or tried.

Obs. 3. According to the charges recorded in MartPol, Polycarp is "the . . . teacher, the father of the Christians." FrgPol does not include "father" in this passage, though the voice of the narrator does employ that metaphor in describing Polycarp, (c) 21.[190] Like MartPol, FrgPol does include the modifying phrase "[of] [the] Christian[s]," though in the latter it modifies only "teacher" and not "father." Apparently neither of the terms used in MartPol to modify "teacher" ("impious," MPol; "of Asia," HE) is included in FrgPol.

Obs. 4. Given the information included in Obs. 3, it might be noted that the charges recorded in the Eusebian tradition of MartPol link Polycarp to a geographic locale, "Asia." With the inclusion of "this city"—presumably Smyrna, (b) 10—the list of charges in FrgPol links Polycarp even more closely to a given locale.

Obs. 5. As is evident throughout FrgPol, particularly in the descriptions on page (c) and in the dialogue and narrated action of page (e), the portrayal of Polycarp is consistent with various motifs and phrases associated with the ideal teacher within both contemporary Christian and philosophical school traditions. Some of these motifs may be evident in this list of charges, as is discussed below.

(d) 8 [hi]s magic

Obs. 1. Among the charges leveled against Polycarp is that he possesses or practices "magic." This charge has no parallel in MartPol or any other literature on Polycarp.

Obs. 2. What is "magic"? In an important discussion of "Magic and the Study of Magic," Sue Garrett regards as "accurate" the assessment of Morton Smith "that ancient wonder-workers were labelled one way by

190. See above, comments on (c) 16–21.

their supporters and another way by their enemies. . . ."[191] In the Greco-Roman world, what was approvingly labeled a "miracle" or "great deed" might disapprovingly be called "magic." Regardless of the activity or activities it connoted, "magic" held social meaning and suggested intent.

In the discussion below, Obs. 3 considers extant descriptions of Polycarp and other early Christians in light of activities which were labeled "magic" in the ancient world. Obs. 4 pursues the findings of Obs. 3, including discussion about social meaning and intent.

Obs. 3. VPol 10 records that "many persons who were sick and afflicted with devils were restored to sound health" by Polycarp.[192] VPol also records at least two visions that Polycarp experienced, and appears to suggest that there were more.[193]

On the matter of visions, MartPol reports that Polycarp received a vision while in bed, "in a trance,"[194] while FrgPol (f) 1–5 narrates a similar event, though no report of a "trance" survives. Both the MartPol and FrgPol narratives report that Polycarp is able to foretell the manner of his impending death following the vision. Healing the sick, doing exorcisms, receiving visions, and foretelling future events are activities associated with magic in the ancient world.[195]

Obs. 4. The activities which VPol, MartPol, and FrgPol ascribe to Polycarp are ones associated with Jesus, the apostles, and other Christians within earliest Christian literature. It is perhaps not surprising that the charge of magic is relatively common in pagan polemic against the Christians.[196] Further, Christian literature from at least the middle of the second century records magic as a charge under which Christians were prosecuted. Among the many extant, dramatic statements by an apostle facing

---

191. Susan R. Garrett, *The Demise of the Devil* (Minneapolis: Fortress Press, 1989) 24. Among the works of Morton Smith cited by Garrett is *Jesus the Magician* (San Francisco: Harper and Row, 1978). For a discussion of the distinction or equation of "miracle" and "magic," see also Georg Luck, *Arcana Mundi: Magic and Occult in the Greek and Roman Worlds* (Baltimore: Johns Hopkins University Press, 1985) esp. 135–140; and David Aune, "Magic in Early Christianity," *ANRW* 2.23.2 (1980).

192. Tr. Lightfoot, *Apostolic Fathers* 2.3.493.

193. VPol 10, 17, 27.

194. MPol 5.2 = HE 4.15.10; "in a trance," BAGD 576.

195. See Luck, *Arcana Mundi*, esp. 133–159, 161–225, 227–305; also below, Obs. 4A.

196. See Stephen Benko, "Pagan Criticism of Christianity during the First Two Centuries A.D.," *ANRW* 2.23.2 (1980) 1055–1118, esp. 1061, 1075–1076, 1090–1091, 1102; also, Morton Smith, *Jesus the Magician*, esp. 21–67.

imminent execution is that of Thomas: "I thank you, Lord, that for your sake I was called a sorcerer and a magician."[197]

Given the descriptions of Polycarp and his tradition as preserved in FrgPol, from what activities might the charge of magic have arisen, and what might it indicate?

A) DIVINATION. In 157 CE (possibly the same year as Polycarp's trial),[198] Apuleius was tried in North Africa for using magic to seduce a woman older, and wealthier, than he.[199] In his *Apology,* Apuleius states, "It is a common and general error of the uninitiated to bring the following accusations against the philosophers."[200] What is the correlation between "the philosophers" and "accusations" of magic?

In Philostratus' *Life of Apollonius of Tyana* 6.11, the reader is told that "the faculty of foreknowledge" (προγιγνώσκειν) distinguishes the philosopher. In 8.7, Apollonius, in his own defence against the charge of being a magician or "wizard" (γοής),[201] argues that he is being tried under the simplistic notion that magic is the foretelling (προειπεῖν) of events. At the beginning of the work, 1.2, the same argument is made through the voice of the narrator. Further, in 5.12 the narrator is at pains to distinguish his hero by declaring that Apollonius "was gaining foreknowledge not from wizardry, but from that which the gods revealed."

It appears that Philostratus, writing in the early third century, is aware that a charge of magic based on the simple notion that an individual who foretells the future is a magician remains viable. But if that notion were true, his Apollonius suggests, then any number of eminent philosophers would have to face the same charge: "What then will Socrates say here of the lore which he declared from his demonic genius? Or what would

---

197. *Acts of Thomas* 107; see also 20, 21, 96, 98, 102, 104.

198. See T. D. Barnes, "Pre-Decian Acta Martyrum," *JTS* 19 (1968) 510–514; for bibliography, see Introduction, n. 5.

199. For the possibility that Apuleius' chief accuser may have been a Christian, see Apuleius, *Apol.* 56, and Benko, "Pagan Criticism of Christianity during the First Two Centuries A.D.," 1091.

200. *Apol.* 27; tr. H. E. Butler, *The Apologia and Florida of Apuleius of Madaura* (Oxford: Clarendon Press, 1909; repr. Westport, Conn.: Greenwood, 1970) 57; see similarly *Apol.* 3.

Reference to the ignorance of the accuser is similarly employed in Christian literature; see the *Martyrdom of Apollonius* 38: "he was despised by the uneducated, like the righteous and the philosophers who preceded him." In MartPol (MPol 10.1 = HE 4.15.21), Polycarp asserts that the proconsul is "acting with ignorance."

201. According to Luck, *Arcana Mundi,* 21, "The term *goeteia* is a synonym for *mageia,* but has even more negative undertones."

Thales and Anaxagoras . . . say, of whom one foretold a plenteous crop of olives, and the other not a few meterological disturbances?"[202]

Returning to Apuleius, the reader is informed that indeed, Socrates and others actually were suspected of activity associated with magic. In *Apol.* 27, after providing a list of prominent philosophers who were charged with being a *magus,* Apuleius states,

> a similar suspicion attached to the "purifications" of Empedocles, the "demon" of Socrates and the "good" of Plato. I congratulate myself therefore on being admitted to such distinguished company.[203]

Further, in *Apol.* 42, Apuleius relates: "For this we know is the prize of magical incantations, namely divination and prophecy."[204] In the early imperial period, philosophy and magic are associated through the activity of divination (foretelling the future).[205]

Apuleius' association of "divination" and "prophecy" is telling. FrgPol and MartPol are consistent in reporting that Polycarp foretells the future following a vision he had received. MPol is most explicit in stating that Polycarp spoke "prophetically." The charge of engaging in magic as found in FrgPol is another distinction that the portrait of Polycarp in FrgPol shares with contemporary depictions of philosophers and teachers. The incident of Polycarp's dream and the following interpretation may have suggested magical activity to a pagan or Jewish critic, as well as to a Christian hagiographer.

B) VIRGINITY. In the *Acts of Paul and Thecla* and the *Acts of Thomas,* magic is associated with promoting chastity. In the former, chapter 15, the crowd calls for the removal of "the magician" Paul because "he corrupted all our wives" and "does not permit the virgins to marry." In the *Acts of Thomas* 96, when the husband of Mygdonia learns of her refusal to engage in sexual relations, he immediately suspects Thomas' influence: "for I heard that that magician and deceiver teaches this."

In FrgPol, Polycarp is associated with "the apostle" John who is specially graced with "virg[inity]."[206] In the extant text there is nothing stated

---

202. Tr. Conybeare, *The Life of Apollonius of Tyana* 2.321.

203. Tr. Butler, *The Apologia and Florida of Apuleius of Madaura,* 57–58.

204. Ibid., 77.

205. Besides those texts already mentioned above, see also *The Life of Apollonius of Tyana* 4.35, 3.41. For further examples of "the equivalence between philosophus and magus" as recorded by ancient authors, see MacMullen, *Enemies of the Roman Order,* 110 n. 16.

206. (b) 2; see above, comments on (b) 2–6.

directly about Polycarp's own preaching or practice regarding chastity, though his adherence to the "canons" of John is mentioned in (c) 12. MartPol is quiet on the subject. But elsewhere in the literature on Polycarp the connection is made.

VPol 14, for example, states that Polycarp "was careful to deliver reasoned exhortations on the subject of continence and virginity,"[207] while according to VPol 9, Polycarp was himself unencumbered by "the fetters of marriage." In an encomium on Polycarp attributed to John Chrysostom,[208] Polycarp is remembered as one who "subdued and enslaved the body . . . for he remains eternally the righteous one."[209]

In his own letter to the Philippians, Polycarp appears less severe than is suggested by these later descriptions. He does, however, include such commands as "the virgins must walk in a blameless and pure conscience" (Pol. *Phil.* 5). It may be Polycarp's association with chastity—either through his own teaching or via his relationship to John, or some combination thereof—that gives rise to the charge of magic in FrgPol.

Obs. 5. In the *Acts of John by Prochorus,* John is repeatedly accused of being a magician. There are three reasons given for the charge. The first is stated by the crew of the boat on which John is traveling, who suspect him of "wishing to take the boat's cargo and depart" (10.1–4), while the third is given by a (rival?) magician who simply tells those gathered, "[John] is deceiving you through magical delusions" (98.14–15).

In the second episode involving charges of magic against John, the people of Ephesus, via a formal letter to the emperor Trajan, state that "[John and Prochorus], while preaching certain new teachings, overturned the temples of the greatest gods through magical skill" (45.5–6).[210] Such a charge recalls the account of the destruction of the Artemis temple in AJn 37–44 (in which no accusation of "magic" is made). It also resembles an item in the list of charges in MartPol ("the destroyer of our gods"; MPol 12.2 = H.E. 4.15.26) which is absent from the text of FrgPol. As in FrgPol, and unlike MartPol, the charges are presented before the hero has been apprehended.

207. See similarly VPol 9, 16.

208. Published by A. Hilgenfeld, "Des Chrysostomos Lobrede auf Polykarp," *ZWT* 45 (1902) 569–572.

209. From the Greek text as found in ibid.

210. See similarly 81.9–11. In 47.5 John is again called a "magician," but no basis for the charge is given.

(d) 8–11 while he [---][---] them neither to give tribu[te ---] [--- n]or to worshi[p the] god[s] of the emperor.

Obs. 1. In the parallels to this sentence within MartPol, the verb used of Polycarp's activity is "teach." The verb is lacking in FrgPol except for the first letter, kappa. There is no Sah verb beginning with ⲕ meaning "teach."

Obs. 2. In FrgPol, there is a grammatical object ("gods of the emperor") following the verb "worship." Further, there is a lacuna following "give tribute" and preceding "[n]or." Since a conjunction or negative reinforcer is not expected preceding "[n]or," and since an object following "give tribu[te]" would create a parallelism with "god[s] of the emperor" in the following phrase, the missing text is probably the object of the verb "give tribu[te]."

The MartPol parallels include no grammatical object following either "offer" or "worship." The verb "offer" (θύω) often appears without an object as a kind of technical term.[211] However, a cognate of "offer" does appear in MPion 8:4 followed by an object: "therefore make an offering to the absolute ruler."

The same Greek loanword used within the verb construction in FrgPol, "give tribu[te]," appears in *The Life of Apollonius of Tyana* 7.4, followed by the objective genitive, to describe the offering made on the emperor's behalf: "the tribute (φορά) of Domitian." Plutarch's *Antony* 24.3–5 includes colorful descriptions of "all Asia" making tribute to Antony.

The original reading of FrgPol may have been: "while he persuades them neither to give tribute to the emperor nor to worship the gods of the emperor."

Obs. 3. There is in FrgPol no parallel to the phrase "the destroyer of our gods," which in MartPol immediately precedes the charge that Polycarp "teaches many neither to sacrifice nor to worship."

(d) 11–15 Hero[d], after he had heard these thin[gs, was] very angry. And he o[r]dered that he be brought to him i[n] order that

211. See also the *Martyrdom of Carpus, Papylus, and Agathonice,* and MPion; in the Church Histories, see HE, esp. book 8, and Sozomen, esp. 3.17.2.

> he might kill him. Aft[e]r the sibli[ngs] knew [that] he was being sought after in order to be killed

Obs. 1. In MartPol it is not Herod but "the whole crowd" which calls for the apprehending of Polycarp (MPol 3.2 = HE 4.15.6 = Boh 63.14–19). No order by Herod to apprehend Polycarp is recorded in MartPol.

Obs. 2. The unnamed recipient of Herod's order would most likely have been the body of *diogmitae* who were under the control of the *eirenarch.*[212]

Obs. 3. This comment about Herod's anger is unique within the extant literature on Polycarp. In Matt 2:16 in the Sah NT, upon realizing that the magi have evaded him, Herod becomes "very angry" (ϭⲱⲛ̄ⲧ ⲉ̄ⲙⲁⲧⲉ) and orders all children in Bethlehem to be killed (ⲙⲟⲟⲩⲧ=). Scholars have long recognized in MartPol apparent quotations from, or allusions to, accounts of Jesus' passion.[213] Even Dehandschutter, who is cautious about ascribing particular items in MartPol to canonical Gospel sources, nevertheless recognizes that "in general, there is little question that the idea of imitation [of Christ] plays an important role in the acts of the martyrs of the Second Century (and beyond), . . . imitation is the *Leitmotiv* of the martyrological literature."[214]

Of the Herod in MartPol Leslie Barnard (196) writes:

> there is only a faint resemblance between the position of Herod, the captain of police in Smyrna, who takes Polycarp into custody, and that Herod whose part in the passion drama was confined to mockery and who pronounced Jesus innocent of the charges brought against him (Luke 23:15). Surely a later redactor would have secured a better parallel.

Has FrgPol's description of Herod as one who becomes "very angry" and wants to "kill" Polycarp been colored by a "better parallel" derived not from

212. See above, (d) 2–3, Obs. 2; see also MPion 15.

213. The current discussion remains shaped, in large part, by Campenhausen, *Bearbeitungen und Interpolationen des Polykarpmartyriums,* esp. 7–16, and Barnard, "In Defence of Pseudo-Pionius' Account of Saint Polycarp's Martyrdom," esp. 193–197.

214. Dehandschutter, "Le martyre de Polycarpe et le développement de la conception du martyre au deuxième siècle," *Studia Patristica* 17.2 (1982) 664; see similarly Delehaye, *Les passions des martyrs,* 21.

Herod Antipas in Luke's passion narrative, but from Herod the Great of Matthew's birth narrative? Further, if one were to narrow the focus on the stated desire to "kill," one might even suggest the influence of the Lukan portrait of Herod Antipas, Luke 13:31b.

Obs. 4. E. A. E. Reymond and J. W. B. Barns, among others, have observed that many of the extant Coptic martyrdoms "abound in passages which may be matched word for word elsewhere."[215] In such martyrdoms, for example, the judge typically becomes "angry"—and often, "very angry"— every time an apprehended Christian, during the trial or in prison, causes a calamity to occur or is miraculously healed of wounds received from torture.[216]

It is notable that the extant text of FrgPol, though recorded in Coptic, shows so few correspondences to Coptic martyrdoms. Even here, the narrative context for Herod's anger—occurring, as it does, pre-trial, even pre-apprehension—is different than would be expected in a Coptic martyrdom.

(d) 18–23 they took him and they hid him somewh[er]e. After they knew again that he was being sought in that place, the siblings tr[a]nsferred him by night and took him to another place.

Obs. 1. The narrative in this section of FrgPol is terse. For a comparison with the relatively discursive parallels in MartPol, see chapter 3.

Obs. 2. In the narrative of FrgPol, Polycarp, as the object of the verb, is consistently acted upon: "they took him," and "the siblings tr[a]nsferred him . . . and took him." For the implications which such activity on the part of Polycarp's followers has on Polycarp's own reaction to the imminent threat of martyrdom, see below comment on (f) 5–7, Obs. 2.

Obs. 3. In the MPol parallels, Polycarp is consistently the subject of the verb: "he went out" (ὑπεξῆλθεν; MPol 5.1) and "he departed"

215. E. A. E. Reymond and J. W. B. Barns, *Four Martyrdoms from the Pierpont Morgan Coptic Codices* (Oxford: Clarendon Press, 1973) 2.

216. See, for example, *Martyrdom of S.S. Paese and Thecla* 59 V ii and 84 R ii and *Martyrdom of S. Shenoufe and His Brethren* 121 R ii; for similar descriptions, see the texts in Budge, *Coptic Texts* vol. 4.

The classic scholarly essay on this literature is Delehaye, "Les martyrs d'Egypt," *AnBoll* 40 (1922) 5–154, 299–364; recently, Theofried Baumeister, "Martyrology," *Coptic Encyclopedia* 5.1549b–1550a.

(μετέβη; MPol 6.1). In the Eusebian text tradition, the status of Polycarp as actor is less clear. In HE 4.15.9, for example, in the place of the indicative verb form of MPol 5.1 stands an optative, which is used by the narrator to indicate the content of the followers' concern: Polycarp "should go out" of the city in order to hide. There is no narrative statement recording that Polycarp did go out. In 4.15.11, the narrator reports that Polycarp is "forced to depart" (ἐκβεβιασμένον μεταβῆναί) to another location. Interestingly, Boh renders both of these instances simply with Polycarp as the subject of a finite verb.[217]

Obs. 4. In MartPol, both of the places in which Polycarp hides are referred to as "farms."[218] FrgPol, as is clear in the translation, is less definitive. Boh includes a close parallel to "farm" for the first location,[219] while referring to the second as simply "the place."[220]

(d) 23–24 [---] once again the Jews knew about th[em].

Obs. 1. The possible restoration provided for the lacuna at (d) 23, "[And] once again" (ⲁⲩⲱ ⲟⲛ), is not exhibited within the extant text. It is, however, employed in Sah NT (John 6:11, Acts 26:6), and is appropriate at this point in the narrative.[221] Further, FrgPol does employ the similar ⲇⲉ ⲟⲛ at (c) 22 and (d) 19.

Obs. 2. According to FrgPol "the Jews" are aware of the movements of Polycarp and his companions. Might this report suggest to the reader that "the Jews" are in pursuit of Polycarp; perhaps even as the unnamed (in the extant text) recipient of Herod's order to seize Polycarp?[222] Or, are "the Jews" privy to information which they will pass along to Herod's forces? In MartPol it is the household slaves from the first hiding

217. "He went out" (ⲁϥϣⲉ ⲉⲃⲟⲗ), Boh 64.8 (cf. HE 4.15.9); "he transferred" (ⲁϥⲟⲩⲱⲧⲉⲃ), Boh 64.25 (cf. HE 4.15.11).

218. First location: τό ἀγρίδιον, MPol 5.1; ὁ ἀγρός, HE 4.15.9. Second location: ἕτερον ἀγρίδιον ("another farm"), MPol 6.1; ἕτερος ἀγρόν ("another farm"), HE 4.15.11.

219. ⲕⲟⲓ, Boh 64.8. W. E. Crum, *A Coptic Dictionary* (Oxford: Clarendon Press, 1939) 92b, does not give "farm" as a definition for this noun, which in the Bohairic dialect means "oftenest . . ., field"; see the translation in Hyvernat, *Acta Martyrum* 2.44, *agrum*.

220. ⲡⲓⲙⲁ (lit., "the place"), Boh 64.25. Unlike MartPol and FrgPol, Boh does not include the modifier "another."

221. See Shisha-Halevy, *Coptic Grammatical Categories*, 165, for the "Colon final" use of ⲁⲩⲱ + enclitic.

222. See above, comment on (d) 11–15, Obs. 2.

place who pass along information about Polycarp's whereabouts (MPol 9:1, HE 4.14.11).

(e) 1–2 [---]they assume[d] the name[---] [---]him, the siblings

Obs. 1. A preceding lacuna of indeterminable size and a lacuna within the passage severely limit the possibility of identifying both the immediate context and the content of these lines.[223]

Obs. 2. Reference to "the name" has particular significance in canonical Gospel material regarding John. As summarized by Alan Culpepper, "the only scene in the synoptic Gospels in which John is named alone as the speaker for the disciples . . . is a pronouncement story that is linked to its context by the phrase 'in your name' (Mark 9:37; Luke 9:48)."[224] It is possible that this section of FrgPol contains a reminiscence or allusion to John.

Obs. 3. Polycarp's letter, as well as other early Christian—and related—sources, discusses "the name" in relation to suffering and persecution. In Pol. *Phil.* 8.2, Polycarp writes: "Let us become imitators, then, of [Christ's] endurance; and if we should suffer on account of [Christ's] name, let us glorify [Christ]." The notion of "suffering on account of [Christ's] name"[225] or "as a Christian"[226] appears early in Christian literature, both within and outside of the New Testament. Reference to "the name" is also extant in the early second-century correspondence of Pliny, governor of Bithynia-Pontus, with the emperor Trajan. Regarding those who call themselves "Christian," Pliny asks whether "the name itself" is punishable.[227]

---

223. Though see below, comment on (e) 2–13, esp. Obs. 1.

224. Culpepper, *John, the Son of Zebedee*, 41.

225. See Acts 5:41, 9:15–16, 15:26, 21:13; also the *Shepherd of Hermas* Sim. 9.28.2; similarly Ign. *Eph.* 3.1.

226. See 1 Pet, esp. 4:15–16.

227. *nomen ipsum, Ep.* 10.96.2. For discussion, see G. E. M. de Ste Croix, "Why Were the Early Christians Persecuted?" *Past and Present* 26 (1963) 6–38, repr. Moses I. Finley, *Studies in Ancient Society* (Past and Present Series; London: Routledge and Kegan Paul, 1974) 210–249, esp. 215; Ste Croix, "Why Were the Early Christians Persecuted: A Rejoinder," *Past and Present* 27 (1964) 28–33, repr. Finley, *Studies in Ancient Society*, 256–262, esp. 259; and A. N. Sherwin-White, "Why Were the Early Christians Persecuted? An Amendment," *Past and Present* 27 (1964) 23–27, repr. Finley, *Studies in Ancient Society*, 250–255, esp. 251.

The "name" referred to within FrgPol may well be "Christ" or "Christian."

Obs. 4. Pliny, in the same letter mentioned above, discusses both (1) those who "denied" they were Christians,[228] and (2) those who "confessed" to being Christians.[229] In the *Shepherd of Hermas* Sim. 9.28.4, the same two options are listed in a consideration of those who are called on to "suffer for the sake of the name": they may "deny" (ἀρνέομαι) or "confess" (ὁμολογέω). The verb of affirmation which one expects to be used in conjunction with "the name" is "confess."[230] That is not what one finds in FrgPol.

Obs. 5. The verb employed within FrgPol, the Greek loanword ὑποκρίνομαι, has as its classic meaning "to answer." During the Hellenistic and Roman periods, however, it increasingly assumes the connotations "pretend," "feign,"[231] or, as it is often interpreted in modern translations, "act hypocritically."

A) Within Christian literature the verb (and, more generally, its root) takes on a decidedly negative connotation. In Gal 2:13, for example, the Sah NT records Paul using the verb to describe those who, in his opinion, "engaged in hypocrisy" through their particular exercise of table fellowship (in the Greek, the cognate noun is employed).[232] Within the second-century Greek literature, the *Shepherd of Hermas* Sim. 9.19.3 uses the verb in its warning against those who "played the hypocrite," while Athenagoras, in a discussion of the "name Christian" within *Supplicatio* 2.3, writes that "no Christians are evil unless they act hypocritically with regard to the teaching." In the Coptic *Discourse on Mary Theotokos by Cyril, Archbishop of Jerusalem,* the voice of Cyril employs the same verb to berate those who "utter the Name of Christ with their mouths only," while "they make a pretence in their hearts."[233]

---

228. *nego, Ep.* 10.96.5, 6; see also 10.97.2.

229. *confiteor, Ep.* 10.96.3.

230. For further examples, see G. W. H. Lampe, *A Patristic Greek Lexicon* (Oxford: Clarendon Press, 1961) 965a and 957a. For an example in Coptic, see *The Testimony of Truth,* Nag Hammadi Codex IX.3.31.23: "if they confess, 'We are Christians.'" "Confess" is employed in FrgPol, though not in conjunction with "the name": ϩⲟⲙⲟⲗⲟⲅⲉⲓ (f) 12–13.

231. See Lampe, *A Patristic Greek Lexicon,* 1450a, and BAGD 845a; contra Philostratus, *Life of Apollonius of Tyana* 2.37, "expound, interpret, explain" as cited in LSJ 1885b.

232. See similarly Luke 20:20, Rom 12:9, 2 Cor 6:6, 1 Tim 1:5, 1 Pet 1:22, Jas 3:17.

233. Tr. Budge, *Coptic Texts* 5.1.61 and 5.2.638.

Within FrgPol, is one to understand that "the siblings" and/or another grammatical subject are engaging in some form of hypocrisy vis-à-vis "the name?"

B) Also within Christian literature, however, the verb may have a positive connotation. In his Thirty-Fifth Catechetical Oration, Gregory of Nyssa discusses how "we assume the salvific burial and resurrection" at baptism.[234] Such a use of the verb is consistent with that found in the second-century historian Appian. In the *Civil Wars* 4.46 he describes how Apuleius and Arrontius first "assumed the character" of military leaders, then collected their respective forces, and finally came to blows.[235] Based on the extant text of FrgPol, one might presume that it is "the siblings" who "assume the name" in a positive sense; perhaps in a manner consistent with that of Polycarp's discussion in Pol. *Phil.* 8:2 about imitating Christ.[236]

Obs. 6. There is another possibility, which is premised in part on the assumption that the three Coptic letters which form the word "name" might here represent two separate Coptic morphemes, the first being composed of two letters, the second, one.[237] Arthur Des Rivières, whose early scholarly association with this text is discussed in the Introduction, recorded the following Latin translation for line 1: *Simulantes actionem.*[238] The notion of "the siblings" "pretending" to engage in a certain "action" or a state of affairs is arguably consistent with the dialogue of pages (e)–(f), in which Polycarp displays his ignorance both that a search for him is already underway and that his companions have already taken him to two separate hiding places.[239] Have "the siblings" neatly concealed their motives through some pretence?

It is possible that FrgPol records that Polycarp's followers "assumed the condition of . . ."; that is, "they acted like. . . ."

234. As cited in Lampe, *A Patristic Greek Lexicon,* 1450b.

235. Tr. Horace White, *Appian's Roman History* (LCL; 1912; repr. Cambridge: Harvard University Press, 1971) 4.217.

236. As quoted in Obs. 3 above.

237. Rather than interpreting the letters ⲣ, ⲁ, and ⲛ as the Coptic noun ⲣⲁⲛ ("name"), one may interpret them as the noun ⲣⲁ, "state" or "condition," followed by an attributive ⲛ- (only the bottom left stroke of this letter is extant; a superlinear stroke may or may not have been present). The use of ⲣⲁ is rarely attested (Crum, *Coptic Dictionary,* 287a) and is not found elsewhere in the extant text of FrgPol.

238. For a description of the collection of Des Rivière's transcriptions and translations, see Layton, *Catalogue of Coptic Literary Manuscripts,* 225–226.

239. (e) 3–6, (f) 5–7, and comments; see also ch. 3.

(e) 2–13 the siblings, to a deserted place. As for hi[m], he was asking them, "Why are you going around with me from place to place?" And they were afraid to tell him lest he forbid them and go alone to the lawcourt. For they had heard him say many times: "It is necessary that I die by the lawcourt

Obs. 1. The context and meaning of this section of text are somewhat obscure. It shares four elements with Luke 4:42–43:[240] (1) location, "a deserted place"; (2) a group of followers which joins the hero; (3) the group is concerned that the hero will "go" from them; (4) the hero responds that "it is necessary" to engage in a certain course of action. In FrgPol steps 3 and 4 are known only through the voice of the omniscient narrator, who describes the concern which is in the (collective) mind of "the siblings." That concern starts to unfold in the narrated action begining with (f) 4–5.

This section may provide another example of the Polycarp tradition adopting motifs associated with Jesus in the Gospels and employing them to describe Polycarp and his actions.[241]

Obs. 2. The prepositional phrase "to a deserted place," as used in FrgPol, probably connotes an elevated "deserted place." The frequently used compound ⲉϩⲣⲁⲓ ⲉϫⲛ̄ may assume either of two distinct, basic meanings, "up onto" or "down upon."[242] The latter, "down upon," is associated particularly with the Bohairic dialect. "Up onto," on the other hand, is typical for the Sah dialect in which FrgPol is preserved. An example from the Sah NT is the introduction to the Sermon on the Mount, Matt 5:1: "But when he saw the crowds, he went up onto the mountain."

MartPol includes no topographical data regarding either of Polycarp's two hiding places. What might the suggestion of elevated topography as found in FrgPol connote? Along the southern outskirts of Smyrna "there runs east and west a broad continuous chain of irregular mountain-masses."[243] Polycarp is associated by local lore with a particular mountain, Mt. Mastousia or the Two Brothers, which is located within this chain; it is

240. See also Mark 1:35–38.

241. See also above comment on (d) 11–15, Obs. 3.

242. Thomas O. Lambdin, *Introduction to Sahidic Coptic* (Macon, Ga.: Mercer University Press, 1983) 27; see also Georg Steindorff, *Koptische Grammatik, mit Chrestomathie, Wörterverzeichnis und Litteratur* (Porta Linguarum Orientalum 14; Berlin: Reuther und Reichard, 1894) 161.

243. Cadoux, *Ancient Smyrna,* 8.

one of the traditional locations of Polycarp's tomb.[244] Among the recorded locations for the tomb, this is the only one which lies outside of the city's stadium compound. One imagines that the activities around the tomb which are mentioned in MartPol (MPol 2–3 = HE 4.15.43–4) might have been engaged in more safely at a considerable distance from the city's interior.

Obs. 3. The use of the Greek loanword "lawcourt" (δικαστήριον) as found in FrgPol is unique in the Polycarp tradition.[245] In MartPol, Polycarp is tried in "the stadium."[246]

A) Gary Bisbee, *Pre-Decian Acts and Commentarii,* 121–122, recognizes that it is highly unlikely that either the trial or the execution of Polycarp would actually have occurred in the stadium. FrgPol assumes that a more plausible location, the "lawcourt," is to be the location of the trial.

According to a report by a seventeenth-century author, Thomas Smith, who presumably would not have been familiar with FrgPol, there were visible remains on Smyrna's Mt. Pagos of "what seems to be a *judicatorium,*"[247] that is, a lawcourt.[248] Further, Smith and others identified a building in the immediate vicinity of this *judicatorium* as the "Chapel of St. Polycarp."[249] Consistent with this interpretation of the archaeological evidence, FrgPol associates Polycarp with a "lawcourt" in Smyrna.

---

244. F. G. Holweck, *A Biographical Dictionary of the Saints* (St. Louis: B. Herder, 1924) 822; for more detail about the location, see Cadoux, *Ancient Smyrna,* 8 nn. 2 and 17.

Another site for Polycarp's tomb is in the vicinity of the stadium; see recently George E. Bean, *Aegean Turkey* (rev. ed.; London: John Murray, 1989) 28. The precise location within the stadium compound has varied considerably; for a thorough treatment of references since the seventeenth century, see F. W. Hasluck, "The 'Tomb of S. Polycarp' and the Topography of Ancient Smyrna," *Annual of the British School at Athens* 20 (1913–1914) 80–93, pls. 10 and 11. For a possible reference to Polycarp's tomb in the inscription found at the Church of St. Mary, Ephesus, see Josef Keil, "Johannes von Ephesus und Polykarpos von Smyrna," *Strena Bulciana: Commentationes Gratulatoriae Francisco Bulic* (Zagreb/Split, 1924) 371 n. 8.

245. Besides (e) 9, 13, see also (b) 5 and (e) 19; as noted above, comment on (b) 2–6, Obs. 6, the same word does occur in the Eusebian tradition of MartPol within the narrative about Quintus (HE 4.15.8 = Boh 63.27).

246. στάδιον, MPol 8.3 = HE 4.15.16 = Boh 66.8–9.

247. Thomas Smith, *Septem Asiae Ecclesiarum Notitia* (London: Excudebat T. R., 1676) 36.

248. The Latin term Smith uses is a direct synonym of the Greek loanword employed by FrgPol; Charlton T. Lewis and Charles Short, *A Latin Dictionary* (Oxford: Clarendon Press, 1955; 1st ed., 1879) 1015b.

249. See F. W. Hasluck, "The 'Tomb of S. Polycarp,'" esp. 88–92.

B) As recounted in both Plato and Xenophon, and alluded to by subsequent philosophers and other speakers and writers, Socrates' trial occurred in a "lawcourt." For various philosophers and teachers in the Roman imperial period, who were familiar with the consequences of calling forth the wrath of the State, Socrates' actions surrounding and within his trial provided a model.[250]

A classic expression of this motif from a Christian teacher is provided by Justin, a contemporary of Polycarp, who recalls Socrates' and other philosophers' trials:

> And those [pagan thinkers] who were born prior to Christ, in trying to examine and prove things according to human reason, were led into lawcourts (δικαστήρια) as impious ones and busybodies. Socrates, who was more adamant than all of them in this matter, was charged with the same things that we are.[251]

Such invocation of the accused Socrates is typical in Christian martyr literature as well. For example, in MPion 17, Polycarp's admirer Pionius equates his position with that of Socrates before the Athenian lawcourt.[252] Does the term "lawcourt" indicate the presence in FrgPol of another element familiar within the traditions of moral philosophy and panegyric?[253]

Obs. 4. "The siblings" recall having heard Polycarp say, "it is necessary[254] that I die by the lawcourt." This direct statement regarding the necessity of the death is unique among extant descriptions of Polycarp. It is, however, present in literature related to Polycarp within the narrative of MPion, and it represents a motif familiar within descriptions of the deaths of philosophers. It is also a motif associated with Jesus'

---

250. For a general discussion of the portrayal of Socrates in Hellenistic (including Christian) sources, see Arthur Droge and James D. Tabor, *A Noble Death: Suicide and Martyrdom among Christians and Jews in Antiquity* (San Francisco: HarperSanFrancisco, 1992), esp. ch. 2, "The Death of Socrates and Its Legacy"; Klaus Döring, *Exemplum Socratis: Studien zur Sokratesnachwirkung in der kynisch-stoischen Popularphilosophie der frühen Kaiserzeit und im frühen Christentum* (Hermes: Zeitschrift für klassische Philologie 42; Wiesbaden: Franz Steiner, 1979); and MacMullen, *Enemies of the Roman Order,* ch. 2, "Philosophers."

251. 2 *Apol.* 10.4–5. For a fine example of the motif as used in contemporary pagan literature, see Epictetus, *Dis.* 2.5.18–20.

252. Similarly, the *Martyrdom of Apollonius,* esp. 19 and 41; see also 38.

253. See esp. above, comments to (c) 16–24, (d) 3–4, (d) 8, and several comments below, esp. (f) 7–15, 15–16; see also ch. 3.

254. ϩⲁⲡⲥ = Gk, δεῖ.

prediction of his forthcoming Passion in the canonical Gospels, most frequently in Luke.

A) In MPion it is reported that Pionius "knew, one day before the anniversary of Polycarp's martyrdom, that it was necessary (δεῖ) on that day that [he and a group of followers] would be seized." No reason for this "necessity" is recorded.[255]

B) In Tacitus' *Annals* 15.61, the voice of the narrator speaks of Nero's call for Seneca's "voluntary death" as Seneca's "final necessity" (*ultimam necessitatem*). In Socrates' general understanding of plights such as his own, it is "God" who "would send a certain necessity (ἀνάγκη)," thereby making death inevitable.[256] To his supporter Crito Socrates explains simply, "it is necessary (δεῖ) for me to die now."[257] Similar words from Polycarp's mouth may have elicited memories of Socrates' plight.

C) In the canonical Gospels, Jesus presents the first passion prediction to his followers through the use of the term "necessity" (δεῖ; Matt 16:21, Mark 8:31, Luke 9:22). This is the only such usage in Mark and Matt, though Matt 26:54 suggests a related understanding. Luke employs the term in the context of Jesus' imminent suffering several more times: besides 9:22, see 13:33, 17:25, 24:7, 24:26. In light of the other possible Lukan allusions in this section of FrgPol,[258] the frequency of the Lukan usage is notable.

(e) **14–21** in the manner that the apostle of the Lord told me when he said, 'Since the Lord granted to me that I die on my bed, it is necessary that you die by the law[co]urt

Obs. 1. According to FrgPol the martyr death of Polycarp is so closely associated with the apostle John that it is made necessary by the apostle's own reprieve from a martyr death. Polycarp's enduring of a martyr death fills the lack left by John's reprieve. The notion which informs such an arrangement is summarized by Harald Riesenfeld: "Suffering unto death is a necessary part of an apostle's vocation."[259]

255. For possible reasons, see Fox, *Pagans and Christians,* 472–473, 484–487.

256. Plato, *Phaedo* 62B; similarly Xenophon, *Apol.* 7.

257. *Crito* 43C; for further discussion and citations, see Droge and Tabor, *A Noble Death,* ch. 2.

258. See esp. Obs. 1, above.

259. Harald Riesenfeld, "The Ministry in the New Testament," in Anton Fridrichson et al., *The Root of the Vine: Essays in Biblical Theology* (London: Dacre, 1953) 117; for further discussion see below, ch. 5.

Obs. 2. As is discussed in chapter 5, from early on (at least the second half of the second century) John's hagiographical biography is rich with explanations both as to why this apostle had not had to experience the death of a martyr and why a given activity or divine dispensation might serve as the equivalent of a martyr death in John's case. FrgPol participates in this hagiographical tradition by providing a striking and unique compensation for the lack that was felt in John's career as an apostle vis-à-vis the matter of martyrdom.

Obs. 3. The question arises, if Polycarp dies not only a martyr's, but also an apostle's death, might Polycarp then be considered an apostle? The Greek versions of MartPol are consistent in labeling Polycarp "an apostolic and prophetic teacher, and bishop" (MPol 16.2 = HE 4.15.39). Such use of "apostolic" as a modifier, meaning "having the qualities of an apostle," is extant in other early Christian literature in association with early, prominent figures such as Barnabas and Ignatius.[260]

The only possible instance in the extant literature in which Polycarp is actually labeled "apostle" is in the Boh parallel to the MartPol passage cited above. According to the modern Latin translation of Hyvernat, which I translate into English, the passage reads: "[Polycarp] was teacher and apostle. . . ."[261]

Though a possible—and fascinating, if accurate—rendering, Hyvernat's is arguably not the most likely way the Coptic sentence was intended to be read. The question regarding the Coptic syntax is simply this: Does "apostle" modify "teacher" or stand in apposition to it? A comparison with the Greek clearly suggests the former; that is, the morpheme "apostle" does not stand on its own, but rather modifies "teacher." For a discussion of ⲛ-modifiers and predicative complements, see Shisha-Halevy, *Coptic Grammatical Categories,* 39–40. It is most likely that Boh simply repeats the sentence as found in the Greek versions of MartPol, in which "teacher" is modified by "apostolic."

Obs. 4. In an early tradition about John and a troubled youngster in Smyrna, the apostle offers his own death as a substitute for another. The apostle says to the youth: "Should it be necessary (δεῖ)[262] I will endure your

260. For a handy short list, as well as broader discussion, see Lampe, *A Patristic Greek Lexicon,* 210b.

261. Hyvernat, *Acta Martyrum* 2.49: "qui fuit magister et apostolus et propheta et episcopus totius catholicae Ecclesiae quae est Smyrnae" (Boh 70.28–71.1).

262. Here, in the subjunctive mood.

death willingly, as did the Lord on account of our [death]; on account of you, I will give up my own life" (HE 3.13.17).

Obs. 5. In the *Acts of John by Prochorus* the apostle orders Prochorus to a particular death, using this same motif of "necessity": "Enter Jerusalem, for it is necessary (δεῖ) that you die there" (163.10).

Obs. 6. The verb translated "granted" is a Greek loanword, χαρίζω. In the *Panarion* 79.5.3, Epiphanius uses a cognate noun in describing John's special death as a "gift" (χάρις) from God.[263]

(f) 1–5 ca]rp, as if the bedspread over him were burning. And [w]hen he woke he said to the siblings, "It is necessary that I be burned alive."

Obs. 1. The content (bed furnishings are burning) and interpretation (imminent execution through burning) of the vision in FrgPol are equivalent to those in MartPol. In FrgPol, Polycarp goes on to make a statement in (f) 5–7 which has no parallel in MartPol. Strictly speaking, that statement is not part of the interpretation of the dream and is treated separately below.

Significantly, the immediate context of the dream and interpretation is unique in FrgPol: in MartPol the vision is received at the first hiding place, while in FrgPol it is received at the second.[264]

Obs. 2. FrgPol presents Polycarp's interpretation as a direct quote, as does MPol 5.2. In the Eusebian account the interpretation is given through the voice of the narrator.[265]

Obs. 3. In HE 4.15.10 (= Boh 64.16), before a description of the content of the vision, it is recorded that Polycarp received the vision "at night." In the same two versions, it is stated that after having seen the vision Polycarp "awoke" (ἔξυπνος, Gk; ⲉⲧⲁϥⲧⲱⲛϥ, Boh). The account in MPol contains neither of these details.

In FrgPol, there is probably narrative material from the vision report which is not preserved in the extant text. In the extant text, however, im-

263. Text in Epiphanius, *Ancoratus und Panarion,* ed. Karl Holl (GCS 3.2; Leipzig: J. C. Hinrichs, 1933).

264. See below, comments on (f) 5–7 and (f) 7–15; also see above, ch. 3.

265. Later in the narrative of MartPol, however, when it is reported that the crowd in the stadium calls for Polycarp to be burned, Polycarp's interpretation is recalled in a direct quote; MPol 12.3 = HE 4.15.28, Boh 68.28; for the texts, see ch. 1, register of parallels. It cannot be known if the full text of FrgPol would likewise have recalled Polycarp's words.

mediately following the description of the vision, it is reported that Polycarp "awoke" (ⲛⲉϩⲥⲉ). Presumably in FrgPol, as in the Eusebian tradition of MartPol, Polycarp received the vision while sleeping.

Obs. 4. In FrgPol the interpretation of the vision is simply stated: "It is necessary that I be burned alive." Regarding this sentence, FrgPol finds a direct parallel in the Ps-Pionian branch of the MartPol tradition (MPol 5.2). In the parallel text of the Eusebian tradition Polycarp's words are not presented as a direct quote and an additional modifying phrase, "for Christ's sake," is present (HE 4.15.10, Boh 64.21–22). Further, the account in FrgPol also shares with MPol 5.2 the use of "said," rather than "interpreted" (ὑφερμιμνήσκω; HE 4.15.10).[266]

Obs. 5. In FrgPol there is no attendant commentary regarding the extent of the fire. Simply, the bedding "was burning." In the MPol 5.2, the report includes the (arguably redundant) "by fire," while in the Eusebian tradition the bedding has been burned "completely by fire" (HE 4.15.10, Boh 64.17–18).

Obs. 6. The Eusebian tradition of MartPol contains more detail regarding the description of the bedding: "the spread bunched up under his head," HE 4.15.10; "his pillow," MPol 5.2. Boh, though consistent with the Eusebian tradition in providing a level of detail, appears to differ markedly with HE in the content of that detail: "his bedding which was over him."[267] FrgPol and Boh are consistent in recording that it was the bed furnishings which were over him which Polycarp saw burning.

Obs. 7. As discussed in the comments on (c) 3–5, above, FrgPol is consistent with MartPol and other ancient literature in associating Polycarp with prayer. Early in this century, P. Corssen suggested that Polycarp's vision might have resulted from his prayer.[268] For substantiation of that claim Corssen cited Ignatius' words to Polycarp in Ign. *Pol.* 2.2: "and ask about the invisible things so that they might be revealed to you."

Particularly in light of the possible association of Polycarp with divination, as discussed in the comments on (d) 8, Obs. 4A, above, Corssen's

266. Curiously, Boh 64.19 also employs ϫⲱ, which generally means simply "said."

267. ⲡⲉϥϩⲃⲟⲥ ⲉⲧϩⲓϫⲱϥ, Boh 64.16–17; Hyvernat relegates the literal reading of the Coptic to a note ("quae [erat] super eum") and translates the passage, "vestem suam qua erat indutus"; *Acta Martyrum* 2.44.

268. Corssen, "Die Vita Polycarpi," 283.

suggestion is pertinent. Unfortunately, much of the text surrounding the reference to prayer in (c) 3–5 is missing, as is the text immediately preceding this vision report.

(f) 5–7 and I marvel that they have not sought after me as of today.

Obs. 1. Since the Coptic preposition ϣⲁ is generally translated "until," a simple translation of Polycarp's statement might be: "I marvel that they have not sought after me until today." However, the simple translation, "until," is ambiguous: Does Polycarp's statement assume that (1) as of now "they" have begun to search for him, or (2) as of now "they" still have not begun to search for him?

The significant difference in the understanding of the force of the preposition can be seen in the contrast of meaning between the German *bis* ("as far as", "up to"; denoting the end of a period of time) and *bis zu* ("right into"; indicating duration or contemporaneity). In his classic nineteenth-century Coptic grammar, Ludwig Stern includes both ("as far as" and "right into") as possibilities.[269]

Obs. 2. Given the former possibility, that in Polycarp's understanding the period of time in which "they have not sought after me" has already ended, both the preceding and the following dialogue make no sense. Through his question, "Why are you going around with me from place to place?" ([e] 5–6), Polycarp reveals that he is unaware that his movements are being controlled by "the siblings." Meanwhile, through the omniscient voice of the narrator, the reader knows both that (1) a search for Polycarp is on; and (2) far from simply following their leader around, it is "the siblings" who "took" Polycarp to each of the hiding places.

Further, and in a most telling fashion in (f) 7–15, the narrator reports that "the siblings . . . cried . . . knowing that it would be soon that he would be taken from them." Polycarp is not privy to the information about his imminent capture; he must make those with him "swear" to "tell him the reason" for their tears. It is only then that they "confess" their knowledge that a search is on, and consequently, Polycarp becomes aware of the search. Consideration of that section follows.

---

269. Ludwig Stern, *Koptische Grammatik* (Leipzig: T. O. Weigel, 1880) para. 543; the English translations of the German prepositions are from Harold T. Betteridge, ed., *Cassell's German-English, English-German Dictionary* (rev.; London: Cassell, 1978) 118 a–b.

In the narrative, Polycarp believes that up to and including the present time, there is no search on.

(f) 7–15 After he had said these things, the siblings cried knowing that it would be soon that he would be taken from them. He made them swear that they would tell him the reason; and they confessed. Then he bound them not to hide him, beginning from this hour.

Obs. 1. As discussed in the previous comment, according to the narrator "the siblings" have been controlling Polycarp's movements since becoming aware of Herod's search for their leader. Presently, Polycarp assumes control of the situation by (1) holding his retinue to an oath that they not meddle; and (2) choosing to remain at his present location, presumably either in anticipation of the arrival of his captors or until he sees fit to "go alone to the lawcourt" ([e] 9–10) as his followers fear.

Obs. 2. Though Polycarp has known for some time that he must die as a martyr,[270] he has chosen this particular moment in which to meet that fate. According to Philostratus' report, Apollonius of Tyana, while himself in prison, once remarked: "Philosophers must wait for the right opportunities when to die; so that they be not taken off their guard, nor like suicides rush into death, but may meet their enemies upon ground of their own good choosing."[271]

Obs. 3. That Polycarp's circle "cried" and, at least so far as Polycarp supposed, continued to harbor notions of protecting their hero, would appear to be natural human reactions under the circumstances. They also represent motifs familiar within the extant accounts concerning the deaths of notable individuals, sometimes called "*exitus* literature."[272]

A) According to Acts 21:12–14, after the circle of Paul's followers had heard Agabus' prophecy about Paul's impending arrest in Jerusalem, they "urged him not to go up to Jerusalem." Paul's response begins, "What are you doing, weeping and breaking my heart?" It is, perhaps, not surprising that the Sah NT employs the same word for "weep" (ⲣⲓⲙⲉ; Greek, κλαίω)

270. See esp. (e) 10–21.

271. Philostratus, *The Life of Apollonius of Tyana* 7.31; tr. Conybeare, *The Life of Apollonius of Tyana* 2.239.

272. For an introduction to the literature, see Alessandro Ronconi, "Exitus Illustrium Virorum," *RAC* 6.1258–1268, and MacMullen, *Enemies of the Roman Order*, esp. 72–92.

as is found in FrgPol. The description of the actions of Polycarp's circle may suggest an allusion to that of Paul's followers.

Further, the narrator's confirmation that Paul " would not be persuaded" is familiar in the *exitus* literature, and is also discussed in sections (B) and (D) below.

B) After a larger retinue of followers ("all" of whom were crying) left his presence, the younger Cato said to Demetrius and Apollonides:

> So it has been given to you to detain in this life a man of such an age, and by sitting by him in silence to guard him . . . but since I have already decided [what to do], it is necessary (δεῖ) that I be master over those things that I have known to be necessary.[273]

Similarly, according to both Plato and Xenophon, Socrates' students felt sorrow and sadness during their final discussions with the great teacher.[274] Further, according to both Plato and Xenophon, an escape plan was hatched in which Socrates refused to take part.[275]

According to Alessandro Ronconi, it is the account of Socrates' death in Plato's *Phaedo* which serves as "archetype" for later *exitus* literature; one might safely expand that notion to include all of Plato's works on Socrates' trial and final days (*Phaedo, Crito, Euthyphro,* and *Apology*), if not Xenophon's *Apology* as well.[276]

C) Among the non-canonical acts, *The Acts of Andrew,* particularly the "Martyrdom" account, displays most directly the characteristics discussed in (A) and (B) above.[277]

D) The *Synaxarium Alexandrinum* records that those accompanying Polycarp,

> while crying and mourning his departure, said to him: "we will not allow ourselves, Father, to be left behind as orphans; we will give our lives for you." However, he was not able to be detained by them, but leaving, went to the governor. . . .[278]

---

273. Plutarch, *Cato the Younger* 69.1–2.

274. *Crito* 43B–C, Xenophon, *Apol.* 27.

275. *Crito* 44B, Xenophon, *Apol.* 23.

276. Ronconi, "Exitus Illustrium Virorum," 1258; see also Droge and Tabor, *A Noble Death,* ch. 2, "The Death of Socrates and Its Legacy."

277. See Jean-Marc Prieur and Wilhelm Schneemelcher, "The Acts of Andrew," in Schneemelcher, *New Testament Apocrypha,* vol. 2, *Writings Relating to the Apostles,* 101–151, esp. 135–151.

278. My translation from the modern Latin translation in Forget, *Synaxarium Alexandrinum,* 515; for the Arabic text, see Forget, *Synaxarium Alexandrinum* vol. 2; for discussion of kinship language as used herein, see above, comments on (c) 16–24.

On reading this account in light of FrgPol, one wonders: (1) whether the missing text of FrgPol includes such a statement by "the siblings"; (2) does Polycarp, according to a full text of FrgPol, continue "to remain" with his followers until his arrest, or does he "go alone to the lawcourt," as "the siblings" fear in (e) 9–10, and as is indicated here?

Obs. 4. The question of the propriety of going on one's own to the authorities is broached within MartPol. In HE 4.15.8, a certain Quintus, along with unnamed "others," are said "to have rushed recklessly to the lawcourt" (or, "tribunal"; ἐπιπηδῆσαι τῷ δικαστηρίῳ). In MPol 4 the "lawcourt" is not mentioned, but implied in the report that Quintus put pressure on himself and others "to come forward voluntarily" (προσελθεῖν ἑκόντας). Significantly, the actions of Quintus and his companions are condemned by the voice of the narrator in MartPol.

Obs. 5. MartPol includes references to "the hour," both at the point of Polycarp's arrest and at his execution.[279] In the later instance, during his final prayer, Polycarp thanks God that "you have considered me worthy of this day and hour" (MPol 14.2 = ME 4.15.33). The presence of the term "the hour" in MartPol, as well as in FrgPol, may represent parallels to the accounts of Jesus' passion.[280] A far less likely, though interesting, referent, given FrgPol's association of John with Polycarp, is the statement regarding the beloved disciple in John 19:27: "from that hour the disciple took [Mary]. . . ."

(f) **15–16** And he remained, talking with them and consoling them, saying: "Do not be discouraged

Obs. 1. MartPol records no words of Polycarp to his circle following the dream interpretation and preceding his arrest.

Obs. 2. Polycarp's words to the circle of supporters gathered around him, like the reports of their crying and plotting to protect him dis-

---

279. At both times, too, the hero prays; MPol 8:1 = HE 4.15.15, Boh 65.24; MPol 14.2 = HE 4.15.33, Boh 69.26–27 (Boh 69.26–27 does not include the reference to the "cup of Christ" which appears in the MPol and HE parallels). See similarly MPol 2.3 regarding the martyrs' "one hour" of suffering, which has no parallel in the Eusebian text tradition.

280. See Matt 26:45; Mark 14:35, 41; Luke 22:14, 53; John 4:23, 5:28, 12:23, 27, 13:1, 16:32, 17:1; see also Lightfoot, *Apostolic Fathers* 3.3.387, Schoedel, *Polycarp, Martyrdom of Polycarp, Fragments of Papias* 61, 70, and Campenhausen, *Bearbeitungen und Interpolationen des Polykarpmartyriums*, esp. 13.

cussed in the comments on the previous section, contain motifs familiar in the *exitus* literature. Arthur Darby Nock draws on several examples from *exitus* literature and other material to develop a smaller, related category which he calls "consolation literature."[281] This section of FrgPol contains much that is familiar within *exitus* literature generally, and "consolation literature" particularly.

Though it may happen the other way around, usually it falls to the hero, in the face of imminent death, to comfort the surrounding followers.[282] So, according to Tacitus, Seneca responded to his supporters' "tears" through such questions as, "Where are the precepts of your philosophy?"[283] In a similar circumstance Demonax, according to Lucian, quoted some "verses of the heralds" to those accompanying him.[284] Among Socrates' last words, according to Plato's *Apology* 41D, are: "Nothing bad comes upon one who is good, either while living or having died, neither are the activities of that one neglected by God." Socrates' "God," like that of Polycarp in FrgPol, is not one to neglect those who would be in God's charge.

Obs. 3. The Coptic term "discouraged" used herein (ⲟⲩⲱⲗ̄ⲥ ⲛ̄ϩⲏⲧ) is found with a similar meaning in the Sah NT, Col 3:21.[285] In a more parallel context, that of the Last Supper as recorded in the Fourth Gospel, Jesus says to his disciples: "Do not let your hearts be troubled" (John 14.1). A different verb is used therein.[286]

Among Andrew's closing words to his circle in the *Acts of Andrew* 17 are: "And as for the thing that is about to happen to me, let it not disturb you in any way."[287]

(f) **18–21** for it is impossible for the [Lo]rd to abandon his peo[ple], neither will he forget the [---] [--- of hi]s inheritan[ce].

Obs. 1. Polycarp's words of comfort to "the siblings" are taken from Ps 93:14 LXX (94:14).

281. Arthur Darby Nock, *Sallustius: Concerning the Gods and the Universe* (Cambridge: Cambridge University Press, 1926; repr. Hildesheim: G. Olms, 1966) xxx–xxxii.

282. See Tacitus' consideration of Petronius' death, *Ann.* 16.19.

283. Tacitus, *Ann.* 15.52; see also *Ann.* 16.24–35 regarding the final days of Thrasea.

284. Lucian, *Demonax* 65; tr. A. M. Harmon, *Lucian* (LCL; 1913; repr. Cambridge: Harvard University Press, 1971) 173. According to Nock, "Poetic quotations are a constant feature of . . . consolations," *Sallustius,* xxx.

285. Gk, ἀθυμέω.

286. Gk, ταράσσω; Coptic, ϣⲧⲟⲣⲧⲣ̄.

287. The same Greek verb is used here as is found in John 14:1.

Obs. 2. The reading of FrgPol and the extant Sah versions[288] differ in two ways: the negation of the first proposal, and the grammatical object of the second proposal.

A) Negation. FrgPol uses the introductory ⲟⲩⲁⲧϭⲟⲙ to render the first proposal an impossibility. The Sah versions display the typical ⲛ...ⲁⲛ negation in verse 14a.[289]

Along with the Sah versions, FrgPol employs ⲛ...ⲁⲛ to negate the second proposal, 14b. But where the Sah versions have ⲁⲩⲱ at 14b, the reading of FrgPol is ⲟⲩⲇⲉ.

B) Object. FrgPol includes a more complex grammatical object than do the Sah versions. In the extant text of FrgPol there is a lacuna preceded by the masculine definite article which indicates that there is a substantive, whose grammatical gender is masculine, preceding "[hi]s inheritan[ce]." This substantive is possibly drawn from another biblical source, such as Ps 73:2, "the tribe of your inheritance"; Mic 7:14, "the flock of your inheritance";[290] or Eph 1:18, "the glory of his inheritance."

In summary, the extant Sah versions, with their (A) simple negation, (B) use of the conjunction "and" to introducc the second proposal, and (C) lack of a substantive preceding "his inheritance," are closer to the extant Greek text than is the reading of FrgPol.[291]

Obs. 3. Use of this verse is unique within the literature on Polycarp. Further, with the possible exception of FrgPol, there is no extant Christian literature from the second or third centuries which makes use of Ps 93:14 LXX (94:14).[292] In the fourth century, the verse is cited by Eusebius of Caesarea and Gregory of Nyssa in their exegetical works on the Psalms,[293] while Gregory Nazianzus, in his *Fourth Discourse*, 4.15–16, cites verse 14 as part of a catena of verses displaying "God's consoling" (παρακαλέω).[294]

---

288. For the texts, see ch. 1, register of parallels to (f) 18–21.

289. Though see Wessely, *Griechische und Koptische Texte theologischen Inhalts* 1.46, ⲁⲛ only in 14a.

290. Such a substantive, were it a part of the text, would suggest an allusion which may be extant in Polycarp's own letter: Lightfoot, *Apostolic Fathers* 2.3.332 n. 5 and 473, sees a possible biblical referent in Pol. *Phil.* 6, "turning back the sheep that are gone astray."

291. There are no variants to 93:14 cited in A. Rahlfs, ed., *Septuaginta Societatis Scientarium Gottingensis Auctoritate* X: *Psalmis cum Odis* (Göttingen: Vandenhoeck and Ruprecht, 1931) 244.

292. See *Biblia Patristica*, vols. 1–3.

293. Ibid., 4.177 and 5.221.

294. See Jean Bernardi, ed., *Grégoire de Nazianze: Discours 4–5 contre Julien* (SC 309; Paris: Éditions du Cerf, 1983) 108–109.

Obs. 4. Without parallel in the extant Greek witnesses to MartPol, Boh employs the motif of inheritance in its closing remarks, using the same word as does FrgPol. In Boh 72.18–20 it is stated that "those who hear" the story of the martyrdom of Polycarp become "heirs" with him of the eternal rest.

Obs. 5. The verb "abandon"[295] does appear in MartPol within the narrator's statement that the community, though desirous of the remains of their hero Polycarp, "would never be able to abandon Christ" (MPol 17.2 = HE 4.15.41).

295. Gk, καταλείπω; compare Ps 93:14b LXX, ἐγκαταλείπω.

CHAPTER FIVE

Remembering Polycarp, Remembering John

Hagiography and Rivalry in Asia Minor

As is discussed in chapters 3 and 4, the descriptions and accounts of Polycarp contained in FrgPol tie the martyr very closely to the apostle John. In so doing, this ancient work not only borrows from but also contributes to two broad and varied tradition-complexes, that regarding Polycarp and that regarding John. Though reminiscent of much that is written by and about Polycarp elsewhere, the understanding of Polycarp and, in particular, his death which is contained in FrgPol is quite unique. At the same time, though clearly conversant with much that is familiar within John's hagiographical profile, this text includes particular descriptions about the apostle and a solution to the perceived lack of a martyr's death which is strikingly unique among the reports which have heretofore been recognized as extant.

In this chapter, the matters of (1) Polycarp's place in the traditions regarding John, and (2) John's special death, as it is variously remembered, will be pursued in order to locate this work within the broad traditions regarding each of these two monumental figures. After that, matters of setting and function are broached: How would this work have functioned? What is a likely setting for its composition?

1. John and Polycarp: How Can It Be?

MartPol, which is probably the most familiar extant document regarding Polycarp, does not provide any direct statement about his past, his training, or those who influenced him within a given Christian community or tradition. As is discussed in the comments on (a) 11–12, the one letter of Polycarp which has survived provides ambiguous data for those who would mine it for a clear indication of Polycarp's influence(s). Is there one particular apostle with whom Polycarp can be most directly identified?

Heretofore, scholars have had at their disposal only one hagiographical document dedicated to him which is at pains to place him in a particular tradition. VPol unambiguosly sets Polycarp within a tradition founded by Paul. FrgPol, which also provides direct information about Polycarp's ecclesiastical pedigree, associates him directly with John. While the broad goal of this chapter is to develop an understanding for FrgPol, and for its depiction of John, within the ongoing rivalry between Smyrna and Ephesus, the immediate concern is that of locating a foundation for FrgPol's understanding of John as the apostle in Polycarp's past.

Irenaeus: Confused, Lying, or Proponent of a Tradition

Polycarp's association with John is recorded in several of Irenaeus' writings: AH 3.3.4 (= HE 4.14.1–8), AH 5.33.4 (= HE 3.39.1), the "Letter to Florinus" (HE 5.20.4–8), and the "Letter to Victor" (HE 5.24.11–17). Writing at the beginning of this century, P. Corssen notes, "the authority of Irenaeus indisputably governs the literary tradition."[1] A survey of the history of modern scholarship on the question of Irenaeus' influence over the understanding of Polycarp's Christian pedigree would indicate that Corssen is indisputably correct in his assessment. Irenaeus' record must be dealt with.

B. H. Streeter, who favored the historicity of VPol over Irenaeus' record, dismissed the influential work of J. B. Lightfoot with the charge that the great scholar of the late nineteenth century "accepts unreservedly all that Irenaeus says about Polycarp's relations with the Apostle John."[2] Most recently, Boismard, in arguing that John, the son of Zebedee, might actually have died as a martyr in the early 40s CE, recognizes that an important

1. Corssen, "Die Vita Polycarpi," 299–300.
2. Streeter, *The Primitive Church*, 272–273.

building block in such an argument must be to provide a more nuanced understanding of seemingly unambiguous statements by Irenaeus and, more generally, to indicate that Irenaeus' testimony is itself "very questionable."[3]

Irenaeus as Confused

Irenaeus names no other apostle besides John in his accounts of Polycarp. But, why John? And more pointedly, which John? It is a tribute to the complexity of the debate regarding the identity or identities of John that the following statement by Culpepper makes perfect sense and is, arguably, insightful: "If the Elder was the evangelist, Irenaeus has misunderstood the tradition he received about the apostle. . . ."[4] Elder, evangelist, apostle—three persons, two persons, or one?

Though thorough consideration of the matter is beyond the scope of this study, the issue of John's identity must be considered insofar as it relates to Polycarp and, more generally, to traditions about John's activity in Asia Minor. Two prominent scholars, William Schoedel and C. K. Barrett, the former identified with scholarship on Polycarp and the latter with Johannine studies, have concluded that Irenaeus may simply be confused about which John influenced Polycarp. Writes Barrett: "while one may admit the truth of Irenaeus' views on youthful memory as regards vividness, they may well be questioned as regards accuracy. That Irenaeus, in good faith, made a mistake is a possibility to be taken very seriously."[5] Similarly, for Schoedel, Irenaeus' association of Polycarp with the apostle John "rests on a misunderstanding."[6]

Within the debate on Irenaeus' representation of John, the account of the second-century bishop Papias, as preserved by Eusebius in HE, looms large. Within a passage which is controversial for, among other things, its

3. Boismard, *Le Martyre de Jean*, 77; see also 67 for the following explanation of Irenaeus' use of John in the "Letter to Florinus": "if Irenaeus mentioned John more specially, it is not because Polycarp had known John more than the other apostles, but perhaps simply because the witness of John was more important than that of the other apostles in order to convince Florinus."

4. Culpepper, *John, the Son of Zebedee*, 124.

5. Barrett, *The Gospel according to St. John: An Introduction with Commentary and Notes on the Greek Text* (2d ed.; Philadelphia: Westminster Press, 1978) 105.

6. Schoedel, *Polycarp, Martyrdom of Polycarp, Fragments of Papias*, 3; following Alan H. McNeile, *An Introduction to the Study of the New Testament* (2d ed., rev. C. S. C. Williams; Oxford: Clarendon Press, 1953) 282–284; see also R. H. Charles, *A Critical and Exegetical Commentary on the Revelation of St. John* (ICC; New York: Charles Scribners Sons, 1920) xlix.

arguably illogical narrative structure and its confusing manner of labeling groups, Papias mentions a certain "John the Elder" (HE 3.39.3–4).

That use of "elder" is not the first in this short passage. "Elders" are mentioned before the naming of several "disciples." All of these "disciples" are familiar from (among other places) Gospel accounts, and one of them is John. Following the list of familiar "disciples" another group is identified in which there are two members, a certain "Aristion" and "John the Elder." Both the group of familiar "disciples," and the following group of which one is called "the Elder," are referred to as "disciples of the Lord."

One must ask, does Papias present three groups (unnamed "elders," named "disciples," and an unlabeled group of two named individuals, one of which happens to be called "the Elder") or two groups ("elders" and "disciples," with the latter category sandwiched between two descriptions of the former; or "elders" and "disciples," with the latter group expanded to include individuals not familiar from Gospel accounts) or one group (variously identified as both "disciples" and "elders")? Further, informed in part by one's answer to that question, one may then ask, does Papias present distinct and distinguishable Johns, or simply one John? If one opts for two Johns, and if one assumes that Irenaeus might have been subject to confusion, then one finds a possible solution to that which Schoedel terms Irenaeus' "misunderstanding."

The influential figure about whom Polycarp spoke, with the young Irenaeus and others, might have been John the Elder. As summarized by Alan McNeile, whose own work may have influenced both Schoedel and Barrett, the confusion might have arisen because Irenaeus was "mistaken in the recollections from boyhood" or—as is substantiated by the canonical *Acts* and even elsewhere in Irenaeus' own writings—because Irenaeus, like other ancient writers, simply confused personages who share the same name.[7]

As for the broader issue succinctly stated in Culpepper's statement about "Elder . . . evangelist . . . apostle," a viable solution is most difficult to substantiate given the conventions of historiographical method and the ambiguity of the data. The Johannine scholar Rudolf Schnackenburg, who believes that "the two Johns in the quotation from Papias should be kept apart," is likewise cautious about the Fourth Gospel: "The question as to who the beloved disciple was . . . is without a solution"; and, "whether the

7. McNeile, *An Introduction to the Study of the New Testament*, 283; see also Charles, *A Critical and Exegetical Commentary*, xlix.

'presbyter John'. . . is to be brought into any kind of connection with the beloved disciple of the Johannine church, is scarcely to be determined."[8] Three Johns, two Johns, or one? For Schnackenburg the answer is, most probably, three. For Culpepper, as indicated in the statement quoted above, two is a possibility. For Irenaeus, the answer is one. If confusion is indeed the explanation for Irenaeus' understanding of the role of John in Asia Minor, then it is an explanation which rings true for the contemporary student of the matter. The matter is confusing.[9]

Irenaeus as Liar

Immediately prior to asking "which John?" I presented the question "why John?" Another possibility for understanding Irenaeus' treatment of John is to cast Irenaeus as one who consciously presents false information in order to forward his own agenda. Near the beginning of this century, the influential scholar E. Schwartz wrote vividly in Latin about the "the guile (*dolo*) of Irenaeus" who "imposed . . . a lie (*mendacium*) that Polycarp was a disciple of John the apostle." Another scholar, P. Corssen, wrote no less vividly in German about Irenaeus' "bold lie" (dreiste Fälschung).[10] Recently Helmut Koester has written pointedly about "a fiction that Bishop Irenaeus of Lyons created."[11] Strong words indeed.

It must be observed that Irenaeus' "lie," if it is such, is as complex and subtle as it is simple (one John), involving such distinguishable "lies" as the apostle John's advanced age, his presence in Asia Minor, and his authorship of the Fourth Gospel and other New Testament literature, as well as the matter of contact with Polycarp. As explained by Streeter, the reason for Irenaeus to forward such an agenda is simple and clear: "To Irenaeus, Polycarp was the link between himself and the apostolic tradition."[12]

Culpepper writes descriptively of Irenaeus' ambitious objectives: "In his writings Irenaeus sought to refute the heresies of Marcion, the Gnostics,

8. Schnackenburg, *The Gospel according to Saint John* 1.81; 3.383, 386; Schnackenburg's "presbyter John" and he whom I refer to as "the Elder John" are, of course, the same person—scholars variously transliterate (Schnackenburg) or translate (as herein) the Greek word meaning "elder."

9. For further discussion, see Hengel, *The Johannine Question*, esp. 1–31.

10. Schwartz, *De Pionio et Polycarpo*, 33; Corssen, "Die Vita Polycarpi," 302. In response to Corssen, who favored the historicity of VPol, A. Hilgenfeld turned the same phrase against that document: A. Hilgenfeld, "Eine dreiste Fälschung in alter Zeit und deren neueste Verteidigung," *ZWT* 48 (1905) 444–458.

11. Koester, "Ephesos in Early Christian Literature," 138.

12. Streeter, *The Primitive Church*, 99.

the Montanists, and probably Gaius . . . Drawing on scripture and tradition, Irenaeus gave the church a powerful anti-Gnostic theological synthesis."[13] It is notable that Irenaeus' presentation of John shores up both pillars of his two-fold foundation, scripture and tradition. Via a direct association with the great Polycarp, who himself had direct contact with John, Irenaeus enhances his own status as a—perhaps, the—legitimate, living spokesperson for a particular Christian tradition. Via confirmation of apostolic authorship for the Fourth Gospel, "the battle for the fourfold Gospel," which Irenaeus favored, "was won."[14]

And on the other hand, as Boismard notes, any move in the direction of removing the apostle John from Asia Minor "ruins the authority of the Fourth Gospel" for Irenaeus. Further, it severs the association with Polycarp which then, in turn, weakens Irenaeus' authority as an interpreter of John for Florinus.[15]

Irenaeus as Proponent of a Tradition

Regardless of whether one judges Irenaeus as confused, willfully fabricating evidence, or some combination thereof, one might consider that, even as early as the time of Irenaeus' writing, there may have been no one account of Polycarp's predecessor(s) and mentor(s).[16] Further, and more to the point, many and varied accounts of John's activity provide the basis for recognizing the existence of both pre-Irenaean and para-Irenaean traditions about the ministry of the apostle John in Asia Minor and, specifically, in Smyrna.

From at least the middle of the second century, John the Apostle is depicted as having actively engaged in a ministry in Asia Minor which includes, in some reports, ordaining bishops. AJn, for example, places the apostle in Asia Minor and describes his active ministry there. It is regrettable that much of the narrative around John's stay at Smyrna is lacking from the extant text of AJn.[17] One would like to know more about how John's ministry in and around Polycarp's city was described.

---

13. Culpepper, *John, the Son of Zebedee*, 123.

14. Ibid., 127.

15. Boismard, *Le Martyre de Jean*, 77; see also 67.

16. See, for example, the list of early Smyrnaean bishops in the *Apostolic Constitutions* 7.46: Through the second bishop, a certain "Strateas, son of Lois," an association with Paul is suggested (see 2 Tim 1:5), while through "Ariston," a name which is seemingly shared by both the first and third bishops, Johannine Christianity may be suggested (see Cadoux, *Ancient Smyrna*, 314–315, who believes "Ariston" is the equivalent of Papias' "Aristion").

17. See Junod and Kaestli, *Acta Iohannis* 2.524, and Schäferdiek, "The Acts of John," 191–192.

Tertullian, who writes after Irenaeus, states in *On the Prescription against the Heretics* 32.2. that "Polycarp was established at the Church of Smyrna by John just as, at Rome, Clement was ordained by Peter." In response to Hengel's assertion that Tertullian "spins out the remark by Irenaeus in a tendentious way,"[18] one might suggest that Tertullian, who is himself conversant with traditions about the activity of another apostle—Paul—in Asia Minor,[19] is portraying a John consistent with both Irenaeus' reports and the greater Johannine traditions of which Irenaeus' reports are a part.

But even if Tertullian can be charged with a simple spinning out of an Irenaean account, Clement of Alexandria cannot. The sheer length and level of detail of the extended account of "John the Apostle" which is recorded by Clement makes clear that it rests on far more than statements like those found in Irenaeus. Indeed, according to Clement's own testimony, that which he records is "an account [which has been] handed down . . . and guarded in memory."[20] At the beginning of this account is the record that "the Apostle John," after serving his term of exile on Patmos, settled in Ephesus, "and used also to go, when called on, to the neighboring districts of the gentiles, in some places ordaining (καθίστημι) bishops, in others uniting whole churches, and in others appointing (κληρόω) a given individual pointed out by the Spirit."[21]

Clement preserves a tradition about an active ministry of John which includes, among other things, ordaining bishops. In light of that tradition one might raise up the suggestive language of the *Muratorian Canon* which, in discussing the apostle John, mentions "his own bishops."[22] A reasonable understanding is that the text is referring to bishops (purportedly) ordained by John.

18. Hengel, *The Johannine Question*, 153 n. 90. Certainly it is consistent with Tertullian's agenda to recognize an apostle at the foundation of important local Christian communities; for commentary on the origin of the churches in the cities named in Rev 1–2, see *Adv. Marc*. 4.5.2: "We have also the churches fostered by John . . . [which], tracing their line of bishops to its beginning, stand on John as their founder."

19. See *On Baptism* 17 for Tertullian's comments on the origin of the *Acts of Paul and Thecla*.

20. Clement, *Quis Dives Salvetur*, as recorded in HE 3.23.6. On the potential antiquity of this particular tradition regarding John, Koester has suggested that "the story may come from a time before Polycarp became bishop of [Smyrna]" (Koester, "Ephesos in Early Christian Literature," 138).

21. Clement, *Quis Dives Salvetur*, as recorded in HE 3.23.6.

22. *Muratorian Canon* 10; for translation of *Muratorian Canon* 10–16, see above comment on (a) 11–12, Obs. 6.

Even Irenaeus' own letter to Florinus suggests, if not confirms, an understanding regarding the activity of the apostle John which is broader and earlier than Irenaeus' own written account. It is significant that Irenaeus prefaces his own reminiscences of Polycarp and John by reminding Florinus, "While I was still a youth I saw you in Asia Minor with Polycarp . . . attempting to be pleasing to [Polycarp]" (HE 5.20.5). As Culpepper writes, "Since he appeals to Florinus's memory of their shared experience [with Polycarp], it is most unlikely that Irenaeus would have fabricated any of this. Presumably, Florinus's memory was as clear as Irenaeus's."[23]

If Irenaeus' childhood memories regarding Polycarp's association with John were confused then so, apparently, were Florinus'. More broadly, as suggested by Schnackenburg, it may not be individual, but corporate memories which lie at the root of Irenaeus' testimony: "Irenaeus may have been misled from the start by the error of the Church of Ephesus."[24] Schnackenburg's suggestion, if correct, provides further confirmation that Irenaeus' testimony is part of a greater and broader tradition.

In sum, the rhetorical posturing within Irenaeus' letter to another of Polycarp's students indicates that a local reminiscence of Polycarp's association with the apostle John predates Irenaeus. In light of the evidence provided by AJn and the tradition preserved by Clement of Alexandria, if not the *Muratorian Canon,* Tertullian, and Polycrates[25] as well, it is evident that Irenaeus' work stands within a broader tradition about John's ministry in Asia Minor.

Whatever the debt that FrgPol may owe to Irenaeus, either directly or indirectly, for the idea of Polycarp's association with John, it may also be indebted to Irenaeus for the very notion of (the perceived need for) an identifiable line of apostolic succession through John. In his well-known study on apostolic succession, Arnold Ehrhardt, after observing that "Irenaeus . . . insisted on apostolic succession," writes: "and his witness is less valuable for the history of the doctrine before his time than for its formation in subsequent times."[26] The raw material needed for a narrative about John and Polycarp may have been in place before Irenaeus; the codification of the significance of a direct line of succession from the apostle John through Polycarp may arguably be linked directly to Irenaeus.

---

23. Culpepper, *John, the Son of Zebedee*, 126.

24. Schnackenburg, *The Gospel according to Saint John* 1.81.

25. See HE 5.24.2–3, in which Eusebius quotes Polycrates, who regards John, "who was lying on the Lord's chest," to be among the "great stars who are sleeping in Asia."

26. Ehrhardt, *The Apostolic Succession in the First Two Centuries of the Church*, 109.

C. K. Barrett, who was unaware of FrgPol, writes: "It is impossible to doubt that a local biographer would have recounted Polycarp's association with John if he could have found a shred of evidence to suggest it."[27] Such is precisely the lacuna which this ancient work fills in a very unique way through an extended narrative piece. Drawing on particular traditions regarding John's activity in Asia Minor and John's lack of a martyr death, FrgPol develops the association of Polycarp and John to a degree unwitnessed, so far as we know, either before or since. Barrett's comment, as it turns out, is prophetic.

2. Why Is John's Peaceful Death So Troublesome?

The Problem

Within depictions of John which have survived from the early centuries, one can detect a concern about the extent of the sufferings which had been endured by this apostle. According to the prominent tradition, John had died peacefully. Yet, as an "apostle," it would have seemed appropriate that John suffer a martyr's death. As stated by Karl Rengstorf, "participation in the suffering and death of Jesus" is the "essence of the consciousness of the apostolic calling and office."[28]

Eusebius' *Commentary on the Psalms,* which is only partially preserved and, unfortunately, not available in a modern text edition, contains pertinent records of early Christian consideration of the matter. Regarding "the twelve . . . apostles," Eusebius writes that "Aquila was saying, 'Their blood will be honored . . .'" and Symmachus, "'Their blood will be an honor.'" Interestingly, Eusebius goes on to write, "each one endured variously the goal (τέλος) of martyrdom."[29] If Eusebius is preserving actual reports or paraphrasing in a trustworthy manner, then a clear statement of the understanding that each apostle must or would endure martyrdom is traceable (through Aquila) to at least the first half of the second century.

Even given such a general understanding of the martyrdom of apostles, the case of John may involve a unique difficulty. According to Walter Bauer,

27. Barrett, *The Gospel according to St. John*, 105.

28. Karl Heinrich Rengstorf, *Apostolate and Ministry: The New Testament Doctrine of the Office of the Ministry* (tr. Paul D. Pahl; St. Louis: Concordia Publishing House, 1969) 41; similarly, Walter Schmithals, *The Office of the Apostle in the Early Church* (tr. John E. Steeley; Nashville: Abingdon Press, 1969) 47, "It belongs to the nature of the apostolate that the apostle must suffer."

29. *PG* 23, 812C.

it is not necessarily a general understanding of the role of the apostle which gives rise to the compensation stories regarding John's martyrdom, so much as it is "the desire to square Jesus' prediction in Mark 10:39 = Matt 20:23, which had already pointed antiquity to a martyrdom that was in prospect, with the tradition that the apostle had lived long and had not died a violent death."[30]

Regardless of whether they stem from a broader concern for the apostolate, a narrower concern for John, or some combination thereof, a number of direct explanations for John's reprieve from a martyr death are extant from the second century on. Through presenting Polycarp's martyrdom as being necessitated by John's peaceful death, FrgPol sets itself within the prominent tradition about John.

Before examining that tradition, it is important to recognize that there is evidence—perhaps early evidence—that John had, in fact, died as a martyr.

An Alternate Tradition: John as Martyr

It is possible that as early a witness as Papias, whose confusing description of "John the Elder" is discussed above, had confirmed that John, son of Zebedee, died a martyr. Reports of John's martyrdom are extant in two works—a seventh–eighth century epitome of the *Church History* of Philip of Side, and a ninth-century manuscript of the *Chronicon* of George the Sinner—which claim Papias as their authority:

> Papias reports in his second book that John the Theologian and James his brother were killed by the Jews. [Philip of Side, *Church History*, Codex Baroccianus 142]

> For Papias . . . in the second book of the *Sayings of the Lord* says that [John] was killed by the Jews. [George the Sinner, *Chronicon*, Codex Coislinianus 305]

If a report about John's martyrdom had in fact been included in the conveyed text of Papias, which is now known principally through HE 3.39, then it is not known when it might have fallen out, though some scholars have suggested that Eusebius himself is the culprit.[31] Culpepper asks the

30. Bauer, "Accounts," 52.

31. Hengel (*The Johannine Question*, 21), for whom "this often neglected tradition seems to me to be more trustworthy than it is usually supposed to be," suggests that Eusebius might have had his reasons for dropping a report about John's martyrdom. For further discussion see Schoedel, *Polycarp, Martyrdom of Polycarp, Fragments of Papias*, 117–121; H. Latimer Jack-

question, "did [Eusebius] suppress the report in favor of the tradition that the apostle wrote the Fourth Gospel?" That is, if the apostle John had indeed been martyred very early on, say 43–44 CE, then it would have been impossible for him to have composed the Fourth Gospel in the form in which that Gospel has circulated (see esp. John 21:21–23).

In answering his own question, Culpepper recognizes that the explanation of suppression on the part of Eusebius "is difficult to accept since Eusebius assumes the five books of Papias are still available. . . ."[32] The preservation of reports about the martyrdoms of "the twelve . . . apostles,"[33] as contained in Eusebius' *Commentary on the Psalms* (cited above), further complicates any consideration of Eusebius' writings and motives.

At the top of the most recent study of "the martyrdom of John the Apostle," Boismard lists the reports found in Philip of Side and George the Sinner along with a report of John's martyrdom in the early sixth-century Martyrology of Carthage as "the three 'proofs' on which is founded the thesis according to which John the apostle might have died a martyr."[34] In fact Boismard builds his case on much more, and provides exhaustive testimony to the tradition that John had died as a martyr, perhaps as early as 43–44 CE.[35]

With Boismard's recent work, that which H. Latimer Jackson stated in 1918 rings even more true today: it "is no longer possible"[36] to ignore evidence indicating a persistent tradition that John, son of Zebedee, had died as a martyr. Simply, two disparate traditions about John's death must be recognized. That said, there is no dismissing the overwhelming testimony to the fact that from at least the second century onwards John was regularly depicted as one who had not died as a martyr.[37] It is this prominent tradition which FrgPol engages, and within which it is to be understood.

---

son, *The Problem of the Fourth Gospel* (Cambridge: Cambridge University Press, 1918) 142–150, "Excursus I: The Death of John Son of Zebedee"; and Zahn, *Apostel und Apostelschüler*, 103 n. 1. For further bibliography, see Kaestli, "Le rôle des textes bibliques dans la Genèse et le développement des légendes apocryphes: Le cas du sort final de l'apôtre Jean," *Augustinianum* 23 (1983) 320 nn. 4–5.

32. Culpepper, *John, the Son of Zebedee*, 155.

33. Among whom are included "the sons of Zebedee"; *PG* 23, 812C.

34. Boismard, *Le Martyre de Jean*, 10.

35. Ibid., 10–13 and throughout. I do not find in Boismard's work any consideration of the statements in Eusebius' *Commentary on the Psalms*.

36. Jackson, *The Problem of the Fourth Gospel*, 150.

37. Kaestli, "Le rôle des textes bibliques," 320, writes: "This tradition [of John's martyr death] has been completely supplanted by the legend of the longevity of the apostle and of his natural death in Ephesus."

The Prominent Tradition and Attempts at Compensation

Both of the central components of the prominent tradition—recognition of the longevity of the apostle John's life, as well as compensation for John's lack of a martyr death—are evident by the end of the second and the beginning of the third centuries. For example Tertullian, in a discussion of the "apostolic churches" (*ecclesiae apostolicae*), writes as follows about the church at Rome:

> How fortunate is the church to whom the apostles have poured out all of their teaching along with their blood: where Peter undergoes suffering like that of the Lord; where Paul is crowned in a death like that of John (the Baptist); where the apostle John, being submerged in boiling oil did not suffer [harm], and was afterwards exiled to the island.[38]

For Origen it is not any gruesome torture miraculously endured, but simply the exile itself which accounts for John's "martyrdom" (μαρτύριον).[39]

The second-century AJn has been discussed previously in this chapter and several times in the Commentary. In AJn 113, the elderly apostle, who has already stepped down into the grave which he asked "the youths" (οἱ νεανίσκοι) to prepare for him (111), prays to "you who have guarded me until this hour for yourself, pure and untouched from intercourse with a woman, who appeared to me when as a youth I was wanting to be married . . . who took me from a bitter death. . . ." The complex address, quoted here only in part, is followed by a petition or, more precisely, a series of petitions, which begins: "Now, therefore, since I have completed the program (οἰκονομία) to which I have been entrusted (πιστεύω) by you. . . ." In AJn it is clear that John's peaceful death at an advanced age is no aberration, it is the divinely appointed outcome of a life's program dutifully fulfilled; John is an excellent apostle.[40]

Concern about John's peaceful death continues through the centuries. Augustine of Hippo is puzzled by reports he has received about miraculous

---

38. *On the Prescription against the Heretics* 36.3; for comments, see R. F. Refoulé, ed., and P. de Labriolle, tr., *Tertullien: Traité de la prescription contre les hérétiques* (SC 46; Paris: Éditions du Cerf, 1957) 137–138.

39. Origen, "Commentary on Matthew" 16.6 (commenting on Matt 20:20–24, the request on behalf of the sons of Zebedee). For a report of the exile of "the apostle" John to the island of Patmos, see Clement, *Quis Dives Salvetur* 42.2., discussed above.

40. For the full narrative of John's final words, prayer, and death, see AJn 111–115; for a discussion of other, related (second-century) traditions, see Junod and Kaestli, *Acta Iohannis* 1.156–158.

dust at the site of John's tomb[41] and reasons that such a wonder likely has as its purpose "to commend the value of [John's] death, since it was not commended by martyrdom (since he did not suffer persecution for the faith of Christ)."[42] As the tradition of John's peaceful death continues to develop through late antiquity and into the medieval period, he is associated with prominent biblical figures such as Elijah and the Virgin Mary, who, it was believed, departed from earthly life neither violently nor in a natural way.[43]

There is also this fascinating statement about John as "martyr" in the classic medieval work of Jacob of Voragine, *The Golden Legend,* 8:

> For there are three kinds of martyrdom: the first is willed and endured, the second willed but not endured, the third endured without being willed. Saint Stephen is an example of the first, Saint John of the second, the Holy Innocents of the third.[44]

When the notion of a martyrdom which is "willed but not endured" might first have been formulated for John is not known.[45]

The Prominent Tradition, the Gospels, and Polycarp

The overt statement of Polycarp's martyrdom as compensation for John's peaceful death as found in FrgPol is unique among the extant sources. But, more broadly understood, the notion that Polycarp's death is associated with John's death—at least as the latter was foretold by Jesus in the Synoptic record—is indicated in the narrative of MartPol.

In the final prayer in MartPol (MPol 14.2 = HE 4.15.33–34), Polycarp assumes that his imminent martyrdom will allow him "a share . . . in the cup of your Christ." As reported by Dehandschutter,[46] scholars have long recognized the phrase, "the cup of your Christ," as an allusion to canonical

41. For a description of this dust, see Schäferdiek, "Acts of John," 258.

42. Augustine, *Tractate* 124, "On the Gospel of John," 3.

43. For the influence of biblical (and related) traditions, see Kaestli, "Le rôle des textes bibliques"; see also Martin Jugie, *La mort et l'assomption de la Sainte Vierge: Etude historico-doctrinale* (Studi e Testi, 114; Vatican City: Biblioteca Apostolica Vaticana, 1944), Excursus D: "La mort et l'assomption de Saint Jean l'Évangeliste."

44. William Granger Ryan, tr., Jacobus de Voragine, *The Golden Legend: Readings on the Saints* (Princeton: Princeton University Press, 1993) 1.50.

45. According to Ryan, ibid., xiv, "The Golden Legend is basically the work of a compiler"; J.- B. M. Roze, *La légende dorée de Jaques de Voragine* (Paris: Edouard Rouveyre, 1902) 1.xv–xvi, has identified several sources from the first through the thirteenth centuries.

46. Dehandschutter, *Martyrium Polycarpi*, 252.

Gospel material, including Mark 10:35–40 (par. Matt 20:20–23), the request by[47] James and John, the sons of Zebedee.

In the Gospel accounts, that request elicits the following response from Jesus: "The cup that I drink you will drink" (Mark 10:39, NRSV); "You will indeed drink my cup" (Matt 20:23, NRSV). Jesus is noncommittal in answering the actual request, stating only that heavenly privilege "is for those for whom it has been prepared (ἑτοιμάζω)" (Mark 10:40, Matt 20:23). Had it been "prepared" for James and John? The Synoptic report does not say.

Recently these verses have been cited by Boismard to suggest the likelihood that John did meet an early death.[48] Others such as Bauer, who is quoted above, would see this Gospel material as precisely the catalyst for the compensation component in the prominent tradition regarding John's peaceful death.

Regarding ancient Christian understandings of Polycarp's death vis-à-vis the prominent tradition about John, what is of interest is the scope of the allusion in Polycarp's prayer. If one makes the supposition that the phrase "the cup of your Christ" in MartPol directs the reader's attention to the first quote of Jesus cited above (Mark 10:39; Matt 20:23), then one ought further to consider whether the second quote cited, Jesus' statement about preparation, is also alluded to in Polycarp's final prayer. According to MartPol, Polycarp states within his prayer that God has "prepared beforehand" (προετοιμάζω) for Polycarp to "be received among [the number of martyrs] in your presence this day." What is a potentiality in the Synoptic story about James and John—Jesus cannot say that it will have been "prepared" for them—is actualized in MartPol: Polycarp is confident that his place has been "prepared beforehand."

Does Polycarp's final prayer, as recorded in MartPol, bear witness to an understanding of Polycarp's martyrdom in which Polycarp, in his manner of death, accomplishes something that John did not? It is impossible to say, since MartPol indicates nothing about John as martyr or as one who experienced a peaceful death. Nonetheless, if one approaches MartPol with the assumption that John has not died a martyr, then one will likely learn that Polycarp accomplished what John has not: Polycarp has drunk

---

47. Or, on behalf of; see Matt 20:20.

48. Boismard, *Le Martyre de Jean,* 78; see also Jackson, *The Problem of the Fourth Gospel*, 142–150; Kaestli, "Le rôle des textes bibliques," 320–323, includes a short consideration of both the Synoptic and the Johannine passages.

from the "cup" of martyrdom; further, his place in the afterlife was "prepared beforehand" by God.

There is a second potentially relevant Gospel pericope which speaks not to manner of death, but to longevity of life. Toward the close of the Fourth Gospel, in response to Peter's request for information about his fellow disciple, Jesus replies:

> If it is my will that [the beloved disciple] remain until I come, what is that to you? . . . So the rumor spread quickly that this disciple would not die. Yet Jesus did not say to [Peter] that [the beloved disciple] would not die, but, "If it is my will that he remain until I come, what is that to you?" (John 21:21–23, NRSV)

Does this passage furnish information regarding the longevity of John's life?

In light of modern scholarship on the text, there is no readily available answer to the question. The pericope may or may not furnish information about the lifespan of the beloved disciple; that character may or may not be John. In approaching an area of study in which "the questions are numerous and so too the answers—numerous and embarrassing,"[49] one must, at best, be tentative.

In light of FrgPol, it is interesting that in a recent assessment of this pericope Richard J. Cassidy writes, "Jesus strikingly foretells . . . that [the beloved disciple] will not experience a martyrdom."[50] Further, it is notable that in a classic article on the matter, Maurice Goguel states the intent of this pericope as follows: "the author would persuade his readers that if the beloved disciple had not . . . suffered martyrdom, this was not because he was inferior, but because the Lord had disposed otherwise."[51] Some attempt at compensation appears to be evident.

Rudolf Bultmann, in his classic commentary on the Fourth Gospel, does not disagree with the understanding that the beloved disciple lived to a great age, but he feels that "it is hardly likely that vv. 20–22 are a defence of the belittling of the beloved disciple on the ground that he did not suffer a martyr's death"; rather, the precipitating problem was "that the idea arose

---

49. Hans-Martin Schenke, "The Function and Background of the Beloved Disciple in the Gospel of John," in *Nag Hammadi, Gnosticism, and Early Christianity* (ed. Charles W. Hedrick and Robert Hodgson; Peabody, Mass.: Hendrickson, 1986) 115.

50. Richard J. Cassidy, *John's Gospel in New Perspective: Christology and the Realities of Roman Power* (Maryknoll: Orbis Books, 1992) 74.

51. Maurice Goguel, "Did Peter Deny His Lord?" *HTR* 25 (1932) 17.

that he would remain alone until the parousia."[52] Nevertheless George R. Beasely-Murray, who translated Bultmann's work into English and then wrote his own commentary, proceeds in the vein of Goguel: "By the time chapter 21 was written and the Gospel went into circulation both disciples had died, [Peter] with the glory of martyrdom and [the beloved disciple] with a peaceful end at Ephesus (we would certainly have heard to the contrary had it been otherwise)."[53]

Whatever the precipitating events which may lie behind the narrative of John 21, however ancient readers might have understood Jesus' words in that chapter, and whoever the beloved disciple was or might have been, two points are of interest: at least by the time of Irenaeus, the apostle John was considered to be "the beloved disciple"; at least by the time of the *Acts of John* (150–160 CE), John was considered to have lived to an old age and died peacefully. By the second half of the second century, the prominent tradition about John and the descriptions within the Fourth Gospel were informing each other. Such cross-fertilization may have influenced the portrait of John in FrgPol, though one can undertand the extant text of FrgPol, and the prominent tradition which it engages, independently from John 21.

Beasely-Murray suggests that the problem or conflict behind John 21 may be a kind of rivalry:

> Is it reasonable to suggest that this presentation of the relations of Peter and the Beloved Disciple, to the Lord and to each other, was made for the benefit of the churches which were inclined to exalt one over against the other? The tendency to favor one apostle more than another is seen in the Corinthian correspondence of Paul . . . (1 Cor 3:3–4).[54]

It is indeed reasonable to approach portrayals of apostolic and other prominent figures in such a manner as Beasely-Murray suggests, not only in light of such evidence as is provided by the early chapters of 1 Cor, but more specifically in light of a history which can be plotted between and among Christian communities. Regardless of its efficacy in the matter of John 21, such an approach illumines FrgPol.

---

52. Rudolf Bultmann, *The Gospel of John: A Commentary* (tr. and ed. G. R. Beasely-Murray; Philadelphia: Westminster Press, 1971) 716.

53. George R. Beasely-Murray, *John* (Word Biblical Commentary 36; Waco, Tex.: Word Books, 1987) 410.

54. Ibid.

In FrgPol, it is because of a lack in John's hagiographical biography that someone else must die a martyr's death. The martyr Polycarp becomes a kind of surrogate for the apostle John; he endures the martyr death on John's account. What context might have given rise to such an understanding of Polycarp's martyrdom?

3. Smyrna versus Ephesus: John, Polycarp, and a Rivalry Both Sacred and Profane

Under Roman Imperial Rule

The ongoing rivalry among several prominent cities in western Asia Minor is well attested in the ancient sources.[55] As George Bean writes: "where once the support or the hostility of Ephesus or Smyrna could make or mar the fortunes of a Hellenistic King, the cities were now reduced to striving merely for titles and honours: 'First and greatest Metropolis of Asia,' 'Four times temple-warden of the emperors,' such are the phrases proudly repeated in the official inscriptions."[56] Another current writer, Anthony D. Macro, considering "the proud display of grandiose titles on coins or insciptions or both," puts it thus: "Warfare was now waged by propaganda and advertisement."[57]

To one who experienced such "striving" firsthand, the philosopher Dio Chrysostom, the cities involved seemed driven by "vanity and self-deception and empty, foolish pride"; their goal of gaining rank among their neighbors being merely "an ass's shadow."[58] For our purposes it is relevant

55. Besides the works engaged in the discussion below, see R. Merkelbach, "Der Rangstreit der Städte Asiens und die Rede des Aelius Aristides über die Eintracht," *Zeitschrift für Papyrologie und Epigraphik* 32 (1978) 287–296; Magie, *Roman Rule in Asia Minor*, esp. 599, 635; Cadoux, *Ancient Smyrna*, esp. 274–275, 291–294; and Joachim Marquardt, *Römische Staatsverwaltung* (Leipzig: Hirzel, 1881) 1.343–346.

56. Bean, *Aegean Turkey*, 17; for inscriptional evidence, see GIBM 3.153–155 and *CIG*, nos. 3199, 3202–3205; also, an inscription published fairly recently in which there is evidence of an erasure, likely indicating a disagreement about whether Ephesus, under Caracalla, was "two times" or "three times" a temple warden, in Dieter Knibbe, Helmut Engelmann, Bülent İplikçioğlu, "Neue Inschriften aus Ephesos XI," *Jh* 59 (1989) 165–168, no. 5.

57. Macro, "The Cities of Asia Minor under the Roman Imperium," *ANRW* 2.7.2 (1980) 658–697, 683.

58. 34.47, 48; tr. J. W. Cohoon and H. Lamar Crosby, *Dio Chrysostom* (LCL, Dio Chrysostom, 3; 1940; Cambridge: Harvard University Press, 1961) 381, 383. "Smyrnaeans with Ephesians" appears as the third and final pair of quarreling citizens which Dio lists.

that among the rivalries which Dio has in mind is that between Ephesus and Smyrna. In a classic treatment of the economic history of "Roman Asia Minor," T. R. S. Broughton writes simply, "[Smyrna's] rivalry with Ephesus was proverbial. . . ."[59]

Though observers both ancient and modern might find such "warfare . . . by propaganda" to be "trivial," it was a very serious matter, as is evidenced, for example, by the fact that it was "expensive," sometimes to the point of being "deleterious to the financial welfare of the cities."[60] Of course the reason a city would expend such effort promoting itself or trying to check the "propaganda" with which a rival city promoted itself was precisely because of the wealth and power which heightened status could bring. Steven Friesen has recently reiterated the notion that "the reason that political rivalry continued after the loss of autonomy . . . was . . . competition for material resources"; further, in commenting on five particular cites, including Smyrna and Ephesus, Friesen writes: "The use of municipal titles in coins and inscriptions suggests that the primary function of such titles was to influence perceptions of status and order among the larger cities. . . ."[61] Simply stated, matters pertaining to wealth and power were worthy of the "warfare" of "propaganda."

When the emperor Tiberius sought a location suitable for the building and maintaining of a new cult site, Smyrna and Ephesus were among the cities petitioning for yet another temple. As Tacitus reports, the representatives of Smyrna, who worked diligently to establish, among other things, "the antiquity" (*vetustas*) of their city, were finally successful in gaining the temple for their city (*Annals* 4.56).[62] Yet, according to *Annals* 3.61, the senate was so troubled by the "acrimony of the discussion" which pervaded all the cities' presentations that it "passed a number of resolutions . . . and the applicants were ordered to fix the brass records actually inside [their

59. Broughton, "Roman Asia," 742.

60. Macro, "The Cities of Asia Minor," 683.

61. Friesen, "The Cult of the Roman Emperors in Ephesos: Temple Wardens, City Titles, and the Interpretation of the Revelation of John," in Koester, *Ephesos*, 238, 240. For a representative list of such titles, see Broughton, "Roman Asia," 740–744.

62. *Annals* 4.56; tr. John Jackson, *Tacitus: The Annals, Books IV–VI, XI–XII* (LCL, Tacitus, 4; 1937; Cambridge: Harvard University Press, 1970) 101. For discussion of the report in Tacitus' *Annals*, see Edwin M. Yamauchi, *The Archaeology of New Testament Cities in Western Asia Minor* (London: Pickering and Inglis, 1980) 57, and Merkelbach, "Der Rangstreit der Städte Asiens," 287.

existing] temples, both as a solemn memorial and as a warning not to lapse into secular intrigue under the cloak of religion."[63]

Smyrna's early victory over Ephesus in the imperial propaganda wars was fairly short-lived. Beginning with Vespasian (69–79), it would seem that emperors generally favored Ephesus over Smyrna and other cities.[64] Dieter Knibbe has referred to the second century generally as a "golden age" for Ephesus,[65] while Friesen, commenting specifically on the establishment of the "Temple of the Flavian Sebastoi" in Ephesus, writes: "The innovation that began Asia's temple of the Sebastoi in Ephesos changed the public discourse of religion and identity in the eastern Mediterranean for centuries to come."[66]

Ephesus had gained the upper hand.[67] Needless to say, that "enhanced the rivalry with Smyrna."[68] As described by Macro, "Ephesus' assumption of the title 'First and greatest Metropolis of Asia' caused such ill-feeling with Smyrna that the Emperor . . . felt the need to intervene."[69] Actually that particular incident, which occurred in the middle of the second century under Antoninus Pius (138–161), is somewhat more complicated.

It seems that Smyrna, in a formal letter addressed to Ephesus, had neglected to include a certain title appropriate for that city; most likely, "First and greatest Metropolis of Asia." At the formal request of Ephesus, which felt snubbed by its rival, the Emperor intervened.[70] It is noteworthy that several years following this episode, the famous rhetorician Aelius Aris-

---

63. Tr. Jackson, *Tacitus: The Annals, Books 1–III* (LCL, Tacitus, 3; 1931; Cambridge: Harvard University Press, 1969) 623. According to Broughton, "Roman Asia," 709, the episode is significant because "the lines of future rivalry among the cities . . . were already being drawn."

64. Dieter Knibbe and Bülent İplikçioğlu, "Neue Inschriften aus Ephesos VIII," *Jh* 53 (1981–1982) 90.

65. Dieter Knibbe and Wilhelm Alzinger, "Ephesos vom Beginn der römischen Herrschaft in Kleinasien bis zum Ende der Principatszeit," *ANRW* 2.7.2 (1980) 775.

66. Friesen, "The Cult of the Roman Emperors in Ephesos," 232, 236.

67. Which is not to say that Smyrna did not continue to enjoy the attention of emperors; see Broughton, "Roman Asia," 744–745, regarding Hadrian and Marcus Aurelius.

68. Erich Lessing and Wolfgang Oberleitner, *Ephesos: Weltstadt der Antike* (Vienna: Carl Ueberreuter, 1978) 52c; see also Dieter Knibbe, "Neue Inschriften aus Ephesos I," *Jh* 48 (1966–1967) 1–22, 19–29.

69. Macro, "The Cities of Asia Minor," 683.

70. GIBM 3.154b and 155a, no. 489; see recently Knibbe and İplikçioğlu, "Neue Inschriften aus Ephesos VIII," 90, no. 6, "Die erste und gröste Metropole Asiens"; also Henri Grégoire, "Epigraphie chrétienne II: Inscriptions d'Ephèse," *Byzantion* 1 (1920) 714.

tides, who was himself variously claimed by Smyrna, Ephesus, and Pergamum,[71] delivered an oration "Concerning Concord,"[72] in which he called on these three cities to end their rivalries.[73]

Under Christian Rule

After the transition to Christian imperial rule, Smyrna formally fell within the jurisdiction of the Bishop of Ephesus, the Metropolitan of Asia.[74] The archaeologist Clive Foss would receive no argument from the ancient Smyrnaeans for writing this comment on the matter of church governance: "Smyrna was evidently a worthy rival of Ephesus, whose ecclesiastical primacy she constantly attacked."[75] In an incident in Ephesus in 441, several Smyrnaeans apparently shouted words or slogans offensive to Ephesus; they were then pardoned against the Ephesians' will.[76] In 451, following a successful course of political maneuvering, Smyrna became an autocephalous bishopric.[77] It was not until the ninth century, however, that the bishop of Smyrna would attain the status of "Metropolitan."[78]

John and Polycarp in an Ephesian Inscription

Among the many discoveries which archaeologists have made in Ephesus are two inscribed marble tablets found in the immediate vicinity of the Church of St. Mary, which have been dated to the time of Justinian.[79] The texts of both fragments are incomplete and badly damaged.

---

71. Not an unusual honor; according to Yamauchi, *The Archaeology of New Testament Cities in Western Asia Minor*, 164 n. 6, "athletes and famous rhetors were claimed by adoptive cities." Homer was claimed by more than one city, among them Smyrna; see Cadoux, *Ancient Smyrna*, 75.

72. English translation in Charles A. Behr, *P. Aelius Aristides: The Complete Works* (2 vols.; Leiden: E. J. Brill, 1981) 2.26–44.

73. For further discussion see Merkelbach, "Der Rangstreit der Städte Asiens," and Cadoux, *Ancient Smyrna*, 274–275.

74. Clive Foss, *Ephesus after Antiquity: A Late Antique, Byzantine and Turkish City* (Cambridge: Cambridge University Press, 1979) 5.

75. Clive Foss, "Archaeology and the 'Twenty Cities' of Byzantine Asia," *American Journal of Archaeology* 81 (1977) 482a.

76. IvE 4.189–190, no. 1352; the same inscription is cited by Foss, *Ephesus after Antiquity*, 16.

77. For a consideration of the "struggle" at the Council of Chalcedon in which the representatives of Smyrna fortuitously sided with the Bishop of New Rome (Chalcedon), see Keil, "Johannes von Ephesos und Polykarpos von Smyrna," 369.

78. *Oxford Dictionary of Byzantium* 1919b–1920a.

79. IvE 1a.281–284, no. 45, "Kaiserbrief (?) über Johannes von Ephesos und Polykarp von Smyrna," 281; all translations, including text restorations, in the discussion below are based on the text edition found on 282–283. This ancient text was earlier edited and de-

Foss, consistent with others who have commented on the text, assumes that it was occasioned by a "dispute . . . [which] seems to have arisen from a claim of the church of Smyrna to the higher rank of Metropolis."[80] That may be right. Regardless, what appears clear is that the inscribed text is at pains to clarify John's status in response to claims which have been made about Polycarp.

As summarized earlier in this century by the eminent archaeologist Josef Keil, the first tablet, Frg. A, is "concerned solely with the person of St. John."[81] Therein John is variously described as "disciple [of God, more] beloved [than] al[l (others)]," "the first, who reclined on [God's] chest," "the theo[logian]," "the son of thunder," and "[most holy a]postle."[82] Twice within the extant text there is evidently direct reference to the "[honor]" of which John is worthy.[83]

Frg. B begins with a consideration of Polycarp, of whom it is said, "but he himself would never accept [the heightened glo]ry of the apostles and the disc[iples]."[84] Of course, regardless of what amount of glory Polycarp may or may not find appropriate, the text of FrgPol casts him as one who suffers an apostle's martyrdom. Had attempts been made, perhaps by the Smyrnaeans—who are mentioned in Frg. B[85]—to bestow "heightened glory" on Polycarp? The Ephesian inscription suggests as much. Why else would the proposition ("That he would never accept [the heightened glo]ry") be made—no less, inscribed?

scribed by Keil, "Johannes von Ephesos und Polykarpos von Smyrna"; see also Grégoire, "Epigraphie chrétienne II," 712–716, and L. Robert et al., eds., *Supplementum Epigraphicum Graecum* vol. 4 (Amsterdam: A. W. Sijthoff, 1929) 99–100, no. 517.

80. Foss, *Ephesus after Antiquity*, 6; similarly IvE 1a.281; Francois Halkin, "Inscriptions grecques relatives a l'hagiographie: L'Asie Mineure" (in Halkin, *Etudes d'épigraphie grecque et d'hagiographie byzantine* [London: Variorum Reprints, 1973], essays nos. 5 and 6) 80; Keil, "Johannes von Ephesus und Polykarpos von Smyrna," esp. 371–372; Grégoire, "Epigraphie chrétienne II," esp. 714–715.

81. Keil, "Johannes von Ephesos und Polykarpos von Smyrna," 371.

82. A.2–4, 6–7,15; my translation is based on the restored text as found in IvE 1a.282–283.

83. "to be deemed [wort]hy of such [honor]," A.1–2; "And such is the magnitude [of his honor]," A.10–11.

84. B.6–7.

85. "Sm[yrnaeans]," B.7; there is a second reference to Smyrna at B.11 according to the restored text as found in Keil, "Johannes von Ephesus und Polykarpos von Smyrna," 370, Grégoire, "Epigraphie chrétienne II," 713, and L. Robert et al., *Supplementum Epigraphicum Graecum* 4.100.

The Harris Fragments on Polycarp as a Smyrnaean Document

When Smyrna, under the emperor Tiberius, sought to bolster its petition for consideration as a temple site, its officials researched and presented evidence for the "antiquity" of their city. As noted recently by Vasiliki Limberis, that strategy had changed little by the time of the first ecumenical councils, though it had been adapted to the Christian circumstance: "Rome, Ephesos, and many other cities stressed apostolic foundation as the criterion for honor, precedence, and position."[86] Indeed, as Oscar Cullman points out in his classic study on Peter, that strategy is even evident among Christian communities from at least the latter half of the second century. Citing Roman accounts of Peter's burial and Polycrates' description of various prominent figures associated with Asia (in HE 5.24.2–9),[87] Cullman writes: "It is true that a purely topographical tradition is not free from the influence of partisan interests."[88]

For Ephesus, the tracing of a glorious Christian antiquity was an easy endeavor: it was a church which could claim to have been founded by Paul, to have hosted Paul and his entourage for an extended period of time, and to have been led by Paul's companion Timothy;[89] further, as described by Keil, it could claim an even "greater flowering . . . with John, a personality of the highest reputation and far-reaching influence."[90] For its part, Smyrna's great hero was Polycarp. Keil observes that in a simple comparison of Christian origins, "the proportion of power between the two old rivals was very uneven."[91]

In the context of the ongoing rivalry between Smyrna and Ephesus, the strategy evident in FrgPol appears to fit a Smyrnaean agenda. That agenda might be stated as follows: identify a vulnerable point in the prominent tradition on John (the lack of a martyr death and need for compensation) and capitalize on it by transferring the martyr death which had been accounted to John onto Polycarp.

---

86. Limberis, "The Council of Ephesos: The Demise of the See of Ephesos and the Rise of the Cult of the Theotokos," in Koester, *Ephesos*, 334.

87. John among them.

88. Cullman, *Peter: Disciple, Apostle, Martyr* (Library of History and Doctrine; 2d ed., tr. Floyd V. Filson; London: SCM Press, 1962) 120.

89. Interestingly, Timothy is also named in the inscription from St. Mary's, along with the title "the apostolic one" (B.8). Polycarp is similarly identified as "apostolic" in MartPol; see ch. 4, comments on (e) 14–21, Obs. 3.

90. Keil, "Johannes von Ephesos und Polykarpos von Smyrna," 369; similarly Dieter Knibbe, "Ephesos," PW, Suppl. 12.293–295. See also Knibbe and Alzinger, "Ephesos vom Beginn der römischen Herrschaft in Kleinasien bis zum Ende der Principatszeit," 783.

91. Keil, "Johannes von Ephesos und Polykarpos von Smyrna," 368.

Josef Keil, who was unaware of FrgPol, wrote of Ephesus and Smyrna: "it would be astonishing if the old rivalry between the two cities should not have been repeated, in some form, in the Christian era."[92] Of course, the evidence of the Ephesian inscription shows that it was repeated. FrgPol quite likely represents another expression of that rivalry.

When FrgPol may have been written, and whether it played a direct or indirect role in eliciting the response extant in the inscription from St. Mary's, is unknown. Nonetheless, probable *termini* can be established. FrgPol cannot reasonably have been produced before both the prominent tradition about John's peaceful death (including the perceived need for compensation) and the tradition about Polycarp's relationship with John had been established. Positively stated, FrgPol could have been produced as early as the beginning of the third century; there is nothing in the extant text of FrgPol that would not have been available to a writer/compiler at that time.

On the other hand, the inscription at St. Mary's is reasonably explained as a reaction to some heightening of Polycarp's status which poses a (perceived) threat to the status of John. There is no extant ancient text, save FrgPol, which can reasonably be understood to accomplish that. Given the available data, it is not unreasonable to assume that FrgPol, or something very like FrgPol, was composed and circulating either before or during the turmoil which resulted in the publishing of the inscription at St. Mary's. It is likely that FrgPol, or something quite like it, had been composed and been circulating in and around Smyrna by the early- to mid-sixth century.

If FrgPol was produced in or around Smyrna between the third and sixth centuries, then it was almost certainly composed in Greek. When a Greek text of FrgPol might have been translated into Sahidic cannot, of course, be known. According to Bruce Metzger, "about the beginning of the Third Century portions of the New Testament were translated into Sahidic."[93] As the codices within the so-called Nag Hammadi Library attest, a broad array of literature had been translated from Greek into Sahidic by the end of the fourth century.[94] The translation might have been made at any point after composition in Greek.

92. Ibid.

93. Bruce Metzger, *The Text of the New Testament: Its Transmission, Corruption, and Restoration* (3rd ed.; New York: Oxford University Press, 1992) 79.

94. The books found near Nag Hammadi were "buried around 400 C.E."; see James M. Robinson, Introduction, in idem, ed., *The Nag Hammadi Library in English* (3rd ed.; San Francisco: Harper and Row, 1988) 2.

OR.7561, no. 55r
British Library

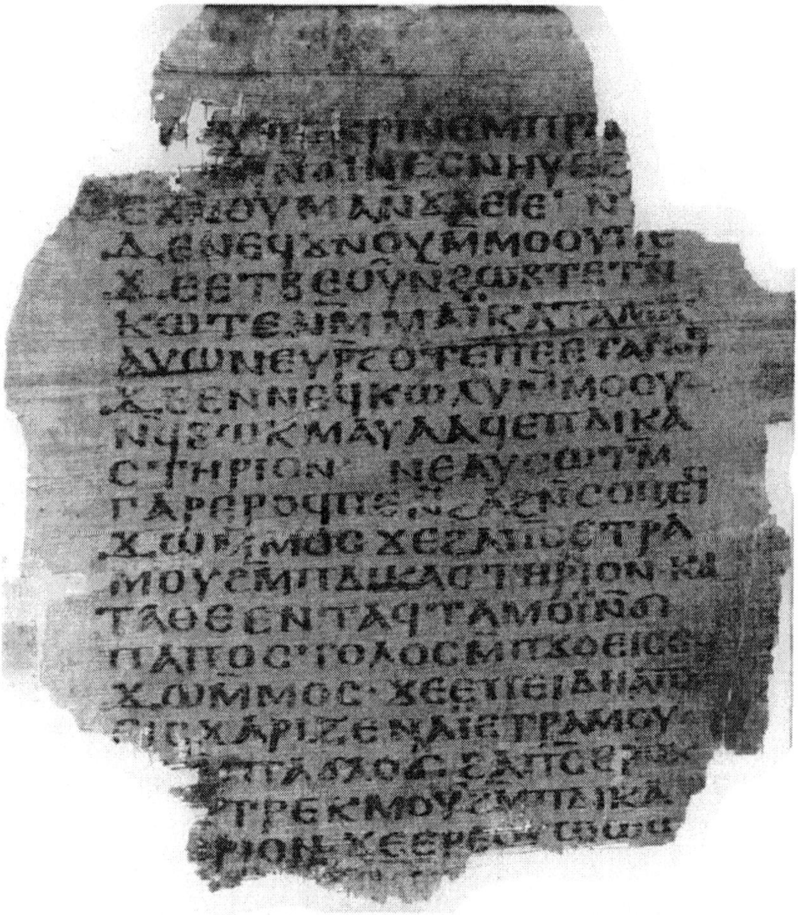

OR.7561, no. 55v
British Library

OR.7561, no. 56r
British Library

OR.7561, no. 56v
British Library

OR.7561, no. 63r
British Library

OR.7561, no. 63v
British Library

OR.7561, no. 64r
British Library

OR.7561, no. 64v
British Library

Bibliography

I. Primary Sources: Individual Authors or Works

Acts of Andrew and Matthias. Die lateinischen Bearbeitungen der Acta Andrea et Matthiae apud Anthropophagos: Mit sprachlichen Kommentar. Edited by Franz Blatt. Giessen: Alfred Töpelmann, 1930.

Acts of John. Acta Iohannis. 2 vols. Translated by Eric Junod and Jean-Daniel Kaestli. Corpus Christianorum, Series Apocryphorum, nos. 1–2. Turnhout: Brepols, 1983.

"The Acts of John." Translated, with introduction and notes, by Knut Schäferdiek. In *New Testament Apocrypha.* Vol. 2, *Writings Relating to the Apostles, Apocalypses, and Related Subjects.* Edited by Wilhelm Schneemelcher and translated by R. McL. Wilson, 152–209. Louisville: Westminster/John Knox, 1992.

Acts of John by Prochorus. In *Acta Joannis.* Edited by Theodor Zahn, 3–165. Erlangen: Andreas Deichert, 1880.

Aelius Aristides. *Orations XVII–LIII.* Vol. 2, *P. Aelius Aristides: The Complete Works.* Translated by Charles A. Behr. Leiden: E. J. Brill, 1981.

———. *P. Aelii Aristidis Opera Quae Exstant Omnia.* Edited by Charles A. Behr. Leiden: E. J. Brill, 1976.

Apostolic Constitutions. Didascalia et Constitutiones Apostolorum. Edited by Francis Xavier Funk. Paderborn: Ferdinand Schoeningh, 1905.

Appian. *Appian's Roman History.* 4 vols. 1912. LCL, 1971.

———. *Prooemium; Iberica; Annibaica; Libyca; Illyrica; Syriaca; Mithridatica; Fragmenta.* Vol. 1, *Appiani Historia Romani.* Edited by P. Vierick and A. G. Roos, with corrections and addenda by E. Gabba. Academia Scientarum Germanica Berolinensis. Leipzig: B. G. Teubner, 1962.

Apuleius. *The Apologia and Florida of Apuleius of Madaura.* Translated by H. E. Butler. 1909. Reprint, Westport, Conn.: Greenwood Press, 1970.

———. *L'Apologia (La Magia), Florida*. Torino: Unione, 1984.

Artemidorus. *Artemidori Daldiani: Oneirocriticon Libri V.* Leipzig: B. G. Teubner, 1963.

Athanasius. *Epistula ad Episcopos Aegypti et Libyae. PG* 25.537–593.

———. *Orationes Tres contra Arianos. PG* 26.12–468.

Chronicon Paschale: 284–628 AD. Translated by Michael Whitby and Mary Whitby. Translated Texts for Historians, no. 7. Liverpool: Liverpool University Press, 1989.

Clement of Alexandria. *Stromata Buch I-VI*. Edited by Otto Stählin. GCS, no. 15, Clemens Alexandrinus, no. 2. Leipzig: J. C. Hinrichs, 1906.

———. *Stromata Buch VII und VIII; Excerpta ex Theodota; Eclogae Propheticae; Quis Dives Salvetur; Fragmente*. Edited by Otto Stählin and Ludwig Früchtel. 1909. GCS, no. 17, Clemens Alexandrinus, no. 3. Berlin: Akademie Verlag, 1970.

Didascalia Apostolorum in Syriac. 2 vols. Edited by Arthur Vööbus. CSCO, nos. 401, 407, Scriptores Syri, nos. 175, 179. Louvain: Secrétariat du CSCO, 1979.

Didascalia Apostolorum: The Syriac Version Translated and Accompanied by the Verona Latin Fragments. Translated by R. Hugh Connolly. Oxford: Clarendon Press, 1969.

Dio Chrysostom. *Dio Chrysostom*. 5 vols. LCL, 1932–1956.

Epiphanius. *Ancoratus und Panarion*. 3 vols. Edited by Karl Holl. GCS, nos. 25, 31, 37. Leipzig: J. C. Hinrichs, 1915–1933.

———. *The Panarion of St. Epiphanius, Bishop of Salamis*. New York: Oxford University Press, 1990.

Epistula Apostolorum. Gespräche Jesu mit seinen Jüngern nach der Auferstehung: Ein katholisch-apostolisches Sendschrieben des 2. Jahrhunderts, nach einem koptischen Papyrus des Institut de la Mission Archéol. Francaise au Caire unter Mitarbeit von Herrn Pierre Lacau, derzeitigem Generaldirektor der Agypt. Museen. Edited and translated by Carl Schmidt. TU 43. Leipzig: J. C. Hinrichs, 1919.

"The Epistula Apostolorum." Translated by C. Detlef G. Müller. In *New Testament Apocrypha*. Vol. 1, *Gospels and Related Writings*. Edited by Wilhelm Schneemelcher and translated by R. McL. Wilson, 249–284. Louisville: Westminster/John Knox, 1991.

Eunapius. *Philostratus and Eunapius: The Lives of the Sophists*. LCL, 1922.

Eusebius. "Commentary on Psalms." *PG* 23, 24.10–75.

———. *The Ecclesiastical History of Eusebius Pamphili, 265–339, Bishop of Caesarea: Syriac Text, Edited from the Manuscripts in London and St. Petersburg, with a Collation of the Ancient Armenian Version by Adalbert Merx*. 1898. Edited by William Wright and Norman McLean. Amsterdam: Philo Press, 1975.

———. *The Ecclesiastical History*. 2 vols. LCL, 1932.

———. *Kirchengeschichte*. Edited by Eduard Schwartz. 1914. Leipzig: J. C. Hinrichs, 1955.

Gospel of Thomas. John S. Kloppenborg, Marvin W. Meyer, Stephen Patterson, Michael G. Steinhauser, *Q - Thomas Reader*. Sonoma: Polebridge Press, 1990.

Gregory of Nazianzus. *Discours 4–5 Contre Julien*. Edited and translated by Jean Bernardi. SC, no. 309. Paris: Les Éditions du Cerf, 1983.

Gregory Thaumaturgus. *Grégoire le Thaumaturge, Remerciement a Origène suivi de La Lettre d'Origène a Grégoire*. Edited and translated by Henri Crouzel, S.J. SC, no. 148. Paris: Les Éditions du Cerf, 1969.

Irenaeus. *Contre les hérésis*. 5 vols (in multiple parts). 1952. Edited and translated by Adelin Rousseau and Louis Coutreleau, S.J., and (vol. 5 only) Charles Mercier. SC, nos. 100, 152, 153, 210, 211, 263, 264, 293. Paris: Les Éditions du Cerf, 1969–1979.

Jacob of Voragine. *Jacobus de Voragine, The Golden Legend: Readings on the Saints*. 2 vols. Translated by William Granger Ryan. Princeton: Princeton University Press, 1993.

———. *Legend Aurea Vulgo Historia Lombardicadicta: Ad Optimorum Librorum Fidem Recensuit*. Edited by Th. Graesse. Dresden: Arnod, 1846.

———. *La légende dorée de Jacques de Voragine*. Translated by J.-B. M. Roze. Paris: Edouard Rouveyre, 1902.

Jerome. *Die Chronik des Hieronymus*. Edited by Rudolf Heim and Ursula Treu. GCS, Eusebius Werke, no. 7. Berlin: Akademie Verlag, 1984.

———. *Hieronymus: Liber De Viris Inlustribus; Gennadius: Liber De Viris Inlustribus*. Edited by Ernest Cushing Richardson. Leipzig: J. C. Hinrichs, 1896.

John Chrysostom. "Homilia in S. Ignatium." Quoted in *The Apostolic Fathers, Clement, Ignatius, and Polycarp*. Edited and translated by J. B. Lightfoot, 2.1.157–166. 1890. Reprint, Peabody, Mass.: Hendrickson, 1989.

Justin. *Justin, Philosoph und Märtyrer: Die Erste Apologie*. Edited by Karl Bayer. Munich: Kösel, 1966.

"Kaiserbrief (?) über Johannes von Ephesos und Polykarp von Smyrna." In IvE 1a. Edited by Hermann Wankel, no. 45, 281–284. Inschriften Griechischer Städte aus Kleinasien, no. 11.1. Bonn: Rudolf Habelt, 1979.

Kerygma Petri. "The Kerygma Petri." Translated, with introduction and notes, by Wilhelm Schneemelcher. In *New Testament Apocrypha*. Vol. 2, *Writings Relating to the Apostles, Apocalypses, and Related Subjects*. Edited by Wilhelm Schneemelcher and translated by R. McL. Wilson, 34–41. Louisville: Westminster/John Knox, 1992.

Lucian. *Demonax*. In *Lucian* 1.141–173. LCL, 1913.

Mark. Das Markusevangelium Saïdisch: Text der Handschrift PPalau Rib. Inv.-Nr. 182 mit den Varianten der Handschrift M 569. Papyrologica Castroctaviana, Studia et Textus, no. 4. Barcelona: Papyrologica Castroctaviana, 1972.

Michael Glykas. "Epistola XVI . . . Utrum Beatus Joannes Evangelista Morti Concesserit, sive non." *PG* 158.899–904.

Muratorian Canon. "The Codex Muratorianus." Edited by E. S. Buchanan. *JTS* 8 (1906–1907): 537–545.

Origen. *Origenes Matthäuserklärung*. GCS, no. 40, Origenes, no. 10. Leipzig: J. C. Hinrichs, 1935.

Philostratus. *The Life of Apollonius of Tyana*. 2 vols. Translated by F. C. Conybeare. LCL, 1912.

———. "The Lives of the Sophists." *Philostratus and Eunapius: The Lives of the Sophists*. LCL, 1922.

Photius. *Bibliothecque*. 2 vols. Edited and translated by René Henry. Collection Byzantine. Paris: Société D'Edition "Les Belles Lettres," 1959–1960.

(Pseudo-)Pionius. "Life of Polycarp." In *The Apostolic Fathers*. Edited and translated by J. B. Lightfoot, 2.3.423–468, 488–506. 1890. Reprint, Peabody, Mass.: Hendrickson, 1989.

Pistis Sophia. Edited by Carl Schmidt and translated by Violet MacDermot. NHS, no. 9. Leiden: E. J. Brill, 1978.

Plato. *Euthyphro, Apology, Crito, Phaedo, Phaedrus*. 1914. LCL, 1971.

Pliny. *Letters and Panegyricus*. 2 vols. LCL, 1969.

Plutarch. *Antony*. In *Plutarch's Lives* 9.137–332. 1920. LCL, 1968.

———. *Cato the Younger*. In *Plutarch's Lives* 8.235–412. 1919. LCL, 1969.

Psalms. *The Earliest Known Coptic Psalter: The Text, in the Dialect of Upper Egypt, Edited From the Unique Papyrus Codex Oriental 5000 in the British Museum*. Translated by E. A. Wallis Budge. London: Kegan Paul, Trench, Trübner and Co., 1898.

Roman Martyrology. *The Roman Martyrology: Published by Order of Gregory XIII, Revised by Authority of Urban VIII and Clement X, Augmented and Corrected in 1749 by Benedict XIV*. Translated by Raphael Collins. Westminster, Md.: Newman Bookshop, 1946.

Strabo. *The Geography of Strabo*. 8 vols. LCL, 1917–1932.

Synaxarium Alexandrinum. Translated into Latin by J. Forget. CSCO, no. 78, Scriptores Arabici, no. 12. Louvain: L. Durbecq, 1953.

"Synaxarium Ecclesiae Constantinopolitanae." In *Propylaeum ad Acta SS. Novembris*. Edited by Hippolyte Delehaye. *Acta Sanctorum* 64.

Tacitus. *The Annals*. 3 vols. Translated by John Jackson. 1931–1937. LCL, Tacitus, vols. 3–5. 1969–1970.

Tertullian. *Adversus Marcionem*. 2 vols. Edited and translated by Ernest Evans. Oxford: Clarendon Press, 1972.

———. *Traité de la prescription contre les hérétiques*. Edited by R. F. Refoulé, O.P., and translated by P. De Labriolle. SC, no. 46. Paris: Les Éditions du Cerf, 1957.

Xenophon. *Apology*. In *Xenophon* 4.637–663. 1923. LCL, 1978.

II. Primary Sources: Collections

Aland, Kurt, et al., eds. *Nestle-Aland: Novum Testamentum Graece*. 1979. Stuttgart: Deutsche Bibilgesellschaft, 1983.

Balestri, G. I., and H. Hyvernat. *Acta Martyrum II: Textus*. 1924. CSCO, no. 86, Scriptores Coptici, no. 6. Louvain: L. Durbecq, 1953.

Bihlmeyer, Karl. *Die Apostolischen Väter: Neuarbeitung der Funkschen Ausgabe*. Sammlung Ausgewählter Kirchen- und Dogmengeschichtliche Quellenschriften, Series 2, no. 1.1. Tübingen: J. C. B. Mohr (Paul Siebeck), 1924.

Boeckhius, Augustius, et al. *Corpus Inscriptionum Graecarum*. 4 vols. Berlin: G. Reimeri, 1828–1877.

Budge, E. A. Wallis. *Coptic Texts*. 1910–1915. Reprint, New York: AMS, 1977.

DuBois, Dom Jacques, and Geneviève Renaud. *Édition pratique des martyrologes de Bede, de l'anonyme lyonnais et de Florus*. Paris: Éditions du Centre National de la Recherché Scientifique, 1976.

Goodspeed, Edgar J. *Die ältesten Apologeten: Texte mit kurzen Einleitung*. Göttingen: Vandenhoeck and Ruprecht, 1914.

Horner, G. (unacknowledged). *The Coptic Version of the New Testament in the Northern Dialect, Otherwise Called Memphitic and Bohairic, with Introduction, Critical Apparatus, and Literal English Translation*. 4 vols. Oxford: Clarendon Press, 1898–1905.

———. *The Coptic Version of the New Testament in the Southern Dialect, Otherwise Called Sahidic and Thebaic, with Critical Apparatus, Literal English Translation, Register of Fragments, and Estimate of the Version*. 7 vols. Oxford: Clarendon Press, 1911–1924.

Hyvernat, H. *Acta Martyrum II: Versio*. CSCO, no. 125, Scriptores Coptici, Series 3, no. 2. Louvain: L. Durbecq, 1950.

Klostermann, Erich. *Reste des Petrusevangeliums, Der Petrusapokalypse, und des Kerygma Petri*. Vol. 1, *Apocrypha*. Kleine Texte für Theologische und Philologische Vorlesungen und Ubungen, no. 3. Bonn: A. Marcus und E. Weber, 1908.

Knibbe, Dieter, and Bülent İplikçioğlu. "Neue Inschriften aus Ephesos VIII." *Jh* 53 (1981): 87–150.

Knibbe, Dieter, Helmut Engelmann, Bülent İplikçioğlu. "Neue Inschriften aus Ephesos XI." *Jh* 59 (1989): 161–138.

Kürzinger, Josef. *Papias von Hierapolis und die Evangelien des Neuen Testaments*. Eichstätter Materialien, no. 4. Regensburg: Friedrich Pustet, 1983.

Layton, Bentley, ed. *Nag Hammadi Codex II, 2–7, together with XIII, 2, Brit. Lib. Or.4926(1), and P.OXY. 1, 654, 655, with Contributions by Many Scholars*. NHS, no. 20. Leiden: E. J. Brill, 1989.

Lipsius, Richard Adelbert (vol. 1), and Maximilian Bonnet (vols. 2–3), eds. *Acta Apostolorum*. 3 vols. 1891–1903. Hildesheim: Georg Olms, 1972.

Musurillo, Herbert. *The Acts of the Christian Martyrs.* Oxford: Clarendon Press, 1972.

Newton, C. T., et al. *Collection of Ancient Greek Inscriptions in the British Museum.* 6 vols. Oxford: Clarendon Press, 1874–1916.

Parrott, Douglas M., ed. *Nag Hammadi Codices V, 2–5 and VI with Papyrus Berolinensis 8502, 1 and 4.* NHS, no. 11. Leiden: E. J. Brill, 1979.

Reymond, E. A. E., and J. W. B. Barns. *Four Martyrdoms From the Pierpont Morgan Coptic Codices.* Oxford: Clarendon Press, 1973.

Robinson, James M., ed. *The Nag Hammadi Library in English.* 3rd ed. San Francisco: Harper and Row, 1988.

Schneemelcher, Wilhelm, ed. *New Testament Apocrypha.* Vol. 1, *Gospels and Related Writings*, translated by R. McL. Wilson. Louisville: Westminster/John Knox, 1991. Vol. 2, *Writings Relating to the Apostles, Apocalypses, and Related Subjects*, translated by R. McL. Wilson. Louisville: Westminster/John Knox, 1992.

Seiber, John H., ed. *Nag Hammadi Codex VIII.* NHS, no. 31. Leiden: E. J. Brill, 1991.

Till, W., and H.-M. Schenke. *Die gnosticschen Schriften des koptischen Papyrus Berolinensis 8502.* 2d ed. TU 60. Berlin: Akademie, 1972.

Wessely, Carl. *Griechische und Koptische Texte theologischen Inhalts.* Studien zur Paleographie und Papyruskunde, no. 9. Amsterdam: Hakkert, 1966.

Wright, W., ed. and tr. *Apocryphal Acts of the Apostles, Edited from Syriac Manuscripts in the British Museum and Other Libraries.* 2 vols. London: Williams and Norgate, 1871.

III. Secondary Sources

Akurgal, Ekrem. *Ancient Civilizations and Ruins of Turkey: From Prehistoric Times until the End of the Roman Empire.* Istanbul: Mobil Oil Türk A.S., 1969.

Aland, Kurt, and Barbara Aland. *The Text of the New Testament: An Introduction to the Critical Editions and to the Theory and Practice of Modern Textual Criticism.* Translated by Erroll F. Rhodes. Grand Rapids: Wm. B. Eerdmans, 1987.

Andrea Palladio: The Churches of Rome. Translated, with commentary, by Eunice D. Howe. Binghamton, N.Y.: Medieval and Rennaissance Texts and Studies, 1991.

Aumer, Joseph, and Karl Felix Halm. *Catalogus Codicum Manu Scriptorum Bibliothecae Regiae Monacensis II.4: Verzeichniss der orientalischen Handschriften der k. Hof- und Staatsbibliothek in München mit Ausschlus der herbraeischen, arabischen und persischen.* Munich: Palm, 1875.

Aune, David. "Magic in Early Christianity." *ANRW* 2.23.2 (1980).

Bacon, B. W. "John and the Pseudo-Johns." *ZNW* 31 (1932): 132–150.

Badcock, F. J. *The History of the Creeds*. London: SPCK, 1938.

Barnard, Leslie W. "In Defense of Pseudo-Pionius' Account of Polycarp's Martyrdom." In *Kyriakon: Festschrift Johannes Quasten*. 2 vols. Edited by Patrick Granfield and Josef A. Jungmann, 1.192–204. Münster: Aschendorff, 1970.

Barnes, T. D. "Pre-Decian Acta Martyrum." *JTS* 19 (1968): 510–514.

Barrett, C. K. "The Apostles in and after the New Testament." In *Svensk Exegetisk Arsbok*, vol. 21. Edited by Harald Riesenfeld. Lund: C. W. K. Gleerup, 1956.

———. *The Gospel according to St. John: An Introduction with Commentary and Notes on the Greek Text*. 2d ed. Philadelphia: Westminster Press, 1978.

———. *The Signs of an Apostle: The Cato Lecture, 1969*. Philadelphia: Fortress Press, 1972.

Bauer, Walter, "Accounts [of the Apostles in Early Christian Tradition]." In *New Testament Apocrypha*. Vol. 2, *Writings Relating to the Apostles, Apocalypses, and Related Subjects*. Edited by Edgar Hennecke and Wilhelm Schneemelcher and translated by R. McL. Wilson, 35–74. Philadelphia: Westminster Press, 1965.

Baumeister, Theofried. "Martyrology." *Coptic Encyclopedia* 5.1549b–1550a.

Bean, George E. *Aegean Turkey*. 2d ed. 1979. Reprint, London: John Murray, 1989.

Beasley-Murray, George R. *John*. Word Biblical Commentaries, no. 36. Waco, Tex.: Word Books, 1987.

Bell, Nancy R. E. *Lives and Legends of the Evangelists, Apostles and Other Early Saints*. London: George Bell and Sons, 1901.

Benko, Stephen. "Pagan Criticism of Christianity during the First Two Centuries A.D." *ANRW* 2.23.2 (1980): 1055–1118.

Bienert, Wolfgang A. "The Picture of the Apostle in Early Christian Tradition." In *New Testament Apocrypha*. Vol. 2, *Writings Relating to the Apostles, Apocalypses, and Related Subjects*. Edited by Wilhelm Schneemelcher and translated by R. McL. Wilson, 5–27. Louisville: Westminster/John Knox, 1992.

Bisbee, Gary A. *Pre-Decian Acts of Martyrs and Commentarii*. Harvard Dissertations in Religion, no. 22. Philadelphia: Fortress Press, 1988.

Boismard, M.-É. *Le Martyre de Jean L'Apôtre*. Cahiers de la Revue Biblique 35. Paris: J. Gabalda, 1996.

Bosio, Guido. "Policarpo." In *Biblioteca Sanctorum*. Edited by Filippo Caraffa, 985–988. Rome: Instituto Giovanni XXII della Pontificia Universita Lateranense, 1968.

Bouriant, U. "Notes de voyage, 1: Catalogue de la bibliotheque du couvent d'Amba Helias." *Recueil de travaux relatifs a la philologie et a l'archéologie égyptiennes et assyriennes* 11 (1889): 131–138.

Bousset, Wm. "Platons Weltseele und das Kreuz Christi." *ZNW* 14 (1913): 273–285.

Braun, F.-M. *Jean Le Théologian et son évangile dans l'église ancienne*. Paris: J. Gabalda, 1959.

Brind'Amour, Pierre. "La date du martyre de Saint Polycarpe (le 23 Février 167)." *AnBoll* 98 (1980): 456–462.

Brockhoff, Wilhelm. *Studien zur Geschichte der Stadt Ephesos, vom IV. nachchristlichen Jahrhundert bis zu ihrem Untergang in der ersten Hälfte des XV. Jahrhunderts*. Inaugural Dissertation. Jena: G. Neuenhahn, 1905.

Broughton, T. R. S. "Roman Asia." In *An Economic Survey of Ancient Rome*. Vol. 4, *Africa, Syria, Greece, Asia Minor*. Edited by Tenney Frank. 1938. Reprint, New York: Octagon Books, 1975.

Brown, Peter. *The Cult of the Saints: Its Rise and Function in Latin Christianity*. Haskell Lectures on History of Religions, no. 2. Chicago: University of Chicago Press, 1981.

———. "The Rise and Function of the Holy Man in Late Antiquity." In *Society and the Holy in Late Antiquity*. Peter Brown, 103–152. Berkeley: University of California Press, 1982. (First published in *JRS* 61 [1971]: 80–101.)

Brown, Raymond E. *The Community of the Beloved Disciple*. New York: Paulist Press, 1979.

Brune, Lucien. *L'antica serie di ritratti papali della basilica di S. Paolo fuori le mura*. Rome: Pontificio istituto di archeologia cristiana, 1934.

Bultmann, Rudolf. *The Gospel of John: A Commentary*. Translated and edited by G. R. Beasely-Murray. Philadelphia: Westminster Press, 1971.

Bürchner, L. "Smyrna." PW. 2d series. 5.727–765.

Buschmann, Gerd. *Martyrium Polycarpi—Eine formkritische Studie: Ein Beitrag zur Frage nach der Entstehung der Gattung Märtyrerakte*. Beihefte zur Zeitschrift für die neutestamentliche Wissenschaft und die Kunde der älteren Kirche, no. 70. Berlin: Walter de Gruyter, 1994.

———. *Das Martyrium des Polykarp*. Kommentar zu den Apostolischen Vätern, no. 6. Göttingen: Vandenhoeck and Ruprecht, 1998.

Cadoux, Cecil John. *Ancient Smyrna: A History of the City from the Earliest Times to 324 A. D.* Oxford: Basil Blackwell, 1938.

Camelot, P. Th., O.P. *Ignace d'Antioche, Polycarpe de Smyrne: Lettres, Martyre de Polycarpe*. SC, no. 10. Paris: Les Éditions du Cerf, 1969.

Campenhausen, Hans Frhr. von. *Bearbeitungen und Interpolationen des Polykarpmartyriums*. Sitzungsberichte der Heidelberger Akademie der Wissenschaften, Philosophisch-Historische Klasse, no. 3. Heidelberg: Carl Winter, 1957.

———. *Polykarp von Smyrna und die Pastoralbriefe*. Sitzungsberichte der Heidelberger Akademie der Wissenschaften, Philosophisch-Historische Klasse, no. 2. Heidelberg: Carl Winter, 1951.

Cassidy, Richard J. *John's Gospel in New Perspective: Christology and the Realities of Roman Power*. Maryknoll: Orbis Books, 1992.

Cave, Wm. *Apostolici: Or, the History of the Lives, Acts, Death, and Martyrdoms of Those Who Were Contemporary with, or Immediately Succeeded the Apostles*. London: 1716.

Chapman, John. *John the Presbyter and the Fourth Gospel*. Oxford: Clarendon Press, 1911.

Charles, R. H. *A Critical and Exegetical Commentary on the Revelation of St. John*. 2 vols. ICC. New York: Charles Scribners Sons, 1920.

Clebsch, Wm. A. *Christianity in European History*. New York: Oxford University Press, 1979.

Collins, John J. "Sibylline Oracles." In *The Old Testament Pseudoepigrapha*. Vol. 1, *Apocalyptic Literature and Testaments*. Edited by James H. Charlesworth, 392. Garden City, N.Y.: Doubleday, 1983.

Coquin, René-Georges. "Le catalogue de la bibliothèque du couvent de Saint Elie 'du Rocher.'" *BIF* 75 (1975): 207–239.

Corssen, P. "Die Vita Polycarpi." *ZNW* 5 (1904): 266–302.

Crum, Walter E. *Coptic Ostraca: From the Collections of the Egypt Exploration Fund, the Cairo Museum and Others*. London: The Egypt Exploration Fund, 1902.

———. "Eusebius and Coptic Church Histories." *Proceedings of the Society of Biblical Archaeology* 24 (1902): 68–84.

———. *Monastery of Epiphanius at Thebes*. 2 vols. New York: Metropolitan Museum of Art, 1926.

———. *Theological Texts from Coptic Papyri*. Anecdota Oxoniensia, Semitic Series, no. 12. Oxford: Clarendon Press, 1913.

Cullmann, Oscar. *Peter—Disciple, Apostle, Martyr: A Historical and Theological Study*. 1953. 2d ed. Translated by Floyd V. Filson. London: SCM, 1962.

Culpepper, R. Alan. *John, the Son of Zebedee: The Life of a Legend*. Studies on Personalities of the New Testament. Columbia: University of South Carolina Press, 1994.

Dehandschutter, B. "Le martyre du Polycarpe et le développement de la conception du martyre au deuxième siècle." *Studia Patristica* 17.2 (1982): 659–668.

———. "The Martyrium Polycarpi: A Century of Research." *ANRW* 2.27.1 (1993): 485–522.

———. *Martyrium Polycarpi: Een Literair-Kritische Studie*. Bibliotheca Ephemeridum Theologicarum Lovaniensum, no. 52. Leuven: Leuven University Press, 1979.

Delehaye, Hippolyte, S.J. *Cinq lecons sur la méthode hagiographique*. Subsidia Hagiographica, no. 21. Brussels: Société des Bollandistes, 1934.

———. *The Legends of the Saints: An Introduction to Hagiography*. Translated by V. M. Crawford. 1907. Notre Dame, Ind.: University of Notre Dame Press, 1961.

———. "Les martyrs d'Egypte." *AnBoll* 40 (1922): 5–154, 299–364.

———. *Les passions des martyrs et les genres littéraires*. 2d ed. Brussels: Société des Bollandistes, 1966.

Des Rivières, Arthur. "Lettre à M. A. C. Harris d'Alexandrie sur divers fragments de papyrus coptes de sa collection." *BIF* 5 (1906): 88–91.

Devos, Paul. "'ΜΕΓΑ ΣΑΒΒΑΤΟΝ' chez Saint Epiphane." *AnBoll* 108 (1990): 293–306.

Dewailly, L.-M. *Envoyés du père: Mission et apostolicité*. Paris: Éditions de L'Orante, 1960.

Dibelius, Martin, and Hans Conzelmann. *The Pastoral Epistles*. Translated by Philip Buttolph and Adela Yarbro. Hermeneia Series. Philadelphia: Fortress Press, 1972.

Diels, Hermann. *Doxographi Graeci*. 1879. Berlin: Walter de Gruyter, 1929.

Drijvers, Hans J. W. "The Saint as Symbol: Conceptions of the Person in Late Antiquity and Early Christianity." In *Concepts of Person in Religion and Thought*. Edited by Hans G. Kippenberg, Yme B. Kuiper, and Andy F. Sanders, 137–157. Religion and Reason, no. 37. Berlin: Monton de Gruyter, 1990.

Ehrhardt, Arnold. *Apostolic Succession in the First Two Centuries of the Church*. London: Lutterworth Press, 1953.

———. *The Framework of the New Testament Stories*. Manchester: Manchester University Press, 1964.

Elliott, Alison Goddard. *Roads to Paradise: Reading the Lives of the Early Saints*. Hanover, N.H.: University Press of New England, 1987.

Esbroeck, Michel van. "La passion arménienne de S. Gordius de Césarée." *AnBoll* 94 (1976): 357–386.

Feltoe, C. L. "St. John and St. James in Western 'Non-Roman' Kalendars." *JTS* 10 (1909): 589–593.

Fieger, Michael. *Das Thomasevangelium: Einleitung, Kommetar, und Systematik*. Neutestamentliche Abhandlungen, Neue Folge, no. 22. Münster: Aschendorff, 1991.

Fiore, Benjamin, S.J. *The Function of Personal Example in the Socratic and Pastoral Epistles*. Analecta Biblica, no. 105. Rome: Biblical Institute Press, 1986.

Foss, Clive. "Archaeology and the 'Twenty Cities' of Byzantine Asia." In *History and Archaeology of Byzantine Asia Minor*. Clive Foss, essay no. 2. Aldershot: Variorum, 1990. (First published in *American Journal of Archaeology* 81 [1977]: 469–486.)

———. *Ephesus After Antiquity: A Late Antique, Byzantine and Turkish City*. Cambridge: Cambridge University Press, 1979.

Fox, Robin Lane. *Pagans and Christians*. San Francisco: Harper and Row, 1986.

Friesen, Steven. "The Cult of the Roman Emperors in Ephesos: Temple Wardens, City Titles, and the Interpretation of the Revelation of John." In *Ephesos: Metropolis of Asia: An Interdisciplinary Approach to its Archaeology, Religion, and Culture*. Edited by Helmut Koester, 229–250. Harvard Theological Studies Series, no. 41. Valley Forge: Trinity Press International, 1995.

Funk, Robert W., Roy W. Hoover, and the Jesus Seminar. *The Five Gospels: The Search for the Authentic Words of Jesus*. New York: Macmillan, 1993.

Gamble, Harry Y. *The New Testament Canon: Its Making and Meaning*. Philadelphia: Fortress Press, 1985.

Garrett, Susan R. *The Demise of the Devil: Magic and the Demonic in Luke's Writings*. Minneapolis: Fortress Press, 1989.

Goguel, Maurice. "Did Peter Deny His Lord?" *HTR* 25 (1932): 1–27.

Goodenough, E. R. *The Archaeological Evidence from the Diaspora*. Vol. 2, *Jewish Symbols in the Greco-Roman Period*. Bollingen Series, no. 37. New York: Pantheon Books, 1953.

Goodspeed, Edgar J. *The Twelve: The Story of Christ's Apostles*. Philadelphia: John C. Winston, 1957.

Grégoire, Henri. "Épigraphie chrétienne II: Inscriptions d'Ephese." *Byzantion* 1 (1924): 710–716.

———. "La véritable date su martyre de S. Polycarpe (23 Février 177) et le 'Corpus Polycarpianum.'" *AnBoll* 69 (1951): 1–38.

Hackel, Sergei, ed. *The Byzantine Saint: University of Birmingham 14th Spring Symposium of Byzantine Studies*. San Bernadino: Borgo Press, 1983.

Haenchen, Ernst. *Die Botschaft des Thomasevangelium*. Theologische Bibliothek Töpelmann series, no. 6. Berlin: Alfred Töpelmann, 1961.

Hagiographie, cultures et sociétés, IVe–XIIe siècles: Actes du colloue organisé a Nanterre et a Paris, 2–5 Mai 1979. Centre de Recherches sur l'Antiquité Tardive et le Haut Moyen Age, Université de Paris, no. 10. Paris: Études Augustiniennes, 1981.

Halkin, Francois. "Inscriptions grecques relatives a l'hagiographie: L'Asie Mineure." In *Études d'épigraphie grecque et d'hagiographie byzantine*. Francois Halkin, essays nos. 5 and 6. London: Variorum Reprints, 1973. (First published in *AnBoll* 71 [1953]: 74–99, 326–354.)

———. "Le prologue inédit de Nicétas, Archeveque de Thessalonique, aux Actes de l'apotre saint Jean." In *Études d'épigraphie grecque et d'hagiographie byzantine*. Francois Halkin, essay no. 7. London: Variorum Reprints, 1973. (First published in *AnBoll* 85 [1967]: 16–20.)

———. *Recherches et documents d'hagiographie byzantine*. Subsidia Hagiographica, no. 51. Brussels: Société des Bollandistes, 1971.

Harnack, Adolf von. *Geschichte der altchristlichen Litteratur bis Eusebius*. 3 vols. Leipzig: J. C. Hinrichs, 1893–1904.

———. *Der Kirchengeschichtliche Ertrag der Exegetischen Arbeiten des Origines zum Hexateuch und Richterbuch*. TU 42.3. Edited by Adolf von Harnack and Carl Schmidt, 1–96. Leipzig: J. C. Hinrichs, 1918.

———. *The Mission and Expansion of Christianity in the First Three Centuries*. Translated and edited by James Moffat. 1908. Reprint, New York: Harper Torchbooks, 1962.

———. *Die Zeit des Ignatius und die Chronologie der antiochischen Bischöfe bis Tyrannus nach Julius Africanus und den späteren Historikern nebst einer Untersuchung über die Verbreitung der Passio S. Polycarpi im Abendlande.* Leipzig: J. C. Hinrichs, 1878.

Harrison, P. N. *Polycarp's Two Epistles to the Philippians.* Cambridge: Cambridge University Press, 1936.

Harvey, W. Wigan. *Sancti Irenaei, Episcopi Lugdunensis, Libros Quinqe Adversus Haereses: Textu Graeco in Locis Nonnullis Locupletato, Versione Latina cum Codicibus Claromontano ac Arundeliano denuo Collata, Praemissa de Placitis Gnosticorum Prolusione, Fragmenta Necnon Graeca, Syriace, Armeniace, Commentatione Perpetua et Indicibus Variis.* 2 vols. Cambridge: Cambridge University Press, 1857.

Hasluck, F. W. "The 'Tomb of S. Polycarp' and the Topography of Ancient Smyrna." *Annual of the British School at Athens* 20 (1913–1914): 80–93.

Head, Thomas. *Hagiography and the Cult of the Saints.* Cambridge: Cambridge University Press, 1990.

Hengel, Martin. *The Johannine Question.* Translated by John Bowden. London: SCM Press, 1989.

Hilgenfeld, Adolf. "Des Chrysostomos Lobrede auf Polykarp." *ZWT* 45 (1902): 569–572.

———. "Eine dreiste Fälschung in alter Zeit und deren neueste Verteidigung." *ZWT* 48 (1905): 444–458.

Hillmer, M. R. "The Gospel of John in the Second Century." Th.D. diss., Harvard Divinity School, 1966.

Holl, Karl. *Der Osten.* Vol. 2, *Gesammelte Aufsätze zur Kirchengeschichte.* Tübingen: J. C. B. Mohr (Paul Siebeck), 1928.

Holweck, F. G. *A Biographical Dictionary of the Saints, with a General Introduction on Hagiology.* St. Louis: B. Herder, 1924.

Jackson, H. Latimer. *The Problem of the Fourth Gospel.* Cambridge: Cambridge University Press, 1918.

Jameson, Anna. *Sacred and Legendary Art.* Edited by Estelle M. Hurll. Boston: Houghton, Mifflin and Co., 1896.

Jones, A. H. M. *The Cities of the Eastern Roman Provinces.* 2d ed. Oxford: Clarendon Press, 1971.

Jugie, Martin. *La mort et l'assomption de la Sainte Vierge: Étude historico-Doctrinale.* Studi e Testi, no. 114. Vatican City: Biblioteca Apostolica Vaticana, 1944.

Junod, Eric. "Origène, Eusèbe et la tradition sur la répartition des champs de mission des apôtres." In *Les actes apocryphes des apôtres.* Edited by Francois Bovon et al., 233–248. Publications de la Faculté de Théologie de l'Université de Genève. Geneva: Labor et Fides, 1981.

———. "La virginité de l'apôtre Jean: recherche sur les origines scripturaires et patristiques de cette tradition." In *Lectures anciennes de la Bible.* 113–135.

Cahiers de Biblia Patristica, no. 1. Strasbourg: Centre d'Analyse et de Documentation Patristiques, 1987.

Junod, Eric, and Jean-Daniel Kaestli. *L'histoire des actes apocryphes des apôtres du IIIe au IXe siècle: Le cas des Actes de Jean*. Cahiers de la Revue de Théologie et de Philosophie, no. 7. Geneva: Revue de Theologie et de Philosophie, 1982.

Kaestli, Jean-Daniel. "Le rôle des textes bibliques dans la Genése et le développement des légendes apocryphes: La cas du sort final de l'Apôtre Jean." *Augustinianum* 23 (1983): 319–336.

———. "Les scènes d'attribution des champs de mission et de départ de l'apôtre dans les actes apocryphes." In *Les actes apocryphes des apôtres*. Edited by Francois Bovon et al., 249–264. Publications de la Faculté de Théologie de l'Université de Genève. Geneva: Labor et Fides, 1981.

Karwiese, Stefan. "The Church of Mary and the Temple of Hadrian Olympios." In *Ephesos: Metropolis of Asia: An Interdisciplinary Approach to Its Archaeology, Religion, and Culture*. Edited by Helmut Koester, 311–320. Harvard Theological Studies Series, no. 41. Valley Forge: Trinity Press International, 1995.

Kasser, Rodolphe. *L'Évangile Selon Thomas: Présentation et commentaire théologique*. Paris: Éditions Delachaux et Niestlé, 1961.

Keil, Josef. "Johannes von Ephesus und Polykarpos von Smyrna." *Strena Bulciana: Commentationes Gratulatoriae Francisco Bulic*. Zagreb/Split, 1924.

Kiley, Mark, et al., eds. *Prayer from Alexander to Constantine: A Critical Anthology*. New York: Routledge, 1997.

Knibbe, Dieter. "Ephesos." PW. Supplement. 12.248–297.

Knibbe, Dieter, and Wilhelm Alzinger. "Ephesos vom Beginn der römischen Herrschaft in Kleinasien bis zum Ende der Principatszeit." *ANRW* 2.7.2 (1980): 748–830.

Koester, Helmut. "Ephesos in Early Christian Literature." In *Ephesos: Metropolis of Asia: An Interdisciplinary Approach to Its Archaeology, Religion, and Culture*. Edited by Helmut Koester, 119–140. Harvard Theological Studies Series, no. 41. Valley Forge: Trinity Press International, 1995.

Koester, Helmut, ed. *Ephesos: Metropolis of Asia: An Interdisciplinary Approach to Its Archaeology, Religion, and Culture*. Harvard Theological Studies Series, no. 41. Valley Forge: Trinity Press International, 1995.

Kraabel, Alf Thomas. "Judaism in Western Asia Minor under the Roman Empire, with a Preliminary Study of the Jewish Community at Sardis, Lydia." Th.D. diss., Harvard University, 1968.

Kümmel, Werner Georg. *Introduction to the New Testament*. Rev. ed. Translated by Howard Clark Kee. Nashville: Abingdon Press, 1984.

Lambdin, Thomas O. *Introduction to Sahidic Coptic*. Macon, Ga.: Mercer University Press, 1983.

Lampakes, Georgios. *ΟΙ ΕΠΤΑ ΑΣΤΕΡΕΣ ΤΗΣ ΑΠΟΚΑΛΥΨΕΩΣ*. Athens: Th. Tzabella, 1909.

Layton, Bentley. *Catalogue of Coptic Literary Manuscripts in the British Library Acquired since the Year 1906*. London: British Library, 1987.

———. *The Gnostic Scriptures: A New Translation with Annotations and Introductions*. Garden City, N.Y.: Doubleday, 1987.

———. *The Gnostic Treatise on Resurrection from Nag Hammadi*. Harvard Dissertations in Religion, no. 12. Missoula: Scholars Press, 1979.

———. "The Recovery of Gnosticism—The Philologist's Task in the Investigation of Nag Hammadi." *SecCent* 1 (1981): 85–99.

———. "Towards a New Coptic Palaeography." In *Acts of the Second International Congress of Coptic Study, Roma, 22–26 September, 1980*. Edited by Tito Orlandi and Frederick Wisse, 149–158. Rome: C. I. M., 1985.

Lessing, Erich, and Wolfgang Oberleitner. *Ephesos: Weltstadt der Antike*. Vienna: Carl Ueberreuter, 1978.

Lightfoot, J. B. *The Apostolic Fathers, Clement, Ignatius, and Polycarp: Revised Texts, with Introductions, Notes, Dissertations and Translations*. 5 vols. 1885–1890. Reprint, Peabody, Mass.: Hendrickson, 1989.

———. "The Name and Office of an Apostle." In *The Epistle of St. Paul to the Gentiles*. J. B. Lightfoot, 92–101. 1865. Reprint, Peabody, Mass.: Hendrickson, 1987.

Limberis, Vasiliki. "The Council of Ephesos: The Demise of the See of Ephesos and the Rise of the Cult of the Theotokos." In *Ephesos: Metropolis of Asia: An Interdisciplinary Approach to Its Archaeology, Religion, and Culture*. Edited by Helmut Koester, 321–340. Harvard Theological Studies Series, no. 41. Valley Forge: Trinity Press International, 1995.

Lipsius, Richard Adelbert. *Die Apokryphen Apostelgeschichten und Apostellegenden: Ein Beitrag zur altchristlichen Literaturgeschichte*. 2 vols. Braunschweig: C. A. Schwetschke, 1883, 1887.

Loewenich, W. von. *Das Johannes-Verständnis im zweiten Jahrhundert*. Beiheft zur Zeitschrift für die neutestamentliche Wissenschaft und die Kunde der älteren Kirche, no. 13. Giessen: Alfred Töpelmann, 1932.

Lucchesi, Enzo. "Deux nouveaux fragments coptes des Actes d'André et Barthélemy (BHO 57)." *AnBoll* 98 (1980): 75–82.

Luck, Georg. *Arcana Mundi: Magic and Occult in the Greek and Roman Worlds*. Baltimore: Johns Hopkins University Press, 1985.

Luttikhuizen, G. P. "The Letter of Peter to Philip and the New Testament." In *Nag Hammadi and Gnosis: Papers Read at the First International Congress of Coptology (Cairo, December 1976)*. Edited by R. McL. Wilson, 96–102. NHS, no. 14. Leiden: E. J. Brill, 1978.

MacMullen, Ramsey. *Enemies of the Roman Order: Treason, Unrest, and Alienation in the Empire*. Cambridge: Harvard University Press, 1966.

Macro, Anthony D. "The Cities of Asia Minor under the Roman Imperium." *ANRW* 2.7.2 (1980): 658–697.

Magie, David. *Roman Rule in Asia Minor: To the End of the Third Century after Christ*. 2 vols. Princeton: Princeton University Press, 1950.

Malherbe, Abraham J. *The Cynic Epistles: A Study Edition*. Society of Biblical Literature Sources for Biblical Study, no. 12. Missoula: Scholars Press, 1977.

———. "Gentle as a Nurse: The Cynic Background of 1 Thess ii." *NovT* 12 (1970): 203–217.

———. *Moral Exhortation: A Greco-Roman Sourcebook*. Library of Early Christianity, no. 4. Philadelphia: Westminster Press, 1986.

Mansfield, J., and D. T. Runia. *Aetiana: The Method and Intellectual Context of a Doxographer.* Leiden: E. J. Brill, 1997–.

Marquardt, Joachim. *Römische Staatsverwaltung*. 3 vols. Leipzig: Hirzel, 1881.

Massaux, Édouard. *The Influence of the Gospel of Saint Matthew on Christian Literature before Saint Irenaeus*. Vol. 2: *The Later Christian Writings*. Translated by Norman J. Belval and Suzanne Hecht, edited with introduction and addenda by Arthur Bellanzoni. New Gospel Studies Series, no. 5/2. Macon: Mercer University Press, 1992.

McNeile, Alan H. *An Introduction to the Study of the New Testament*. Revised by C. S. C. Williams. Oxford: Clarendon Press, 1953.

Meinardus, Friedrich August. *St. John of Patmos and the Seven Churches of the Apocalypse*. New Rochelle, N.Y.: Caratzas Bros., 1979.

Ménard, Jacques-E. *L'Évangile selon Philippe: Introduction, texte-traduction, commentaire*. Paris: Letouzy and Ané, 1967.

———. *L'Évangile selon Thomas*. NHS, no. 5. Leiden: E. J. Brill, 1975.

———. "Les Problèmes de l'Évangile selon Thomas." *Studia Patristica* 14 (1976): 209–228.

———. "La sagesse et le logion 3 de l'Évangile selon Thomas." *Studia Patristica* 10 (1970): 137–140.

Merkelbach, R. "Der Rangstreit der Städte Asiens und die Rede des Aelius Aristides über die Eintracht." *Zeitschrift für Papyrologie und Epigraphik* 32 (1978): 287–296.

Miltner, Franz. *Ephesos: Stadt der Artemis und des Johannes*. Vienna: Franz Deuticke, 1958.

Müller, Hermann. *Aus der Uberlieferungsgeschichte des Polykarp-Martyrium: Eine hagiographische Studie*. Paderborn: Bonifacius, 1908.

———. "Eine Bemerkung zum Martyrium Polycarpi." *TGl* 2 (1910): 669–670.

———. "Das Martyrium Polykarps: Ein Beitrag zur altchristlichen Heiligengeschichte." *RQ* 22 (1908): 1–16.

Nautin, Pierre. "La date du 'De Viris Inlustribus.'" *Revue D'Histoire Ecclésiastique* 56 (1961): 33–35.

Nielson, C. M. "Polycarp and Marcion: A Note." *TS* 74 (1986): 297–299.

Nock, Arthur Darby. *Essays on Religion and the Ancient World: Selected and edited, with an Introduction, Bibliography of Nock's Writings and Indexes*. 2 vols. Edited by Zeph Stewart. Oxford: Clarendon Press, 1986.

———. *Sallustius: Concerning the Gods and the Universe*. 1926. Reprint, Hildesheim: G. Olms, 1966.

Norden, Eduard. "Beiträge zur Geschichte der griechischen Philosophie." *Jahrbücher für classische Philologie* 19 (1893): 365–462.
O'Leary, De Lacy. *The Saints of Egypt*. London: SPCK, 1937.
Parrott, Douglas M. "Gnostic and Orthodox Disciples in the Second and Third Centuries." In *Nag Hammadi, Gnosticism, and Early Christianity*. Edited by Charles W. Hedrick and Robert Hodgson, Jr., 193–219. Peabody, Mass.: Hendrickson, 1986.
Patterson, Stephen. *The Gospel of Thomas and Jesus*. Sonoma: Polebridge Press, 1993.
Pearson, Birger A. *Gnosticism, Judaism, and Egyptian Christianity*. Studies in Antiquity and Christianity, no. 5. Minneapolis: Fortress Press, 1990.
Pervo, Richard I. "Johannine Trajectories in the *Acts of John*." *Apocrypha* 3 (1992): 47–68.
Pococke, Richard. *A Description of the East and Some Other Countries*. 2 vols. London: W. Bowyer, 1745.
Poirier, Paul-Hubert. *La version copte de la prédication et du martyre de Thomas avec une contribution codicologique au corpus copte des acta apostolorum apocrypha par Enzo Lucchesi*. Subsidia Hagiographica, no. 67. Brussells: Société des Bollandistes, 1984.
Polotsky, H. J. *Collected Papers*. Jersusalem: Magnes Press (Hebrew University), 1971.
———. *Grundlagen des koptischen Satzbaus*. 2 vols. American Studies in Papyrology, nos. 28–29. Decatur, Ga.: Scholars Press, 1987, 1990.
Poupon, Gérard. "L'accusation de magie dans les actes apocryphes." In *Les actes apocryphes des apôtres*. Edited by Francois Bovon et al., 71–93. Publications de la Faculté de Théologie de l'Université de Genève. Geneva: Labor et Fides, 1981.
Ramsay, Wm. M. *Historical Geography of Asia Minor*. 1890. Amsterdam: Adolf M. Hakkert, 1962.
———. *The Letters to the Seven Churches of Asia and Their Place in the Plan of the Apocalypse*. New York: Hodder and Stoughton, 1904.
———. *The Social Basis of Roman Power in Asia Minor*. 1941. Amsterdam: Adolf M. Hakkert, 1967.
Reardon, B. P. "Aspects of the Greek Novel." *Greece and Rome* 23 (1976): 118–131.
Rengstrof, Karl Heinrich. *Apostolate and Ministry: The New Testament Doctrine of the Office of the Ministry*. Translated by Paul D. Pahl. St. Louis: Concordia Publishing House, 1969.
Reuning, W. *Zur Erklärung des Polykarpmartyriums*. Darmstadt: C. F. Winter, 1917.
Riesenfeld, Harald. "The Ministry in the New Testament." In *The Root of the Vine: Essays in Biblical Theology*. Edited by Anton Fridrichsen et al., 96–127. Westminster: Dacre Press, 1953.

Rius-Camps, J. *The Four Authentic Letters of Ignatius, the Martyr*. Orientalia Christiana Analecta, no. 213. Rome: Pontificum Institutum Orientalium Studiorum, 1980.

Robert, L., M. N. Tod, and E. Ziebarth, eds. *Supplementum Epigraphum Graecum*. Vol. 4. Amsterdam: A. W. Sijthoff, 1929.

Ronconi, Alessandro. "Exitus Illustrium Virorum." *RAC* 6.1258–1268.

Schenke, Hans-Martin. "The Function and Background of the Beloved Disciple in the Gospel of John." In *Nag Hammadi, Gnosticism, and Early Christianity*. Edited by Charles W. Hedrick and Robert Hodgson, Jr., 111–125. Peabody, Mass.: Hendrickson, 1986.

Scherrer, Peter. "The City of Ephesos from the Roman Period to Late Antiquity." In *Ephesos: Metropolis of Asia: An Interdisciplinary Approach to Its Archaeology, Religion, and Culture*. Edited by Helmut Koester, 1–26. Harvard Theological Studies Series, no. 41. Valley Forge: Trinity Press International, 1995.

Schmithals, Walter. *The Office of the Apostle in the Early Church*. Translated by John E. Steely. Nashville: Abingdon Press, 1969.

Schnackenburg, Rudolf. *The Gospel according to St. John*. Vol. 1, translated by Kevin Smyth (1968); vol. 2, translated by Cecily Hastings, Francis McDonagh, David Smith, and Richard Foley, S.J. (1979); vol. 3, translated by David Smith and G. A. Kon (1982). Reprint, New York: Crossroad, 1990.

Schoedel, William R. "Are the Letters of Ignatius of Antioch Authentic?" *RelSRev* 6 (1980): 196–201.

———. *Ignatius of Antioch: A Commentary on the Letters of Ignatius of Antioch*. Hermeneia Series. Philadelphia: Fortress Press, 1985.

———. "Papias." *ANRW* 2.27.1 (1993): 235–270.

———. "Polycarp, Epistle of." ABD 5.390a–392a.

———. "Polycarp, Martyrdom of." ABD 5.392a–395a.

———. *Polycarp, Martyrdom of Polycarp, Fragments of Papias*. Vol. 5, *The Apostolic Fathers: A New Translation and Commentary*. Edited by Robert M. Grant. Camden, N.J.: Thomas Nelson and Sons, 1967.

———. "Polycarp of Smyrna and Ignatius of Antioch." *ANRW* 2.27.1 (1993): 272–358.

Schwartz, E. *De Pionio et Polycarp*. Göttingen: Officina Academica Dietrichiana, 1905.

———. *Ueber den Tod der Söhne Zebedaei: Ein Beitrag zur Geschichte des Johannesevangeliums*. Abhandlungen der königlischen Gesellschafter der Wissenschaften zu Göttingen, philologisch-historische Klasse, New Series 7.5. Berlin: Weidmann, 1904.

———. "Unzeitgemässe Beobachtungen zu den Clementinen." *ZNW* 31 (1932): 151–199.

Segal, Alan F. "Hellenistic Magic: Some Questions of Definition." In *Studies in Gnosticism and Hellenistic Religions: Presented to Gilles Quispel on the Occasion of his 65th Birthday*. Edited by R. van den Broeck and M. J. Vermaseren, 349–375. Leiden: E. J. Brill, 1981.

Seufert, Wilhelm. *Der Ursprung und die Bedeutung der Apostolates in der christlichen Kirch der ersten zwei Jahrhundert: Eine kritische-historische Untersuchung auf Grund der Schriften des Neu Testaments under der weiteren christlichen Literatur*. Leiden: E. J. Brill, 1887.

Shepherd, Massey Hamilton, Jr. "Smyrna in the Ignatian Letters: A Study in Church Order." *JR* 20 (1940): 141–159.

Sherwin-White, A. N. "Why Were the Early Christians Persecuted? An Amendment." In *Studies in Ancient Society*. Edited by M. I. Finley, 250–255. Past and Present Series. London: Routledge and Kegan Paul, 1974. (First published in *Past and Present* 27 [1964]: 23–27.)

Shisha-Halevy, Ariel. *Coptic Grammatical Categories: Structural Studies in the Syntax of Shenoutean Sahidic*. AnOr 53. Rome: Pontificum Institutem Biblicum, 1986.

Smith, Morton. *Jesus the Magician*. San Francisco: Harper and Row, 1978.

Smith, Thomas. *Septem Asiae Ecclesiarum Notitia*. London: Excudebat T. R., 1676.

Stählin, Otto. *Die Altchristliche Griechische Litteratur*. Munich: H. Beck, 1924.

Ste Croix, G. E. M. de. "Why Were the Early Christians Persecuted?" In *Studies in Ancient Society*. Edited by M. I. Finley, 210–249. Past and Present Series. London: Routledge and Kegan Paul, 1974. (First published in *Past and Present* 26 [1963]: 3–38.)

———. "Why Were the Early Christians Persecuted? A Rejoinder." *Studies in Ancient Society*. Edited by M. I. Finley, 256–262. Past and Present Series. London: Routledge and Kegan Paul, 1974. (First published in *Past and Present* 27 [1964]: 28–33.)

Steindorff, Georg. *Koptische Grammatik, mit Chrestomathie, Wörterverzeichnis und Litteratur*. Porta Linguarum Orientalum 14. Berlin: Reuther and Reichard, 1894.

Stern, Ludwig. *Koptische Grammatik*. Leipzig: T. O. Weigel, 1880.

Streeter, Burnett H. *The Primitive Church: Studied with Special Reference to the Origins of the Christian Ministry*. New York: MacMillan, 1929.

Veter, P. "Über die armenische Ubersetzung der Kirchengeschichte des Eusebius." *TQ* 63 (1881): 250–276.

Wansink, Craig Steven. *Chained in Christ: The Experience and Rhetoric of Paul's Imprisonments*. JSNTS, no. 130. Sheffield: Sheffield Academic Press, 1996.

Ward, Philip. *Apuleius on Trial at Sabratha*. Stoughton, Wis.: Oleander Press, 1969.

Wilson, Stephen. *Saints and Their Cults: Studies in Religious Sociology, Folklore, and History*. Cambridge: Cambridge University Press, 1983.

Wright, Benjamin G., III. "Cerinthus *apud* Hippolytus: An Inquiry into the Traditions about Cerinthus's Provenance." *SecCent* 4 (1984): 103–115.

Yamauchi, Edwin. *The Archaeology of New Testament Cities in Western Asia Minor*. London: Pickering and Inglis, 1980.

Zahn, Theodor, ed. *Acta Joannis*. Erlangen: Andreas Deichert, 1880.

———. *Apostel und Apostelschüler in der Provinz Asien*. Vol. 6, *Forschungen zur Geschichte des neutestamenlichen Kanons und der altkirchlichen Literatur*. Leipzig: Andreas Deichert, 1900.

———. *Geschichte des neutestamentlichen Kanons*. 2 vols. 1888, 1890. Reprint, Hildesheim: Georg Olms, 1975.

———. "Die Wanderungen des Apostels Johannes." *Neue kirchliche Zeitschrift* 10 (1899): 191–218.

Index of Ancient Sources

Biblical Literature

Hebrew Bible

New Testament

Early Christian Literature

Other Ancient Literature

Inscriptions

Index of Modern Authors

Subject Index

Frederick Walter Weidmann is Assistant Professor of New Testament at Union Theological Seminary in New York and author of numerous essays on the New Testament and the Early Christian period.